The American Journalists

THE SPIRIT OF
THE PUBLIC JOURNALS

George Bourne, Editor

ARNO
&
The New York Times

Collection Created and Selected
by Charles Gregg of Gregg Press

Reprint edition 1970 by Arno Press Inc.

LC# 74-125679
ISBN 0-405-01654-9

The American Journalists
ISBN for complete set: 0-405-01650-6

Reprinted from a copy in
The University of Illinois Library

Manufactured in the United States of America

THE

SPIRIT

OF THE

PUBLIC JOURNALS;

OR,

BEAUTIES

OF THE

AMERICAN NEWSPAPERS,

FOR 1805.

Duplex libelli dos est; quod risum movet,
Et quod prudenti vitam consilio monet.

A twofold gift in this my volume lies;
It makes you merry, and it makes you wise.

BALTIMORE:

PRINTED BY GEO. DOBBIN & MURPHY,
No. 4, BALTIMORE-STREET.

1806.

TO THE

EDITORS

OF

NEWSPAPERS

THROUGHOUT THE

UNITED STATES,

AND THEIR

CORRESPONDENTS,

This selection is inscribed,

WITH ALL DUE RESPECT,

BY

The Editor.

PREFACE.

THE volume now presented to the publick may be confidered an original work: the effays and poetry of which it is compofed can be known to very few only, and thofe few may have forgotten them fince they appeared in the diurnal prints: hence it appeared a defirable object to preferve the quintessence of the newspaper in a durable form. No paper of any celebrity in the Union has been omitted in the fcrutiny neceffary to make an impartial felection; ten thoufand at leaft have been carefully perufed, that nothing of value might pafs unnoticed: and the lift of Journals which have been examined in the preparation of this volume includes nearly one hundred vehicles of information.

Eaftern Argus	Bofton Gazette
Freeman's Friend	—— Centinel
Farmer's Cabinet	—— Palladium
Salem Regifter	—— Chronicle
Salem Gazette	—— Democrat

Dartmouth Gazette
Providence Gazette
Hartford Mercury
National Ægis
New England Republican
Connecticut Courant
—— Gazette
Troy Gazette
New York Gazette
—— Mer. Advertiser
—— Daily Advertiser
—— Evening Post
—— Amer. Citizen
—— Com. Advertiser
—— Morn. Chron.
Newark Centinel
Albany Register
—— Gazette
—— Centinel
Farmer's Register
Hudson Bee
—— Balance
Trenton American
—— Federalist
Aurora

Boston Repertory
Providence Phœnix
Wilmington Mirror
—— Museum
Lancaster Journal
Bedford Gazette
Pittsburgh Tree of Liberty
—— Commonwealth
Baltimore American
—— Telegraphe
—— Fed. Gazette
—— Evening Post
Maryland Gaz.
Easton Star
National Intelligencer
Washington Federalist
Alexandria Ad.
—— Expositor
Fred. Town Advocate
—— Herald
Winchester Gaz.
Pet. Intelligencer
—— Republican
Fredericksburgh Ex.
Rich. Gazette

Phil. True American
—— Regiſter
—— Gazette
U. S. Gazette
Poulſon's Advertiſer
Freeman's Journal
Miſſiſſippi Herald
Naſhville Gazette
Poughkeepſie Barometer
Newbury Port Herald
Republican Farmer
—— Spy
Farmer's Muſeum
Charleſton Gazette
—— Times
—— Courier
N. Orleans Gazette
Richmond Argus
—— Enquirer
Norfolk Ledger
—— Herald
Raleigh Regiſter
Geo. Town Gazette
Political Obſervatory
Indiana Gazette
Herkimer Monitor
Savannah Muſeum
Auguſta Chronicle
—— Herald
Halifax Journal
Pittsfield Sun
Portſmouth Oracle
Frankfort Palladium.
Kentucky Gazette
Independent Gazette
Ohio Herald.

It is proper however to remark that the Portfolio, and ſimilar publications as being almoſt or entirely confined to miſcellaneous literature were not reviewed: and it muſt be recollected that three or four of the compoſitions although Engliſh are introduced by particular requeſt, upon the ſuppoſition that they might contribute to the amufement and inftruction of the reader.

That no perfon might be difgufted with this fpecimen of the talents of thofe who write for our daily and weekly chronicles of the times; all political difcuffions, jeus d'esprit and caricatures, although many of them be intrinfically excellent in themfelves, are entirely omitted.

But its purity recommends the volume —whilft many parts of it will produce the "hearty laugh," no one page will excite a blufh in the cheek of modefty, or fanction any impropriety of conduct. Its object is to render vice odious by the lafh of ridicule and the energy of admonition, and virtue lovely by animating all the refined feelings of our nature, and difplaying the enjoyments of the chriftian.

CONTENTS.

THE SPIRIT

OF THE

PUBLIC JOURNALS,

FOR 1805.

THE Public, is a being with many heads, and consequently possesses as many different minds; as those can amply testify who are the *servants of its will*, among whom printers perhaps, are the chief *Butlers and Bakers*. "Give us more foreign intelligence," says the newsmonger, "and let domestic politics alone." "Battle the feds; dash away at the demos," cries the politician; "a fig for your foreign intelligence, unless you can send Emperor Buonaparte into England up to his knees in blood. We do not want to hear about ships spoken at sea—a courier passing through Hampergoscamperdum—Marshal Helter Skelter, holding audience with his serene highness, the landgrave of Lubberdegullion, or the marriage of count Waddletwattle, with her ladyship the duchess of Winkumsquintum; let not your paper detail such unimportant advices."—"Hit the federal or democratic editors," exclaims the third, "nothing I like so well as ſquabbles among editors; there is ſome fun in that." "Let us have another novel," ſays Mrs. Fripple, "I like novels monſtrouſly, eſpecially if there be ſomething ſcareful in them; I would not give a cent for the papers if they had not a novel in them." Novels, ſays old Grouſe—"Nonſenſe! give us ſomething about farming; tell us how to deſtroy the Heſſian fly, or ſomething about fining cider, or wheat upon clover." "I like novels too," ſays miſs Simper; but beſides them I want a good deal more poetry, and a number of queer ſtories about Ann Necdotes; I love to read them, terribly." "All wiſhy-waſhy," ſays Jack Galloper, 'give us the ſport of the turf; tell us about the race between Madam Thornton, and Mr. Flint, and her challenging him after ſhe got beat; that's the dandy."

Thus might we go on ad infinitum, and deſcribe the modes which Mr. Public points out for us to be guided by, in conducting our paper; in anſwer, we can only ſay, that although we conſider our own method beſt, yet, as ſoon as they can all agree upon one plan, we will cheerfully adopt it, and until then, we truſt we may be permitted to jog on in the old way of giving a little of every thing which we conſider the moſt important; for,

"If all the land were paper,
"And all the ſea were ink,"

It would ſtill be impoſſible for us to comply with all the demands of the Public, until thoſe demands became more united.

MODE OF SINGLE COMBAT, IN THE CENTRAL PARTS OF AFRICA.

A moſt obſtinate quarrel had happened between a colonel of the guards, and a capital butcher in Gutty-Gur, concerning the dignity of their reſpective profeſſions; and to make the quarrel ſtill more ſerious, they were both candidates for the affections of the ſame lady. The parties being called before the judges, declared that their rage was ſo great as to be ſatisfied only by an appeal to violence. They were then ſeparated at the diſtance of a "fœtid funk" (about three miles) from each other, each of them being attended by one of the judges and an officer of juſtice, who carried along with him pins, bodkins, knives, ſciſſars, pincers, thumb-ſcrews, and other inſtruments of mutilation and torment. The ſpectators divided themſelves into two parties, and accompanied, according to their affections, one or other of the duelliſts, who now, without ſight of each other, and as it were back to back, began the fierce combat; with pen and ink, which was placed on purpoſe on a table cut out of the ſolid rock, he who gave the challenge, without the leaſt heſitation, wrote to the other the following note:—"Colonel Gog defies Butcher Magog with a pin ſix inches in length thruſt to the very head in one of his thighs." This note being delivered with due ſolemnity into the hands of the judge, the officer of juſtice, (or, as we ſhould ſay, "Jack Ketch,") without ceremony, delay or remorſe, thruſt the pin into Gog's naked thigh to the full extent of what was affirmed in the note of defiance. This note, with the ſeal of the judge now appended to it, in "teſtimonium veritatis," was ſent by a public meſſenger to his rival, Magog, who was attended as well as his adverſary, with his judge and executioner: he not only preſented the part deſignated with ineffable diſdain to the executioner, but without a moment's delay, wrote as follows: "Butcher Magog defies Colonel Gog with a bodkin of a foot in length thruſt through the brawny part of his arm." This terrible billet being duly conveyed to the judge, the executioner at his nod, thruſt the bodkin into the arm of Magog, till its bloody point fairly appeared the other ſide. Magog's challenge, duly ſigned, ſealed and delivered, was not without a viſible effect on the countenance of Gog; nevertheleſs the colonel, plucking up a good heart, held out his bare arm to the executioner, who performed it with a proper bodkin, in the twinkling of an eye. Having done this, and refreſhed himſelf a little, he wrote as follows: "Gog defies Magog with the ſcalp of his head."—Immediately after which he preſented himſelf in the proper attitude; and the judge having nodded aſſent, the ſcalp was carried with due ſolemnity to Magog, who loſt no time in returning the *compliment*.

The enraged butcher was now at a loſs how to continue the conteſt. To ſend an ear, a finger or a toe to his antagoniſt, would be ſkirmiſhing to no purpoſe; and for a foot or a hand, a leg or an arm, he could not *conveniently* ſpare them. He, therefore, in order to put an end, if poſſible, to the combat, wrote the following note: "Magog defies Gog with * * * * *" [Here the book is ſo defaced, it is impoſſible to make out what the defiance was.] This defiance ſtruck the judge with horror; he refuſed his aſſent to what was propoſed, on the ground of its being a new caſe, until he ſhould conſult the *hierophant*, and the other judges. Two of theſe declared their opinion, that to ſettle a diſpute in this manner, by * * * * * * [here is another defect in the book] was a thing altogether unheard of, and prepoſterous; but the chief juſtice, Metlek Ammon, to whoſe opinion the other two judges readily aſſented, obſerved that the whole of the judicial proceeding in queſtion was abſurd, and therefore that one part of it could not be ſet aſide, on account of its abſurdity, rather than another.

The butcher having fortified himſelf with a ſtrong doſe of *jumbu*, (brandy and aſſes' blood,) actually carried his threats into execution; but the colonel, to whom a report had been made of the demurrer juſt mentioned, ſaid, that in ſo tender a point it was impoſſible for him to proceed, and to eſtabliſh a new precedent to all future times, unleſs there had been greater concord, if not entire unanimity, among the judges. The butcher therefore triumphed fairly over the colonel; but to which of the combatants, the victor or the vanquiſhed, the lady who was the ſubject of diſpute, gave a preference, is unknown.

THE HERMIT.

THE ſun was ſunk beneath the ſea-green wave,
The bird of eve began her 'cuſtom'd lay,
When the lorn Hermit left his moſs grown cave;
To wander penſive by the twilight ray.

I too "by lonely contemplation led,"
In the ſame walk had ſhap'd my devious way;
To ſee the ſunbeams ſink in Ocean's bed,
And watch the landſcape, as it fades away.

Mild and dejected, was the Hermit's mien,
Dim was the luſtre of his pale blue eye,
Slow bent his tott'ring footſteps, o'er the green,
And oft his boſom heav'd an heartfelt ſigh.

I trac'd him to the margin of the wood,
Near where the brook the bordering flow'ret laves,
He gaz'd with fix'd attention on the flood,
And ſigh'd his "woe fraught" ſtory to the waves.

"While diſappointment mocks each ling'ring day,
And ſtern misfortune holds her rigid ſway,
Why ſhould my fond, enthuſiaſtic heart,
Regret with each terreſtrial ſcene to part.

"While the lorn cypreſs calls me to the ſhade,
Where 'neath the turf my Adeline is laid,
Why to the Earth ſhould fond affection cleave,
Nor wiſh this ſcene of varied ill to leave?

"Ah! what is life? the viſion of an hour,
Fleet as the wind, and fading as the flow'r;
A fair deluſion all its brighteſt joys,
Its charms but wound us, and its bliſs deſtroys.

" Since it's beſt blessings oft a ſnare conceal,
And thoſe moſt ſuffer who the moſt can feel,
Ye tender ſenſibilities, depart!
And thou, chill apathy poſſeſs my heart!

" I once was bleſt, but ah, the time is o'er!
The painted viſion can delight no more;
Around my path is ſpread a ſable gloom,
Which ſpeaks, my only refuge is the tomb.

" Smooth as thy ſurface, gently flowing ſtream,
Were the firſt days, unhappy Albert knew;
But ſwifter than the light's all-piercing beam,
On wings of wind, th' auſpicious moments flew.

" As fades the Iris in the ambient ſky,
So did the dear, illuſive viſion fly;
As dew-drops vaniſh, 'neath the morning ray,
So did the ſoft deluſion paſs away.

" The ſacred rights of freedom to defend,
I left my cottage and the charms of peace;
And truſted to the *honour of a friend*,
The deareſt treaſure mortal can poſſeſs.

" That *friend* perdition blaſt the *name profan'd*,
Tore from my arms the idol of my ſoul,
Her artleſs truth betray'd, her honour ſtain'd:
She ſipp'd a noxious draught, from pleaſure's bowl.

" Awak'd from guilt's delirium too late,
She ſaw, and trembled at her fallen ſtate;
Then tir'd of life, reſign'd her fleeting breath,
And drank the balſam of conſoling death.

" Since then, though thirty times the rolling globe
Its annual circuit round the ſun have made;
Though thirty times in nature's vernal robe,
I've ſeen the landſcape of the ſpring array'd;

" Yet ev'ry eve, and ev'ry roſy morn,
I've wept, and call'd on Adeline's bleſt ſhade;

"And when the moonbeams trembled on her Urn,
The folemn offering of my love have paid.

"Tir'd of the hackney'd vices of mankind,
Of friendfhip flown, and innocence betray'd;
The world and all its follies I refign'd,
And fought repofe in yonder lowly glade.

"Yet even there, the mem'ry of my grief,
Preys like a vulture on my tortur'd breaft;
Where but in death can Albert find relief?
What but the grave can give the fuff'rer reft?

"But now, methinks, a cheering beam of day,
Breaks through the cloud to chafe my gloom away,
And th' Angel Hope, upborne on wings of love,
Whifpers, " We ftill *may* meet in realms above."

He ceas'd, and rais'd to Heav'n his languid eyes,
And a low figh difmifs'd him to the fkies.

UNCLE JONATHAN'S REFLECTION.

I often think of the words of my uncle Jonathan who was fitting by the firefide one day, and after knocking the afhes out of his third pipe upon the top of the andiron, and very deliberately placing one leg upon the knee of the other,—" boy," fays he, (for I was ftanding directly oppofite to him) " boy," fays he " you have yet feen but little of the world; you know not, as yet, what difficulties and dangers mankind are obliged to encounter, and what thorns and briers are fcattered to entangle them in almoft every ftep of their journey through life. The fruits of the folly and misfortunes of men are continually hanging upon them, and whatever be their vigilance and caution, trouble will ſometimes happen. Youth frequently are free from troubles and perplexities, becauſe they are not expoſed to them; but when they come to act for themſelves, when they are obliged to live by their own labour, and earn their own bread, they will then ſee, that 'man is born unto trouble.'

I muſt confeſs that what uncle Jonathan told me made ſo much impreſſion upon my mind, that I have thought of it ſeveral times ſince, and each time I have ſeen ſome ſtriking inſtance to confirm its truth.

Couſin Peter, who lives but two doors to the eaſt of me, is as clever and induſtrious a man, as ever trod ſhoe-leather, yet he is far from baſking always in the clear ſunſhine of proſperity. He has a decent farm and a comfortable houſe; he labours hard, and lays up wherewith to treat a friend, and ſupport himſelf and family, in foul weather and ſickneſs. But notwithſtanding all this, whenever he enters his houſe, whether with a ſmile upon his countenance or not, it is ten to one but he is laboured over with a broom-ſtick. The fact is, he has gotten a ſcolding wife, and if the Devil ever lived on earth, I believe that a ſcolding wife is one of his daughters. She is continually tormenting and perplexing him; and whether in public or private, he is ſure to bear the laſh of her tongue, if not the laſh of ſomething a little more painful. Finally, ſhe is 'a thorn in his ſide,' which he cannot poſſibly get rid of; and the whole neighbourhood believe that the poor man is born unto trouble.

Neighbour Scrapewell, is another ſtrange character of theſe ſtrange times; he is very far, however, from poſſeſſing all the gentleneſs of my couſin Peter, and far leſs, from indulging his liberality and benevolence. He is continually complaining of poverty, though he has thouſands in the old iron-bound cheſt, which in all probability will fall into the hands of ſome greedy heir, who is now wiſhing for his departure. His wife is as kind a creature as ever lived, and is ever ready to do every good ſervice that lies in her power; and he is ready enough to grant her this liberty, provided it coſt no money. But as ſoon as ſhe begins to mention, or even hint, that a little of his treaſure is wanting, you will ſee him very deliberately riſe from his chair, and with quite an ungracious aſpect, limping acroſs the floor, curſing and reprobating the folly and extravagance of the world —' and women, ſays he, in particular, have continually ſome fooliſh notions in their heads, which, if men have a mind to gratify, will reduce them to poverty at once,—I'll not give away a ſingle farthing of my money,'—and I believe he is as good as his word; for his children went to ſchool ſcarcely a day in their lives; his family are ever deſtitute even of the moſt neceſſary articles, and he would even ſtarve himſelf, if he could thereby add a ſingle cent to his ſtore. Who can doubt that this man and his whole family are born unto trouble?

Tom Rattle was early in youth puffed up with all thofe high notions of pride and dignity which, his becoming heir to a large fortune, would tend to imprefs upon him. At nineteen he married, and he and his lady fcarce ever attempted to make the leaft movement without being attended by a coach and fix, and at leaft half a dozen fervants. Balls, parties of pleafure, and indeed the whole round of fafhionable amufements were punctually attended; fo that in a very fhort time they acquired the name of being very accomplifhed.—But fuch diffipated habits, you muft well know could not be permanent, without an almoft inexhauftible fund to fupport them. This was really the cafe; for after a few years Mr. Rattle's creditors, having repeatedly called, and finding themfelves likely to be cheated out of their dues, came upon him at once, and ftripped him of all his boafted wealth. Thofe who once were his moft flattering courtiers, are now his moft grievous oppreffors, and his former warmeft friends are now his greateft enemies. It is fufficient to obferve, that he was at once thrown from apparently the moft flattering profpects to the moft abject ftate of want; and deftitute and ignorant of bufinefs, he is now left with a wife and family upon his hands, without a friend to affift or to comfort him. He is certainly wretched, and born unto trouble.

I have feen the diftreffes of my fellow creatures, I have pitied them for their misfortunes; and, whenever the truly deferving have come within my reach, as far as my humble circumſtances would allow, I have afforded them relief. Inexperienced as I am, in the ways of life, I have, neverthelefs, ſeen and endured many of its troubles and difficulties.—At an early period, my parents died and left me a patrimony barely ſufficient to complete my education. Since that time, I have been expoſed to all the vices, wickedneſs and temptations of the world ; but, by my own prudence and reaſon, and the advice of a few generous friends, whom fortune has always afforded me, I have been enabled to outride ſtorms and tempeſts, and arrive ſafely to the preſent moment. The want of property and home, abſence from my dear connections, and a little of the hypochondriac withal, ſometimes moſt violently aſſail me, and though people in general imagine me to be one of the wildeſt of their acquaintance, (for I always keep the moſt gloomy ſide to myſelf) yet I have many unhappy hours, and unpleaſant meditations.

But God will aſſuage the wrongs of the aggrieved ; and if we walk in the path of the prudent, and the counſel of the wiſe, we may reaſonably anticipate the ſmiles and the favour of heaven.

THE MOCKING-BIRD.

The ſweeteſt warbler of the ſhady grove,
So oft made vocal by his plaints of love,
Left the wild beauties of the ſcene,
And ſought the buſy haunts of men ;
In ſearch of yet untaſted joys,
Though fond, like them, of glitt'ring toys
Or elſe to kill the tedious hour,
He leaves awhile the nuptial bower,
Where his ſoft mate, fill'd with maternal cares,
The future nurſery of his love prepares.

Perhaps, he flies theſe ſcenes of rapturous bliſs,
Where all the Heaven of faithful love was his,
Till death his deareſt treaſure ſtole,
And deſolated all his ſoul !
The widow'd wand'rer, fond to ſtray ;
Unheedful of his devious way,
It chanc'd the city caught his view,
Fate urg'd him on--away he flew :
Near the deep vale a lonely manſion roſe,
And one fair tree where he might court repoſe.

He gain'd the tree—he ſought the topmoſt ſpray,
Where oft he trill'd his ſoft melodious lay ;
While, as he ſwell'd his downy throat,
And lengthen'd every mournful note,
He ſooth'd his troubled ſoul to reſt,
And huſh'd the tumult of his breaſt ;
Thus, harmony ſuſpended grief,
And ſuff'ring nature found relief,
Some kind indulgent power, his choice might guide,
Its widow'd lord to cheer, to him in fate allied.--

He grateful, liſten'd to the various ſong,
And pray'd him, oft repeat and ſtill prolong,
The ſadly-ſweet, alternate ſtrain,
Nor ſeek his native woods again,
Content, the little warbler ſtay'd,
The tree was good for food—the ſhade

Was grateful, from the noon-tide heat,
There he might chuse his ſhelter'd ſeat,
While ſympathy, beguil'd the live-long day,
For hearts reſpondent—charm their woes away—

Alas! how ſhort-liv'd e'en this *ſhew* of peace,
How evaneſcent! as th' extreme of bliſs!
For now, a ſavage foe appear'd,
With inſtruments of death! prepar'd.
That *men* might praiſe his wondrous ſkill,
'Twas his inhuman ſport to kill!
His murd'rous eye, had mark'd the prize,
His heart had ſaid—The victim dies!
The blameleſs minſtrel, ignorant of guile,
Still chirps and ſings to cheer his heart the while.

With cautious ſteps and ſlow, the fiend drew near,
Th' unconſcious bird, who knew no cauſe of fear,
Purſued his ſoft mellifluous lay,
Still fond to chuſe the topmoſt ſpray;
Satanic joy his foe poſſeſſ'd,
His eye ſuch horrid joy expreſſ'd,
Too certain was his dreadful aim,
Too ſure to quench the vital flame;
For ſee! alas! he falls—he faints—he dies!
On the cold earth, a mangled corſe he lies!

Poor, luckleſs bird! thy deſtiny ſevere,
Wrings from her ſoul, the ſympathetic tear,
Who, long by tyrant man oppreſt,
With thee would gladly ſink to reſt;
This boon denied, ſhe breathes—to feel
Wounds—deeper, than transfix'd by ſteel,
And ſtill repeated by the foe,
Inflicting laſting, deadly woe.—
Thy milder fate, then why ſhould ſhe deplore,
Who in the grave alone, ſhall ſigh and weep no more

BAGATELLES.

A Student at one of our Colleges, ſome years ſince, by the name of Tucker, who was remarkable for large *teeth*, and another by the name of Green, whoſe *noſe* was not the leaſt prominent feature of his face, one day warmly diſputed the point of precedence in Arithmetical knowledge.—As the conteſt grew warmer, and was not likely ſoon to be compromiſed by themſelves, they referred the matter to the deciſion of a ſtudent in the claſs above them. In diſcloſing the diſpute to this arbitrator, they agreed that he ſhould propound a knotty queſtion, and the one who ſhould ſolve it with the moſt expedition, and, in his judgment, with the moſt propriety, ſhould bear the palm. After conſiderable heſitation and unwillingneſs to comply on the part of the Referee, and increaſing importunity on the part of the diſputants, he propoſed the following very ingenious and keenly ſatirical queſtion, which at once ended the conteſt :—

"If Tucker's teeth three ſcore of beef,
"Conſume in half an hour ;
"I pray diſcloſe, what chance Green's noſe
"Would ſtand, if in their power ?"

A virgin of *twenty-five*, was lately throwing out ſome affected ſneers at matrimony, when a grave friend in company obſerved, that "marriages were made in Heaven." Can you tell me, ſir, rejoined the ſly nymph, why they are ſo *ſlow in coming down*.

An American having brought up his ſon to the profeſſion of the Bar, was aſked in what branch of the law he propoſed to diſtinguiſh him.—"Why," ſays the old man, alluding to the Criminal Law, "I believe ſomething in the *hanging line*."

The death of a *Miſer*, was lately announced thus—"On Friday laſt died, Joſiah Braintree, of Bennington, at the age of 98. He retained his *money* to the laſt."

A man obſerving, that there was leſs danger from a wound on board a ſhip, when the ſea was rough, being aſked the reaſon, anſwered, becauſe one *ſurge-on* comes after another exceedingly faſt.

A merchant advertiſed a commodity for ſale, and gave notice that he would take in payment all kinds of *country produce*, except *promiſes!*

A Gentleman by the name of Barryl, in one of the Northern States; made a Speech, in which he ſpoke very loud and long. One of the company not being pleaſed with the harangue, obſerved that an empty *Barrel* always made the greateſt ſound.

A Lawyer in croſs examining a witneſs, aſked him among other queſtions, where he was on a particular day, to which he replied, in company with two friends. "Friends?" exclaimed the Lawyer, "two thieves, I ſuppofe you mean." "They may be fo," replied the witnefs, "for they are both *Lawyers!*"

An old negro by the name of Harry, who lived in New Jerfey fome years ago, commonly made it a practice on holidays, to go round the country begging. One Chriftmas, meeting a Mr. Nicholas G. he thus accofted him—"good morning mafsa G. wifh you melly Clifmus; pleafe gib ole negur fispence dis morning?" Mr. G. who well knew the negro, but determining to have a little fun, replied with fome degree of fternnefs, "who are you?" "Maffa no know me? anfwered the negro, my name Harry; dey call me ole Harry." "Old Harry;" "fays Mr. G. "they call the Devil old Harry." "Yes maffa," replied the negro. "*Some time ole Harry, fome time ole Nick.*"—The wit pleafed, and Harry was folaced with a dollar.

A phyfician had a fkeleton fo fixed, that on entering the room a fpring was touched, when, in an inftant it grafped the perfon entering. A ftranger called on the doctor for fome medical aid, and was fhewn into the room where the fkeleton was; it feized him in a moment—he up with his fift to defend himfelf; but, to his great aftonifhment, he faw the ghaftly figure difengaging itfelf, when he flew from the houfe like lightning. A few days after, meeting the doctor, (who might be called a walking ſkeleton,) coming out of his houſe—"Ah,—are you there! you think I don't know you, with your clothes on? he ſeized the doctor by the throttle, and beſtowing a few hearty whacks; take that for the ſweat you gave me the other day."

Some time ſince, a captain of a veſſel had a quantity of coals to go on board, and as a great number lay ſcattered about the wharf, he thought it would be beſt to get a rake that he might more ſpeedily collect them together, he went into a counting houſe and enquired of the merchant, whether he could have the loan of a *rake* for a few minutes? The merchant ſmiled, and looking ſignificantly round at his clerks, ſaid, I believe I have a number of them, but no one who will readily anſwer your purpoſe; the captain comprehending the pun, replied, I think you are quite right, for neither of them, I ſuppoſe, would wiſh to be "*hauled over the coals.*"

NOTE FROM THE DOGS IN NEW YORK, TO THE PUPPIES IN THE COUNTRY.

The dogs of the city preſent reſpectful compliments to thoſe who live in its vicinity, or who *uſually come into* town, and beg leave to inform them, that after the 1ſt of June next they are under the painful neceſſity of declining the viſits of their ſuburban acquaintances—a law having paſſed which ſubjects to a penalty of ten dollars any dog, however genteel his manners, or important his presence, who may be found collarless in the streets of New York.—The city dogs are extremely sorry to be thus deprived of the endearing company of their friends who *usually come into* town to enjoy a bone, or fight a battle. They sincerely hope that the reign of the *dog days* will soon be over, and that the delightful intercourse at present existing, will not be long interrupted.

In the index to a certain book, containing "the rules that govern our daily conduct," is said to be this odd reference—"Swine—see *Justices of the peace*." Some time since, one of the learned judges of the supreme court was rallying a member of the committee who revised the laws of Vermont, on the singularity of the reference,—when a gentleman present, observed to "his honour" that he recollected one in the same index still more singular, viz. "adultery"—see *Judges of the supreme court*.

THE BLACK-BIRD, IN WINTER.

Poor bird! my heart is truly wae,
Forlorn to see thee wand'rin' sae,
Whar ilka thing's thy mortal fae,
E'en heav'n's vice-gerent—
Unfeelin' man—he waits to slay
Thee like a tyrant.

Aft times whan e'enin' frae her den,
Staw saftly up the dewy glen,
I've seen thee far frae treach'rous men
Thy sonnet singin',
While loud resoundin to thy strain
The groves war ringin'.

But ah ! the times are fadly chang'd ;
The leafy foreft whar thou rang'd
Clean bare by gurly winter fcraing'd,
Nae bield it yie'ls
An' hunger makes thee quite eftrang'd
To open fiel's.

In hoary mift wi' biting breath,
Stern winter reigns in gloomy wrath,
Though calm the air yet fraught wi' death
It brings ftarvation,
An' thou maun feek, to fcape the fcaith,
Som 'ither ftation.

Alas ! before the cottage door,
In humble mood thou's fain to cow'r ;
Though bawdrons crouching to devour,
An' riddle traps,
Await thee ftill, thou looks them o'er
For antrin fcraps.

Yet ah ! in this thou's no thy lane ;
Thy fate is aft the fate o'men,
Wha in their actions fair an' plain,
Nae guile expect
Till driv'n on knaves quite unforefeen
They're fairly wreckt.

Happy thy fate compar'd wi' their's :
Returnin' fpring fhall end thy cares,
But ah ! nae changin' time repairs
The broken heart ;
Still weepin' recollection tears
Wi' double fmart.

WRITTEN AT SEA.

ON the deck, in the filence of night,
I watch'd the pale moon in the weft ;
When the billow reflected her light,
In fancy's gay vifion expreft :

All the woes my fond boſom e'er bore,
From remembrance were ſever'd and free,
And I ſaw not the cloud paſſing o'er,
'Till it figur'd the emblem of me.

While the dim cloud was melting in air,
Her mild ſplendour again I diſcern'd,
Not ſo, I exclaim'd in deſpair,
Have the ſmiles of my ANNA return'd;
As the heavens, my love was o'ercaſt,
But the ſcene is ſtill gloomy and drear,
For the dark ſhade of ſorrow when paſt,
Left the proſpect enſhrin'd in a tear.

MY NATIVE HOME.

O'ER breezy hill or woodland glade,
At morning's dawn or cloſing day,
In Summer's flaunting pomp array'd,
Or penſive moonlight's ſilver ray;
The wretch in ſadneſs ſtill ſhall roam,
Who wanders from his native home.

While at the foot of ſome old tree,
As meditation ſoothes his mind,
Lull'd by the hum of wand'ring bee,
Or rippling ſtream or whiſpering wind,
His vagrant fancy ſtill ſhall roam,
And lead him to his native home.

Though love a fragrant couch might weave,
And fortune heap the feſtive board,
Still mem'ry oft would turn to grieve,
And reaſon ſcorn the ſplendid hoard;
While he, beneath the proudeſt dome,
Would languiſh for his native home.

To him the ruſhy roof is dear,
And ſweetly calm the darkeſt glen.
While pomp, and pride, and power appear,
At beſt the glitt'ring plagues of men;

Unſought by thoſe that never roam,
Forgetful of their native home.

Let me to Summer's ſhades retire,
With meditation and the Muſe,
Or round the ſocial winter fire,
The glow of temper'd mirth diffuſe;
The winds may howl, and waters foam,
I ſtill ſhall bleſs my native home.

And oh, when youth's ecſtatic hour,
And paſſion's glowing noon are paſt,
Should age behold the tempeſt low'r,
And ſorrow blow its keeneſt blaſt,
My ſhade no longer doom'd to roam,
Shall find the grave a peaceful home.

DECEIT.

OH! that the human form ſhould wear,
Deception's garb for pelf;
Or, hated vice, the ſemblance bear,
Of Innocence itſelf!

Almighty Parent! when thy word,
This nice machine began;
Why did this paſſion interlard,
The various pow'rs of man?

Why ſhould the ſeeming graces join,
Its natal horoſcope?
Or, ſober manhood e'er combine,
To blaſt the virgin's hope?

Why ſhe in turn, urg'd by Deceit,
Though robb'd of priſtine worth;
With borrow'd modeſty elate,
In virtue's guiſe walk forth?

And why ſhould hoary age, unwreath
Truth s garland;—once its own?

Or, quaint illufion ftalk beneath,
A fanctimonious frown?

Creative Father! though thy ways
Seem intricate and dark;
Yet Faith's illuminated rays,
Shall cheer the vital fpark.

THE WITHERED ROSE.

How fair wert thou, when firft mine eye
Caught the light tint thy leaves that dreft;
Juft burfting from obfcurity,
To court the zephyr to thy breaft.

To me thou didft recall the time,
When hope and fancy wing'd my days;
When in my joyous youthful prime,
No penfive note e'er mark'd my lays.

Thou too like me wert but half blown,
Ere drooping for thy parent foil,
Thy richeft fragrance far had flown,
And death had ta'en thee as his fpoil.

He bow'd thy unaffuming head,
And paler made thy modeft glow,
Which boafted ne'er the brighteft red,
But fuch a blufh as pale cheeks know.

Thy lively green is faded too,
And thou doft not one trace retain,
Of that fweet flow'r the peafants woo,
To waft its perfume o'er the plain.

Poor Rofe, adieu! may I like thee,
When "death has laid my green head low,"
Have fome fond friend to figh for me,
And mourn for buds that never blow.

WRITTEN WHEN CROSSING THE ATLANTIC.

Great ſcene with awe I hail thy azure wave!
And the great author of thy birth adore,
Who firſt to thee thy wide dominion gave,
Round every iſle, and each indented ſhore.

But oh! what horror does the fearful mind
Aſſail, embarked upon thy trembling foam,
Some fiend he thinks, that comes in every wind,
Denies his courſe; and when returning home,

Danger affrights him on the midnight main,
When drowning cries in roaring waves he hears,
Loſt in deſpair he wiſhes once again,
To tread that ſhore, which danger more endears.

Death in thy gloomy chambers doth reſide,
And thy deep face reflects his horrid form;
Come to my bark! fair ſpirit of the tide,
And guide me from the dæmon of the ſtorm.

BEEF-STEAK AND OYSTERS.

What ſignifies all the diſpute reſpecting the queſtion of ſuperiority in the ancients or moderns? *Sir William Temple*, and *Doctor Bentley* and *Doctor Wotton*, and the *Earl of Orrery*, might have ſhed ink till this time, and never would the ſuperiority of the ancients reſpecting a knowledge of the properties and the right uſe of the OYSTER have been eſtabliſhed to the ſatisfaction of GEORGE WATSON.

I am clearly for the ſuperiority of the moderns. What are the facts? So ſuperſtititious and ignorant were the ancient Greeks and Romans, that they believed oyſters to grow fat with the two firſt quarters of the moon, and become lean with her waning. *Oſtreis et conchyllis omnibus* ſays *Aulus Gellius*, *contigit, ut cum Luna creſcant pariter, pariterque decreſcant:* ſo ſays *Cicero. Gellius* quotes *Lucilius, Luna alit oſtrea*: *Horace* alſo ſays, *naſcentes implent conchylia Lunæ.* It is true they had ſome taſte reſpecting the reliſh of oyſters; and knew how to diſtinguiſh well. What ſays *Juvenal* of the nicely diſcriminating taſte of an oyſter epicure?

> *Circeis* nata forent an
> *Lucrinum* ad ſaxum, *Rutupinove* edita fundo
> *Oſtrea*, calcebat primo deprehendere morsu:

i. e. he could tell at the *firſt taſte* whether they came from the Caietan rocks, the Bay of Lucrinum in Campania, or from Richborough, in Kent county, in England. And *Horace* mentions the great ſuperiority of the Circean oyſters:

> Murice Baiano melior Lucrina peloris,
> *Oſtrea Circæis*, Miſeno oriuntur echini.

So alſo *Pliny*: *Circæis* autem oſtreis neque dulciora neque teneriora, eſſe ulla, &c. In ſhort, it is my opinion, that the Circean oyſters very much reſembled the oyſters at my houſe called the YORK COVE and QU EN'S CREEK. They knew as well as we, that the beſt oyſters are taken from the *coves; optima ſunt oſtrea*, ſays Pliny, *si quando* LACUS *adjacet aut fluvius*; by which, ſays *Caſaubon*, we are to underſtand, the *Cove* oyſters. But what is this to the purpoſe? It only ſhews that the ancients had a reliſh for *raw* oyſters. Shew me that they ever cooked. Where is a treatiſe in Greek or Latin, on *roaſting*, *ſtewing*, *frying*, and other ways of dreſſing oyſters? Here is a proof of *modern* ſuperiority. They had no *houſe set apart* for the particular purpoſe of regaling the lovers of this delicacy. *Juvenal* to be ſure mentions a *bad* lady's eating great oyſters at midnight.

Grandia quæ mediis jam noctibus *oſtrea* mordet; but from the context it may be ſeen that ſhe *bit* them [or rather *ate* them off—*mordet*] at *home*. This is another proof of *modern* ſuperiority. In ſhort, had G. Watſon time to examine the writings of the ancients, (much of which he has forgotten ſince turning his attention to the delightful taſk of pleaſing the palate of a patroniſing public) he might prove in almoſt every way, as it reſpects the oyſter, that the ancients were far, very far inferior to the moderns. One proof more. Did they ever know the union of *beef ſteak* and oyſters? Homer may tell about the *ambroſia* and *nectar* of his un-epicurean gods and goddeſſes, but where in the Iliad will you find a ſyllable relating to beef ſteak and oyſters? It is all folderol; they knew nothing of good living.

Who firſt diſcovered the excellent qualities of the oyſter, and brought into general uſe this firſt of ſhell fiſh; in compariſon with which crabs, lobſters, craw-fiſh and clams, "hide their diminiſhed heads?" Did I know the name of ſuch a "benefactor of the human race," I would build him a *monumentum ære perennius*, made of gold and cemented with oyſter lime.

For *nouriſhment* what equals the oyſter? What ſays "*Willich* on Diet and Regimen," a work that ſhould be in every family? "Oyſters are eaſily digeſted; they may be eaten with great advantage by the robuſt, as well as the weak and the conſumptive; they poſſeſs more *nutritive animal jelly* than almoſt any other." Though G. Watſon's reading is not ſo extenſive as that of thoſe who have read more than he has, yet he muſt acknowledge that neither in Galen, nor in Hippocrates, in Cullen or Boerhaave, has he ever found half a ſyllable againſt the wholeſomeneſs of this ſovereign of bivalved cruſtaceous aquatics. This animal, that lives in a houſe not made with hands, with but one door, for cheapneſs, flavour and ſalubrity,

Bears like the Turk no ſhell-fiſh near his throne.

Come then to the oyſter reſtorateur where ſhall be wanting, neither WINES *red and white*, *roſy faced* BRANDY, *pure unſpotted* GIN, *good old* JAMAICA, *foaming* PORTER, *ſparkling* CYDER, nor *invigorating* BEER.

Cato the Cenſor (and where find we a more rigid moraliſt?) was wont to ſay, as Plutarch informs us, that a few glaſſes of wine, aſſiſted the diſcuſſion of philoſophical ſubjects. Sir John Hawkins ſays of another rigid moraliſt, Doctor Johnſon, that he ſeldom more enjoyed himſelf, than at a well ordered public houſe, with his literary companions. It is the abuſe, not the uſe that injures health, wealth and reputation —Oh conſider the dreadful ravages of intemperance.

This ugly monſter,
" 'Tis ſtrange he hides him in *freſh cup's* ſoft beds,
' Sweet words, yet hath more miniſters than thoſe
' Who draw their ſword in war."

G. Watſon hopes that no one will ſuffer his *glaſs to wear the breeches;* nor even to permit his cheek to be crimſoned beyond the temperate due of Hygeia's roſe.— Thou deſtroying angel intemperance! the ſword and the plague bring but their hundreds, whilſt thou bringeſt thy thouſands to the court of death. What Virgil ſays of the bees may be applied to intemperance.

Triſti languebunt corpora morbo,
Quod jam non dubiis poteris cognoſcere ſignis;
Continuo eſt ægris alius color; horrida vultum
Deformat macies; tum corpora luce carentum
Exportant tectis, et *triſtia funera* ducunt.

But let me draw towards a cloſe, by obſerving that I am a great lover of *peace of mind*, and have a great *affection* for all my fellow-creatures. I hence ſtrive to prevent any injury to my feelings, or the feelings of others. There is nothing that touches G. Watſon's nice ſenſibility ſo quick, as a neglect on the part of his kind cuſtomers, to ſettle all arrears, before leaving his houſe. With all his benevolence towards his friends, he muſt ſay, that he expects a *reciprocation of favours;* this *indiſpenſable* return is PECUNIARY and IMMEDIATE.

THE HUMMING BIRD.

Light wand'rer of the summer ſky,
Whoſe gloſſy plumes of beauteous dye,
To my charm'd ſight in ſhades unfold,
Each lucid tint beſprent with gold.
Oh lovelieſt of the tribes of air,
To yonder od'rous ſhade repair;
For there the lily ſpreads her charms,
And woos thee to her ſnowy arms:
And there the honey-ſuckle blows,
And proudly ſpreads each rival roſe.
Repoſe the mingled blooms beneath,
And ſounds of ſofteſt muſic breathe;
Attention o'er each ſenſe will ſteal;
Each nerve the tender ſtrain ſhall feel;
Of hapleſs love the tale ſhall tell,
And ev'ry note in its fine ſwell.
To my fond heart thy tale relate,
And mourn perhaps thy tiny mate,
By treach'rous human wiles enſnar'd,
And plac'd within the wiry guard,
To prove of abſence ev'ry pain,
And of loſt liberty complain;
Penſive, yet ſweet; the ſong muſt be,
Of love and ſad captivity.
Oh fly not! quit not yet my ſight,
Still reſt thou little airy ſprite!
For ſure thou art of fairy kind,
And for their uſes wert deſign'd.
Oft haſt thou ſooth'd with plaintive ſtrain
Of Oberon, the jealous pain,
Or near the fair Titania's ear,
Charm'd to repoſe her ev'ry care;
The while her ſportive elfin throng,
Hung round enamour'd of the ſong,
  And when within their green retreat,
In muſic dance at eve's ſoft hour,
  They preſs the turf with tiny feet,
Thou art the minſtrel of their bow'r.

LIFE A STREAM.

As through irriguous vales and ſhadowy groves,
A mildly-murmuring ſtreamlet viewleſs roves,
By verdant borders, wins its winding way,
Eſcaping through the fields in Fairy play;
Till rapid force th'increaſing waters gain,
And mingle with the ſwelling main;

Thus may my devious life ſecurely glide,
Far from Ambition's blood-empurpled tide,
By Riches unoppreſſed, its courſe purſue,
Nor mid Law's vortex be abſorbed from view.
When darkneſs veils my evening's cloſing hour,
And nature yields to Time's reſiſtleſs power,
May Death's cold hand my wearied limbs compoſe,
And kindly grant the welcome Tomb's repoſe.

CHARACTERISTICS.

I AM fond of the converſation of intelligent perſons, and am pleaſed when in their company; but my hopes have often been diſappointed, by the peculiarities of ſome who were preſent; who inſtead of permitting the diſcourſe to flow in its proper and unreſtrained courſe, direct it to a particular channel, for their own gratification, or without dwelling upon any ſubject, digreſs with as much celerity and frequency as Mr. Shandy.

Among the foes to the freedom and pleaſure of converſation are thoſe who obtrude remarks on their own profeſſion and occupation. Is Fulvius preſent—if it be only obſerved as a cauſe of regret, that ſome late violation of the public peace, has paſſed without due puniſhment, he inſtantly interrupts you with an air of joy and impatience, and aſks if you were at court yesterday? "Did you ever here such a verdict as the jury found in the action of Detinue, Peters versus Peterson? I consulted Crok Jaq. and all the reporters, and every one is directly, unequivocally and decidedly in favour of the defendant. I advised his counsel to move for a new trial, or move it to the District by Supersedeas." Or is Medicus in the same mixed company, probably you will hear much about sudorifics, stimulants, sedatives, galvanism, &c. &c. and he will talk in so technical a stile, that you will understand him as little as you would an Hindoo.

Religiosus will continually introduce religious topics, as if it were criminal for a divine to enjoy innocent mirth, or as if he thought like the devotees of old, or the Monks of La Trappe, that the Almighty intended us for no other purposes but to think and talk of death.

Scepticus who has lately read several new treatises, will suffer you to listen to nothing but his comments on the futility of ancient systems. He will deny that the Sun is the source of heat, or the reality of objects. He will contend that men are capable of arriving at such a state of perfection as to render all legal restraints unnecessary, or that perhaps in a century hence, ships will sail under the ocean with as much facility as they at present sail on the surface. He cannot be at rest unless the discourse is controversial, and will remind you of these lines of Hudibras—

Who to their own opinions stand fast
Only to have them claw'd and canvast,

And keep their confciences in cafes
As fiddlers do their crowds and bafes,
Ne'er to be us'd but when they're bent
To play a fit for argument.
Difcufs, and fet a paradox,
Like a ftrait boot upon the ftocks,
And ftretch it more unmercifully
Than Helmont, Montaigne, White or Tully."

Pedanticus is a young man, who has read, or rather fkimmed many books. He has few ideas of his own, and has never fuffered reflection to produce many. He cannot give a reafon for an opinion which he advances. He more refembles a common place book, than any thing I know. His defign is to pafs for a man of reading, genius and tafte, and to attain that character, it has been his practice, to note every paffage that ftrikes his fancy, and get it by rote, and by repeating it in every company often, whether it be applicable or not, he has gained the reputation of great erudition, and a prodigious memory. For his quotations there is no peace. There is no end to them, and whenever he appears, you muft either rudely out-talk him, affront him, or remain in profound filence, for he refembles Aaron's rod, he fwallows up every fubject of difcourfe.

Once when two merchants were fpeaking flightly of the price of tobacco, he exclaimed with a fudden ftart, as if out of a profound reverie, "this reminds me of a ftory I read fome time ago" and then proceeded in the narrative contained in the letters of Lord Lyttleton, of the ſtrange being who joined ſome Engliſhmen at a hunting match.

Frothy is a gentleman rather diverting at firſt, but ultimately as troubleſome as the others. He will not relate the moſt trivial incident, without the action and geſture of a public ſpeaker. He formally and laboriouſly proves facts and poſitions, which no one denies. He will harangue, ten minutes to prove that commerce cannot exiſt, unſupported by agriculture, or that the Virginian partridge commonly ſo denominated, has no reſemblance to the Engliſh bird of the ſame name—with all the volubility of ſuperfluity, and all the vehemence of enthuſiaſm; until he almoſt foams at the mouth, like Gil Blas chopping logic at Oviedo.

THE SAILOR BOY.

Dark flew the ſcud along the wave,
  And echoing thunders rent the ſky;
All hands aloft, to meet the ſtorm,
  At midnight was the boatſwain's cry.

On deck flew ev'ry gallant tar,
  But one—bereft of ev'ry joy;
Within a hammock's narrow bound,
  Lay ſtretch'd this hapleſs Sailor Boy.

Once, when the Boatſwain pip'd all hands,
  The firſt was he, of all the crew,
On deck to ſpring—to trim the ſail—
  To ſteer--to reef--to furl or clue.

Now fell diſeaſe had ſeiz'd a form
  Which nature caſt in fineſt mould;
The midwatch bell now ſmote his heart,
  His laſt, his dying knell it toll'd.

" Oh God !" he cried, and gaſped for breath,
" Ere yet my ſoul ſhall cleave the ſkies,
" Are there no parents—brethren near,
" To cloſe, in death, my weary eyes.

" All hands aloft to brave the ſtorm,
" I hear the wint'ry tempeſt roar ;
He rais'd his head to view the ſcene,
And backward fell to riſe no more.

The morning ſun in ſplendour roſe,
The gale was huſh'd, and ſtill'd the wave ;
The Sea-boy, far from all his friends,
Was plung'd into a wat'ry grave.

But HE who guards the Sea-boy's head,
HE who can ſave, or can deſtroy,
Snatch'd up to Heav'n the pureſt ſoul,
That e'er adorn'd a Sailor Boy.

HOPE.

How ſad is friendſhip's parting hour,
When anxious throbs the boſom ſwell,
How fondly memory lingers o'er
The vaniſh'd forms we love ſo well.
Alas ! what anguiſh rends the heart
In that ſad hour when friends muſt part.

Yet young ey'd hope ſhall turn the view,
A cheering ſcene of bliſs to paint,
When ſtarting tears the eyes bedew,
And all expreſſion ſhall be faint,
To mark the joy with which we greet,
That rapturous hour when friends ſhall meet.

TOASTS.

It has been a controverſy of long ſtanding, and was formerly ſubject to much uncertainty, whether the ancient or the modern philoſophers were ſuperior in wiſdom. For a long time the ancients appeared to have the advantage, and were particularly diſtinguiſhed above their rivals for their choice ſayings and profound maxims, in which much deep thought was expreſſed in few words, and the moſt admirable wiſdom couched in ſhort, pithy ſentences. In thoſe times a philoſopher was the moſt popular, as well as the moſt eſtimable of men. The SEVEN SAGES were almoſt worſhipped as divinities; and few, even among the legiſlators and defenders of the country, were honoured like a *Thales*, a *Plato*, or a *Pythagoras*. Their diſcourſes were liſtened to as oracles, and every word that dropped from their mouths, was recorded in the memories not only of their diſciples, but of the common people. From the receſſes of their academic groves, the people of thoſe days were inſtructed in the principles of morals, the government of the paſſions, and the conduct of life; and the influence of their doctrines was diffuſed through the ſtate with wonderful energy. The methods however of the modern ſages are different from thoſe of the ancient. Inſtead of ſhort ſentences and wiſe ſayings, theſe great profeſſors chiefly hold forth in learned lectures on their own inventions, diverſified with ſpirited invectives, and embelliſhed with a profuſion of fictitious narrative: ſo that truth in their diſcourſes, is ſwallowed up and extinguiſhed in a blaze of wiſdom. The happy aſcendency acquired over the community by theſe great maſters, ſeems to be very nearly equal to that of a *So-*

lon or a *Socrates*. From a view of the eminent advantages of modern philofophy, aided by the art of printing, it appears that the fcale has been for fome time turning in favour of the moderns; and I am inclined to think, that in confequence of one extraordinary modern invention, the queftion of relative fuperiority may now be confidered as at reft. The invention I fpeak of is that of TOASTS. This is a fpecies of philofophy properly modern; being unknown to the Greeks and Romans, though fome fuppofe they have difcovered traces of a practice, in fome refpects fimilar, among the Scythians and Gauls. Unknown to the ancient fchools, it is practifed by all the modern. *Epicurus* was ignorant of it; and yet nothing is more familiar to our modern *Epicureans*. *Cato* the ftoic never dreamt of it, and yet all our modern *Catos* are well verfed in this fcience, and have its maxims in their mouths, on all public occafions. The cuftom of TOASTS has now become a great branch of public inftruction, and is doubtlefs the happieft contrivance ever hit on for inculcating general principles. It completely fills up that interval, where fomething appeared ftill wanting to give us a decided fuperiority over the ancients; and while the prefs, manages all the details of doctrine and difcipline, it is referved to our fage toaft-makers to inftruct and refrefh the public mind with great leading truths, couched in the form of maxims, pointed with the fting of the epigram, and carried directly to the brain by the cheerful glaſs. Admirable union of philoſophy and wit; of the *utile* and the *dulci*; where the ſurly *Diogenes* ſhakes hands with the jolly *Ariſtippus*; and where *Anacreon*, crowned with the olive and vine, ſets to muſic the divine words of *Ariſtotle* and *Plato*, while he pours out libations to *Bacchus*! It is here, at ſome public table, on ſome periodical ſolemnity, that modern ſuperiority appears conſpicuous. On ſome jocund day, the philoſophers of all the ſchools aſſemble to eat, to drink, to hold wiſe diſcourſe, and to utter profound oracles, under the diſcharge of cannon accompanied with loud huzzas. All alike glow with the pride of philoſophy. Men of all ſhades of character join in the expreſſion of ſentiments and maxims worthy of the moſt venerable ſages, and ſeal the truth of them with the daſhing of glaſſes, ſwinging of arms, and cheering huzzas, ſometimes three, ſometimes ſix, and at others nine, according to the importance of the toaſt. A ſet number of wiſe ſayings are firſt toaſted in ſucceſſion. Theſe may be called the primary *circle*; which are uſually prepared with wiſe premeditation by the fathers of the ſchools, and are intended to exhibit their grand ſyſtem of doctrine. Then follows the ſecondary *circle*, vulgarly called VOLUNTEERS. They commonly compriſe ſuch eccentric flaſhes of wiſdom and wit as do not neceſſarily belong to the ſyſtem, and yet ſome times ſerve to grace it wonderfully. Theſe are generally given out by the principal teachers: But ſometimes a very humble tyro in philoſophy will put himſelf forward and let fly a VOLUNTEER, that ſhall aſtoniſh the whole company.—Moſt of theſe toaſts of both ſorts, when analyzed, may be found to contain a *definition*, a *plaudit*, a *prayer* and a *curſe*, or ſome one or more of them; and thus conſtituted, they embrace nearly the whole circle of modern philoſophy. The *definition* expreſſes the pure abſtract doctrine, and diſtinguiſhing dogmas of the academy; the *plaudit* is the incenſe offered up to great men—the *prayer* is the invocation of bleſſing—and the *curſe* what ſhall I ſay? What can it be but the voice of NEMESIS the AVENGER thundering in the ears of the wicked.

If all the TOASTS produced within theſe few years and now extant, were collected by ſome able hand, they might be formed into a code of wiſdom, that would remain immortal. Such a code, digeſted with ſkill and accompanied with a learned commentary, would entitle the compiler to the gratitude of his country, and the praiſe of poſterity. To any one ſo inclined, I could mention a few particular toaſts, which for their richneſs, and point would deſerve a volume, or at leaſt a diſſertation.—While we have a ſufficient number of learned toaſt-makers and patriotic toaſt-drinkers, we ought never to deſpair—We ſhall be ſafe, and philoſophy will flouriſh.

CITY LIFE.

I do not know what you meant when you urged me to viſit town; you told me I ſhould findthe folks very clever, and ſee a great many fine things. I partly believed you; and yeſterday paid a viſit to my wife's half ſiſter, Mrs. Tumbleup, who lives in a houſe jammed in among a great pile of houſes, with a door yard about as wide as a carrot-bed. I got to town about ten o'clock in the morning; and on inquiring of a young fellow where ſiſter lived, he told me to ride down —— ſtreet to the corner of the green, turn round the printing office corner, and after going down —— ſtreet to Mr. ——'s, turn round to my left, there ſhe lived at the firſt houſe on the right hand, juſt at the head of ——ſtreet.— "Much obliged to you," ſays I— "now I know juſt as well as I did before" The puppy began laughing; and I was left to inquire again, or find my way alone. The next man I ſpoke to proved a little more civil; he went with me till he could point out the houſe, and then wiſhed me good morning.

I found ſiſter's folks at breakfaſt, late as it was; they ſeemed glad enough to ſee me, but looked crooked at my old boots; and when I aſked where I ſhould turn the old horſe, they went to the door, and pointing down ſtreet told me that Mr.—'s ſtable was there. I thought this plaguy odd, ſeeing I had come *couſining*: however I began to think I muſt do as I was bid; ſo I ſcrambled away through the mud, and ſaw old Sorrel ſafe in a brick ſtable as big as a meeting houſe.

By the time I had got back to ſiſter's and told wife's and children's love to her, and all that, the clock ſtruck twelve. I was glad to hear it; as I had eaten very early breakfaſt, I began to feel pretty ſharp ſet. However I had my longing for my pains; for not a bit of dinner did I ſee till after two o'clock: we then ſat down to a fine looking piece of beef; but it was not half roaſted; ſo that I roſe from the table about as hungry as I ſat down.

After dinner, I was preparing to go down to the water ſide, to do ſome buſineſs for one of my country neighbours, when ſiſter told me I muſt be back by half paſt four to tea. I obeyed her punctually, and judging from our country practice, I hoped I ſhould find ſome butter-cakes, & ham to make amends for my tough dinner. On my return at the tea hour I found ſeveral young folks at the houſe, who, I ſuppoſe, had come there to ſee ſiſter's eldeſt girl Sophy. When I firſt got in, Sophy got up and made a curtſey, and told them that I was Uncle Bruſhwood, and then told who they all were; but I have forgot now, & beſides, I muſt haſten to tell you about my tea ſcrape—the very pickle of all the plagues which this town-viſit has brought upon me.

After we had waited about half an hour, a little negro came out of the kitchen, with a towel tucked under his chin, lugging along a great tin platter as big as a bread-tray; I ſtared like an owl, and could not tell what to make of it.

The platter had about a peck of tea cups on it all full, befides a fugar pot, and I do not know what elfe: and to top off all, the puppy brought it right to me;—I ftarted back—the young folks tittered like a flock of blackbirds —Sifter fcowled, and called out, "Brother don't drink hyfon—I'd forgot it!" The negro then carried it to the reft: they all took a cup off the platter, and firft put a bit of fugar into it, and then drizzled in about three drops of milk out of a little thing no more like a milk cup than a gridiron. They held their tea cup in their hands and began to fip, red hot as it was: Sifter faid, "You'd better try a cup of our hyfon, brother—I guefs you'll like it." I thought I muft do as I was bid again; and fo I tried to work it as the reft did—I got my cup into my hands: but I am fure it was hotter than the reft; for the very faucer burnt my fingers; and at this moment along came the negro with another platter full of bread and butter—And now, had you feen me, you would have pitied me from your very foul.—In one hand I held the tea cup, as hot as a warming-pan; and in the other a great bit of bread and butter; and for my life I could not tell which way to go to work to eat the one or drink the other.—The fweat ran down my face with mere vexation; but at length, as I was doleful-hungry, I made a greedy bite at my bread: in doing this I tilted the tea-cup in the other hand, fo that fifter's hyfon flopped over on my fingers, and fcalded me fo intolerably, that down went bread and butter, tea-cup and all. The butter fide of the bread fell fpat on the knee of my new velvet breeches; and the hyfon, after fcalding my knee to a blifter, run down my boot to my very toes—Up I jumped and capered about the room, like a bell-fheep; the boys and girls ran out of the room, and left fifter and me together. I wiped my velvets, while fhe was picking up the fragments of my tea-cup; and as fhe carried them into the kitchen, I feized my hat, took a French leave, got old Sorrel from the ftable; and after a ride of five hours I got fafe home at ten o'clock at night.

I need not tell you that our folks were dolefully frightened to fee me return at that hour; that if you happen to call pretty foon, you may fee my new velvets half fpoilt; poor me, limping round the houfe with a fcald on my knee as big as a leather apron, and wife fcolding like a bedlamite, becaufe, as fhe fays, I have difgraced the family—However, if I ever go to town *coufining* again, they may fhip me for a jack-afs to the Weft-Indies.

THE LIMNER.

Egotifm is a fault, from which very few of us are exempt. Newfpaper editors, (I mean thofe only who fometimes write paragraphs) and newfpaper effayifts, in particular, are generally egotifts. In a late excurfion I came acrofs a great egotift, who had the appearance and deportment of a gentleman.

I took my ſeat in the mail-ſtage with five other paſſengers, all ſtrangers to me, and who appeared to be but little acquainted with each other. " It is an uncomfortable mode of travelling," ſaid the egotiſt—" I wiſh I had taken my horſe and ſulky. I have juſt bought one of the beſt horſes and the fineſt ſulky in the ſtate." The ſtage plunged into a deep rut with ſuch violence, that every paſſenger was joſtled from his ſeat—" Curſed roads," exclaimed Egomet after he had recovered his ſeat," it puts me in mind of a droll affair I lately had with the road commiſſioners in our town. I convinced them of the neceſſity of attending to their duty." He then told a long ſtory, of which I heard but very little, and ended with ſaying—" I did not want the money myſelf; I gave it to the poor." We paſſed an elegant houſe. " A fine ſituation," remarked one of the paſſengers. " Tolerable", replied Egomet, " but I would not give my houſe in town for five of it. I got mine, a great bargain, too. I knew how the buſineſs was ſituated; and ſo, took advantage—having all the caſh by me." The next thing that drew our attention, was a carriage, with a lady very tranſparently dreſſed. A word was dropped concerning the *lightneſs* of faſhionable female clothing. " Ay," interrupted Egomet, " the lightneſs of female clothing! that reminds me of a funny joke that I gave a lady of the firſt circle the other evening in company. I offered to bet her my gold watch againſt one kiſs, that every article of her drefs could be drawn through my ring"; holding up his hand and difplaying an elegant diamond ring. A gentleman paffed with a very neat cane. Exclaimed Egomet, " if I did not know pofitively that I left my gold-headed cane locked up at home, I could fwear that man had ftolen it."

You may fuppofe, that by this time, we were all convinced that Egomet, was a man of high ftanding; and, thus far, it would appear that he was exceffively oftentatious.—Circumftances, however, foon arofe, which let us into a knowledge of his true character. Egotifm, monftrous Egotifm, was his foible. He chofe to be the hero of every tale. He wifhed to be thought an adept in every thing. We halted for dinner. A roafted pig was brought on. He carved it with great dexterity. " This pig is badly dreffed," faid he—" I always drefs my own pigs at home. I truft nobody elfe with it." A buxom girl waited upon the table. She ftepped out of the room. " I never fee one of thefe tavern-maids, but I think of a curious frolic I once had"————————She came in and interrupted him. After dinner, we heard a noife, at the door. Two fellows were engaged in boxing. They fought badly, and were parted. " Blundering dogs!" exclaimed Egomet, " I could whip a dozen fuch in ten minutes."

In the afternoon, paffing a large field, we heard the report of a gun. A man had fhot a lark. " I am very fond of that fport," faid

Egomet,—" I have a fowling-piece at home that coſt me forty-ſeven guineas in London; and it was cheap enough too, I never miſſed my mark with her but once, and then ſhe was very foul."—Croſſing a ſtream, we ſaw a boy angling for trout. This gave riſe to a tedious ſtory about angling; and thus the whole day paſſed, no perſon having an opportunity to ſpeak but Egomet; and he carefully avoiding every ſubject but himſelf. As I am ſomething of an egotiſt myſelf, you may conclude, I was not a little pleaſed to find that he had got to his journey's end that evening.

GRAVITY.

SIR ISAAC, that ſurpriſing Man,
Long toil'd, with fruitleſs induſtry,
The univerſal Cauſe to ſcan
Ere he diſcover'd GRAVITY.

At length, one day, by chance, he ſpied
An apple falling from a tree;
Then with triumphant joy he cried—
"The thing I ſought for! GRAVITY."

That all things to their centre tend,
Since NEWTON's days the Learn'd agree;
Prince, Stateſman, Soldier, Lover, Friend,
Has each his point of GRAVITY.

Self-intereſt, ambition, love,
Compoſe the mighty Centres three,
Tow'rds which all human creatures move,
With various pow'rs of GRAVITY.

The Judge, who looks ſo ſternly juſt,
So void of partiality,
Like other atoms of frail duſt,
Is biaſs'd oft by GRAVITY.

The Lawyer, who turns black to white,
And *vice versa*, for a fee,
Acknowledges his magic might,
Depends on *golden* GRAVITY.

The sage Physician, to whose skill,
We trust our lives, if sick we be,
(Let his prescription cure or kill)
Owes half his fame to GRAVITY.

The crafty son of Merchandize
Who labours like the busy bee,—
Both when he sells and when he buys,
Puts on the mask of GRAVITY.

As for the poor hard-toiling race,
It needs no great sagacity,
Their plain propensities to trace,
Without the aid of GRAVITY.

But now I find the theme I sing,
Begins to operate on me—
So, Muse, compose thy weary wing,
And sink in silent GRAVITY.

EPIGRAM.

Once two divines, their ambling steeds bestriding,
In merry mood, o'er Boston neck were riding,
At length a simple structure met their sight,
From whence the felon takes his hempen flight,
When, sailor like, he squares accounts with hope,
His all depending on a single rope——
'Ah where, my friend,' cried one, 'where now were *you*,
Had yonder gallows been allow'd its due?'
'*Where*,' said the other in sarcastic tone,
'Why *where*—but riding into town *alone*.'

THE WITLING AND CLOWN.

A Witling of the dashing kind
Ask'd Hodge if he had seen the wind,
"Yes that I have quoth Hodge I vow,"
'I saw a mighty wind just now."

"You *ſaw it* Hodge? it cannot be,"
Replies the man of repartee.
"Pray what was't like? like" quoth the clown,
"T'was like t' have blown my cottage down!"

EPIGRAM.

A Sportſman not leſs keen than he
For quizzing wit and repartee,
One ſtormy night when winds blew high
Eſſay'd on Teague a *hoax* to try;
Aſk'd what he'd take on diſtant tow'r
To face the pelting blaſt an hour.
"Take" quoth he—for wits too old,
"Take" what take? "why take a——
—————— COLD!!"

IMPROMPTU.

SAYS Thomas to George, "of what uſe is a *key*
"But treaſure from thieves to ſecure?
"What then is't if left in full view at the door,
"But rogues to the plunder t'allure?

To the queſtion of Thomas, George nodded "yes,"
"Why then replied Thomas, I ſee,
"The reaſon why each pretty Miſs *on her breaſt*,
"Conſpicuouſly fixes a *key*."

PROMISES IN BUSINESS.

Being a conſcientious tradeſman, and often put to ſhifts and inconvenience to act with entire ſatisfaction to myſelf and cuſtomers, I have had a deal of concern on my mind to find out ſome method to ſerve both them and myſelf to good purpoſe: for I do not like to tell fibs *unleſs I can gain ſome advantage by it.*

The matter is this—I am apt to promiſe to do work within a fixed period, and ſeldom keep my word. Thus a man beſpeaks a pair of boots, and ſays they muſt be done by that day week; willing to oblige him and secure the job, I assure him, upon the honour of a gentleman, that they shall be ready on the *very day*, knowing, notwithstanding, that I have already engaged more work than I can do in six months. My customer calls, exactly at the time, and were I equally punctual, all would be well—but every body knows that the memory of the man who promises is not so *exact* and *strong* as his to whom the promise is made, and so it happens that I have forgotten the boots—and sure it can be no crime to have a bad memory—and if a man cannot remember, how can he? I make my apology accordingly, and *promise* anew—but as my evil genius will have it, time goes on, and the appointed day comes round again, and still the boots are unfinished; disappointment succeeds to disappointment, until at length my customer grows outrageous, and perhaps abusive.—Now what is to be done? I am desirous of obliging every body, and yet satisfy but few. Dick Trim lately affronted me very much. He came to my shop, with a strip of paper in his hand, on which he had noted down the number of times I had deceived him, and even preserved a record of the very words I had used from time to time—and really alarmed me as he read aloud, before my apprentice boys, the catalogue which he had preserved of my transgressions; and after that he pulled a bible out of his pocket, and backed what he had already done with as many scripture quotations, against liars, as made my very hair ſtand on end ; and in my confuſion, being juſt at that time pounding a bit of ſoal leather, I hit my thumb and bruiſed it ſo violently, that I have not been able to do any work ſince—and ſo, having leiſure, I take the liberty of making matters known to you.

This affair ſorely grieved me awhile, but I took comfort on remembering that as to the *hard ſayings* in the Bible, they were uttered expreſsly againſt the Jews—a ſtiff-necked, perverſe generation—more than *ſix thouſand years* ago ; and even that ſuch of them as are in the Teſtament are *very old*, and almoſt *worn out*. But, as Dick affronted me ſo much, and I did not wiſh him to make any more ſuch unmannerly viſits, I got rid of him by making my boys finiſh his boots and take them home ; and I am reſolved, let what will happen, he ſhall never enter my ſhop again; for I will let him know I have as rich relations, and am as good a man, and come of as good a family, and ſupport as good a reputation as he, and am not aſhamed to ſpeak my mind to him, nor meet him any day—only let him keep his ſcrips of paper and his bible to himſelf—and not come troubling his neighbours, who do not want any of his reading.

But I do profeſs, what with one, and what with another, they almoſt put me beſide myſelf. A "cute" old gentleman in our ſtreet, knowing how my cuſtomers vex me with their unreaſonableneſs in expecting me to keep my word, whether it ſuits me or not, has recommended me to get a thing made, which will be a fort of wheel of fortune, and which fhall go flowly round, by internal clock work. To this wheel I am to have as many prizes as I have cuftomers, and as many blanks as I choofe; and when a prize is drawn againft any one's name, the fortunate adventurer fhall have his work done immediately. The advantage, he fays, will be here; that all ftanding an equal chance there will be lefs grumbling among the difappointed, each will be fortunate *fome* day—and I fhall fave my poor brains numberlefs tormenting quandaries, and my tender confcience fome twitches and qualms. At firft, I thought his propofal a piece of queer impudence, or waggery; but having confidered the matter, I am inclined to think well of it, believing it may prove a *convenience*; and would alfo recommend it to the notice of my brother mechanics, and to merchants and others, who have occafion to make and to break a deal of promifes, when dunned either for work or for money; for, it will prove a faving of time, and keep a man from telling fo many fibs; and when any one calls for an anfwer, let him look to the *wheel*, and not bother the mafter of the fhop, who will, of courfe, take care to make the machine move flowly and have a plenty of blanks.

It was but laft week that a merchant's apprentice, a pert, forward chap, who left his boots to be repaired, only a few months before, brought his marking pot and brufh, to my houſe, and receiving the uſual anſwer, without further ado made a long black ſtroke quite acroſs my ſhop wall, and ſaid that every time he came there after, and I told him a lie, he would do the ſame. As I hate ſuch doings, I plainly told him it was fooliſhneſs, and would anſwer no purpoſe, for, ſays I, you will ſoon black the wall all over, and what will you do then? "Do! ſaid the ſaucy youth—why then I will begin to mark with white, and after that with black again, until you get my boots done."

Now I have no reliſh for ſuch nonſenſe, and ſhall abominate his naſty markings, and would almoſt as ſoon have another viſit from Dick Trim, with his ſlip of paper and bible; for they will be like a ſtanding reproach to me every time I look up, and alſo tempt ſome of my other cuſtomers to be equally miſchievous, and if any one ſhould take it in his head to cut a notch on ſome part of my ſhop every time I diſappointed him, I ſhould ſoon ſee an end of ſhop and all, and be literally cut out—and yet I do not know but I am threatened with a worſe evil or plague than them all; for Joe Twiſt ſaid, but laſt night, "Simon, I have called ſo often for the ſhoes I left here to be mended, ſome months ago, that I am reſolved I will call but *once* more."

"Fellow, ſays I, why I do not care if you never call again (for I had his ſhoes and could loſe nothing as I thought)—but he anſwered me, very coolly, that call *once* more he would, and bring his taylors work with him, and not ſtir from my houſe, but *eat*, *drink* and *ſleep* with me, till his ſhoes were mended! Should others hear of Joe's threat, and be like minded, I ſhall ſoon be eaten out of houſe and home, and buſineſs too, and therefore I am determined to do ſomething "right off hand" to get rid of theſe *peſterments;* ſo I have been thinking, that, if ſo be you will get a wheel made for me, and ſend it to my ſhop, I will put it up and try it, and then enter into a *promiſe* to make you a pair of boots.

N. B.—An apprentice wanted; none need apply but of *good character and ſharp*; *fit to look after the wheel.*

CHARACTERISTICS.

Fortunately for mankind, and the harmony of ſociety, our taſtes and inclinations are as various and as different, as our faces and forms. Although we all unite in one great object of purſuit, and all our wiſhes and exertions have happineſs for their end and aim, ſtill, our ideas of the proper means to attain it, are always diſſimilar, and often oppoſite in the extreme. "All Nature's difference, keeps all Nature's peace," ſays the moſt ſenſible of the Engliſh bards. The cauſe of this difference is referred by metaphyſicians and moraliſts to the natural diſpoſitions, talents or bias of the mind, or, to mental habits and propenſities, acquired by education or other accidental circumſtances. But it is not my buſineſs to ſolve this wonderful enigma. In hot weather, it is better to make ourſelves eaſy, and to take logical dogmas for granted, than to puzzle our brains with attempts to penetrate the grand arcana of the mind, or to discover the reason, why it is a useless employment to dispute concerning the difference and variety of our tastes.

My friend *Dan Spondee*, was of opinion, that the great secret, whereby a man may gain universal esteem, consists in gravity. He accordingly marched on through life with a solemn step and serious countenance and descended into the grave with the "austere composure" of a disciple of Diogenes. Peace to his ashes! Yet I have often smiled at his whim, and pitied his affectation, for he had assumed a character that "sat awkwardly about him," and which encumbered and embarrassed him most grievously. His taste was formed very early in life, by living with an old gentleman, for whom, he entertained a degree of respect, that rendered the ancient's words oracular, and even the nod of his head, a subject of high importance. Dan beheld the wig and scarlet cloak of his venerable friend with superstitious awe. The gold-headed cane, was in his opinion an emblem of sanctity and honour, not exceeded by the sceptre of a monarch. If Dan swore by the Morocco slippers of Justus, he esteemed his oath as sacred as the oath of the Celestials by Styx, which bound the Gods with an indispensible obligation. But alas, how vain are human wishes! How are our inclinations and our means at variance ! Poor Dan now lies mouldering in an obſcure corner of a church-yard ; not a ſtone marks his humble grave, and when his few ſurviving friends are no more, Oblivion's ſable cloud ſhall ſettle on his turf, and his name and remembrance be utterly forgotten.

Dick Beeſwax, has a bundle of habits ſticking to him, which will encumber him through life, and prove continual impediments in his progreſs towards the goal of his ambition. His taſte is for the fine arts ; his aim to excel in them all ; and the conſequence is, he is perfect in none. This is a common character ; yet Dick has ſome ſingularities worthy of notice. Does he hear a lady play a number of airs, he is ſure to applaud the worſt. He talks with gravity to children, diſcourſes concerning the belles-letters with a mechanic, and prattles about love and romances with a judge. He once affronted a party of modeſt and reſpectable females, by quoting ſome *ſingle* entendres from a foreign publication, and in defence of his conduct, paid a fine *compliment* to the underſtandings of his offended auditors by declaring, that, the charm of novelty, was like the mantle of charity, and would effectually cover a multitude of ſins. Dick, however, is *diſtinguiſhed*, and he thinks himſelf admired. This is enough for him, and vain would be the taſk of endeavouring to correct his manners, by diſputing with him about the evil tendency of his taſte.

But, in order to prove, that each man has a doating partiality to his own tafte, it is not neceffary to feek for fingular and ftriking examples among the whimfical and eccentric of our fpecies. A candid examination will convince every one of the truth. Shakefpeare fays, with that propriety of thought, and ftrength of expreffion, by which all his writings are characterifed, that " our judgments are like our watches; not two agree, yet each believes his own."

CHARACTERISTIC.

To catch the " manners living as they rife," and to delineate them with a faithful pencil, have employed the labour and attention of the moft diftinguifhed ornaments of literature and fcience. This fubject though varioufly agitated, has not become ftale and uninterefting — In the revolution of time, it prefents to our view many diftinct and difagreeing phafes, interfperfed with individual objects of fufficient importance, to attract our attention and intereft our feelings. To examine and defcribe thofe appearances as they occur in fucceffion; to pourtray the manners of a people, or the character of a nation, is the bufinefs of the impartial and philofopick hiftorian, while to difcufs the cuftoms of a particular place, or the peculiarities of an individual character, falls more exclufively within the province of the obferving effayift; who will always be fortunate if his felection fhould be fo happy, his imagination fo rational & excurfive, and his ſtyle ſo poliſhed and correct, as to enchain the attention of the reader even for a few minutes.

In our intercourſe with the world, it is neceſſary that our habits and manners, ſhould assimilate themſelves to thoſe of the community in which we exiſt. The collective ſenſe of mankind has every where erected a general ſtandard; the admeaſurements of which are to direct us in caſes of doubt and dilemma.

In this reſpect, cuſtom is literally a tyrant; that which has been moſt extenſively ſanctioned, is certainly preferable. It is as cogent an argument in favour of a particular action, as it is in ſupport of the meaning of a given word, to ſay that practice has uniformly eſtabliſhed it. Who is there possessed of a mind ſo penetrating and a judgment ſo infallible as to juſtify him in denouncing all the world beſide; and in aſſerting that his conduct alone is correct and defenſible.

An oſtentatious ſingularity of manner, the invariable indication, of unbounded vanity and a contracted ſoul, is not more reprehenſible than that aſſumed vulgarity of manners, (ironically termed philoſophick) which affects to deride the opinion of the world.

Curius was a man of rather diminutive ſtature, his form poſſeſſed neither the elegance of proportion, nor the grace that is the conſequence of activity; in fact, it was" juſt not ugly." His face devoid both of ſymmetry and regularity of feature, was like his body deficient in maſculine lineaments, and his countenance, though it wanted intelligent expreſſion, had a half-cunning ſelf-ſatisfied caſt, that at once introduced you to his character : and if he ſmiled, your acquaintance with it might be ſaid to be complete.

Had Curius known the celebrated Cheſterfield, he would have regarded him with the moſt abhorrent antipathy; infinitely would he have preferred the awkward ruſticity of a clown to the feminine refinement of the accompliſhed Lord. Roman integrity and Roman simplicity were the eternal themes of his eulogy. I have ſeen him thrill with rapture while deſcanting on the character of Cincinnatus, and if the elegancy of modern times, preſented itſelf in contraſt to his imagination, he would execrate and revile it until overpowered by the conflicting sensations of anger and contempt Should a female wiſh to enſnare him, ſhe would much more certainly inſure ſucceſs by aſſuming the manner and attire of the artleſs tenant of the Hamlet, than by arming herſelf with the bow and quiver of the Cyprian youth, or the Ceſtus of beauty. To have dreſſed and acted in the cuſtomary way, would have been to him the moſt diſtreſſing and mortifying puniſhment. Sooner would he have paſſed for a thief than a faſhionable man. Rather than to have had a brilliant ſeal or a golden key appended to his watch, he would have foregone the uſe of it. In conſequence of this, poor Curius, though highly eſteemed by his friends, (for he had many truly valuable qualities) was pointed at, even ſometimes hiſſed by the boys as he walked along the ſtreets; and to the girls he was a ſource of eternal amuſement. Indeed his remarks, when combined with his truly original manners, had ſomething ſo peculiarly ſingular in them, that they would have put to rout the moſt determined gravity. With the higheſt zeſt for the pleaſures of ſocial converſation—he was frequently diſappointed in his enjoyment. Frequently have I ſeen him leave the moſt delightful circles, diſguſted and chagrined with an half formed determination to ſeclude himſelf for ever.—From theſe unfortunate circumſtances a heart of the moſt ineſtimable value, and a mind that was almoſt amiable in its defects, became nearly inſulated. He might be truly termed a microcoſm. He was ſo disjoined by his habits and manners from the great ſtructure of ſociety as to form no part of the building which he ſeemed deſtined to ornament and ſupport.

MY MOTHER.

WHO fed me from her gentle breaſt,
And huſh'd me in her arms to reſt,
And on my cheek ſweet kiſses preſt?
My Mother.

When ſleep forſook my open eye
Who was it ſung ſweet lullaby,
And rock'd me that I ſhould not cry?
My Mother.

Who ſat and watch'd my infant head
When ſleeping on my cradle bed,
And tears of ſweet affection ſhed?
My Mother.

When pain and ſickneſs made me cry,
Who gaz'd upon my heavy eye,
And wept for fear that I ſhould die?
My Mother.

Who dreſs'd my doll in clothes ſo gay,
And taught me pretty how to play,
And minded all I'd got to ſay?
My Mother.

Who ran to help me when I fell,
And would ſome pretty ſtory tell,
Or kiſs the place to make it well?
My Mother.

Who taught my infant lips to pray,
To love God's holy Book and Day,
And walk in wiſdom's pleaſant way?
My Mother.

And can I ever ceaſe to be
Affectionate and kind to thee,
Who was ſo very kind to me?
My Mother.

Ah! no, the thought I cannot bear,
And if God pleaſe my life to ſpare,
I hope I ſhall reward thy care,
My Mother.

When thou art feeble, old and grey,
My healthy arm ſhall be thy ſtay,
And I will ſooth thy pains away,
My Mother.

And when I ſee thee hang thy head,
'Twill be my turn to watch thy bed,
And tears of ſweet affection ſhed,
My Mother.

For God who lives above the ſkies,
Would look with vengeance in his eyes,
If I ſhould ever dare deſpiſe
My Mother.

FRAGMENT.

MONITOR.

A futile, inconcluſive argument.——
Give me plain ſenſe and unaffected truth;

I disbelieve your fancied, rapturous joys,
Illusions all. Romance and Poesy!—
Vile impositions, formed to cheat mankind
Of money, time, and manly energy.
Oh mention them no more, I hate the sound.

AUTHOR.

'Tis sordid love of gold debases you,
Absorbing every soul-ennobling passion.
The tear of sympathy, the god-like wish,
Th' impassioned glow of sensibility,
That, while it views the miseries of man,
Affords alleviation; these delights
You never knew.

MONITOR.

Nor is it my desire.
The sympathies, the sensibilities,
The tender woes, which affectation feigns,
Are foreign to my heart. I reprobate
That soft, disgusting imbecility,
Which quite emasculates our faculties.
No more pursue deceitful vanities,
Imagination's fascinating pleasures,
Or sportive fancy's fond, illusive wiles;
Abandon such allurements of the mind;
Be my companion, quit these vain delights;
Come, tread with me preferment's flow'ry path,
And leave to madmen Fiction's airy flights.

AUTHOR.

Cease, tempter, cease to censure my pursuits;
For intellectual joys are permanent
And pure. Deceptive, fleeting are the gifts
Of affluence, of elevated station.
When smiling hours exhilarate our lives,
For Fiction's charms increase endeared enjoyments;
Or when calamity diffuses gloom,
And wretchedness; then let imagination
Waft us o'er mountains, groves, and vales of bliss,
Communicating pleasures unalloyed.

Far lovelier the tints, which Fancy's power
Diſplays to pale misfortune's mental view,
Than all the ſcenes of dark reality ;
Far lovelier joyous day's irradiant hues,
Than melancholy night's obſcurity.

THE LITTLE COT.

ROUGH Boreas now comes forth,
Far from the diſtant North,
And coldly whiſtles round our humble dome ;
But we, ſecure, admire
Our comfortable fire,
Poſſeſing joy, a friend, and happy home ;
We look around, and bleſs our obſcure lot,
Pleaſure and mirth within our little Cot.

While ſome poor helpleſs form,
Doom'd to the pelting ſtorm ;
Cold and dejected wanders o'er the plain,
Made white by fleecy ſnow,
Where ſtreams no more can flow,
Being bound by tyrant froſt's deſpotic reign ;
How he would bleſs his comfortable lot,
Cheerful and warm within our little Cot.

The ſocial ſong is ſung,
While mute is ev'ry tongue ;
Attention's paid to ev'ry vocal ſtrain.
That ſpeaks of battle's rage,
Of heroes who engage
In murd'rous war, and ſeek ſuperior fame.
We praiſe each feat and well conſtructed plot,
While ſeated happy in our little Cot.

Toil fills each paſſing day,
But when it fades away,
Nocturnal pleaſures, rural ſports ſucceed :
We envy not the great
Who ride in coach and ſtate,
Convinc'd our life's felicity indeed,

Peace, plenty, innocence, are all our lot,
And ſweet contentment in our little Cot.

WAR AND PEACE.

WHEN the ſweet-ſmiling Moon rolls her orb through
the ſky,
And the white clouds are flying afar,
I rove
Through the grove,
While no danger is nigh,
And with penſiveneſs utter a heart-broken ſigh,
As I think on the horrors of War.

O'er the earth, hoſtile armies, in battle, around
Spread deſtruction and carnage afar;
While blood,
Like a flood,
Stains with crimſon the ground;
And the groans of the dying, unnumber'd reſound;
Oh! the mercileſs horrors of War!

Heav'n haſten the time when the battle ſhall ceaſe,
And dread terror be baniſh'd afar;
When love
Like the dove
With the Emblem of Peace,
Shall return to the Ark, and that wretchedneſs ceaſe,
Which embitters the horrors of War.

Then the vulture Deſpair, from Miſery fly,
And no ill-omen'd grief-bearing ſtar,
Shall keep
Gentle ſleep
From the fatherleſs eye,
Nor diſturb the repoſe of the brave, with a ſigh
For the wide waſting horrors of War.

LINES

Occasioned by overhearing an answer of one of the Turkish Captives in New-York to some questions respecting his wife. The words were :—" She look for me every day ; but I no come."

NOW o'er the darkly heaving main,
Her jet eye bright in sorrow roves,
And still she seeks, but seeks in vain,
The sweling sail of him she loves.

A sail appears—her heart beats high,
And from the lofty terrace see,
The signal flutt'ring to the sky,
Which should have been my guide to thee.

The whisp'ring breeze enamour'd, plays,
'Midst each perfum'd and silken fold,
And hast'ning low, the sun's last rays
Illume each tint, with brilliant gold.

Alas ! in vain—no answ'ring sigh,
Proclaims Abdullah's glad return ?
Yet, as 'twere Mecca's sainted shrine,
Still dost thou watch the surge, and mourn.

Retire, my love ! the ev'ning dew
Will damp thy tresses, as they play ;
Retire ! and in thy dreams review
His image, who is far away.

THE IDLER.

A hungry wolf is not more dangerous to a flock of sheep, nor a cat to a mouse, than an *idle* man is to the industry of a neighbourhood.

A pleasant story is told of a fellow who went into a town-market, and placing himself in the centre thereof that he might be seen by the butchers, began to gape wide his jaws and yawn in a formal manner; when (ſo great is the power of ſympathy) the whole of the butchers, as they ſtood at their ſhambles, began to gape and yawn in concert.

This tale, whether true or falſe, is explanatory of the influence of an *idler* on thoſe within his ſphere. The induſtrious citizen, who views his neighbour lolling indolently in his porch, begins immediately to draw envious compariſons. 'Behold,' ſaith he; 'mine is a life of labour; I toil, and I ſweat; but yonder man, who is no richer than I am, pleaſantly paſſeth away his time, puffing the cares and diſquietudes of the world from him with ſmoke from a ſegar, or an old tobacco-pipe: I will go and do likewiſe.' Fooliſh man! thou hadſt better not.

In the midſt of ſummer, when the meridian rays of the Sun oppreſs by their intenſe heat the whole animal creation, who is there that has not experienced the attractive power of an *idler* as he loiters in the ſhade? "Lo!" crieth one; "there is *Lawrence* ſeated under the ſhadow of yonder building; doubtleſs it is a cool and a refreſhing place; come let us go and ſit with *Lawrence*." Friend, if thou valueſt life, thou hadſt better mind thy buſineſs, and purſue an object more eſtimable than pleaſure and eaſe; that will be profitable to thyſelf, to thy family, thy friends, or the public.

Attracting by his evil example a circle of diſciples around him, the *idler* becomes an important perſonage. He is the inſtrument of VICE and worketh wonders: The group whom the evil influence of his indolence hath collected together, amuse themselves with trifles; serious and weighty topics of discourse are too burthensome for their mind; quips, cranks, and legends only are palatable. When the chief *idler* hath spread himself upon the portico, *Nathan* the carpenter espying him leaveth his work, and flies to him just to have a little chat. Then comes *David* the smith; and *Ephraim* the hatter; and *Barnaby* the scribe. The tale passeth round, and every one is merry—Meanwhile the Sun journeyeth to the west, and the work of *Nathan* and *David* and *Ephraim*, and *Barnaby*, is neglected; and when called for, it is unfinished. Verily if they continue under the enchantment of the *idler*, poverty will overtake them.

The *idler* is generally mischievous: He playeth off tricks, and is always contriving stratagems to render some one ridiculous, in order that he may have a subject for merriment. He gathereth on his memory the tattle of the day, and retaileth it in scraps to regale his companions. A joke is his supreme delight: and ribaldry his highest diversion.

Wherever these *idlers* abound, health, wealth, and virtuous morals decay. They gather together corrupt youth, and lead them very often to drunkenness. Full many a promising citizen has fallen a prey to the vicious practices of an *idler*.

Beware of him, therefore; for his is the

road to poverty, and the path that leadeth to misery.

NOBODY'S COMPLAINT.

Aye Nobody—and why not?—As for my single self, I see no just cause or impediment why my name and a newspaper should not be joined together, in the tenuous bands of scribling wedlock, as any other body. There is your Busybody, and your Anybody, and your Somebody, and your Everybody—each in his turn run the race of typographical notoriety; whilst I, who boast a pedigree as great, nay, being eldest of the Body family, of greater antiquity than either, am doomed to grope through the labyrinths of mere verbal consequence. Against such an unequal distribution of rights among brethren of the same principle, and of the same texture, I solemnly protest and more especially against the unhallowed profanation of my good name and charactre. Yea, in my own proper capacity I am resolved to defend both; and, contrary to a certain dogma of philosophers, prove, that I, *No* body, possess the fundamental principles of a *real* body, or matter! inasmuch as I occupy *space*, to wit, length and breadth; though as for *depth* I do not contend.

All my enemies—that is, all the world, utter daily calumnies on my fame—Ought I not then to avenge it?

Says Goody Gaffer, 'John! you will be the ruin of your family—carousing it every night: Who was with you laſt night?' 'With me, mother—nobody!'

Little maſter lets fall a glaſs—it breaks—in comes the nurſe —'Sirrah! who did this?' 'Nobody!'

Miſs has a lover—he ſtays late—next morning a female friend gets a hint of it—*for the balmy breeze whiſpers theſe things to the ſex*—She calls on her, and after ſome chit-chat, dryly obſerves, 'why really Melinda, you ſeem indiſpoſed to-day—I fear you reſted ill laſt night——Oh! while I think of it, prithee what rude creature kept you up ſo unſeaſonably?' 'Rude! me up! (ſtammering and crimſoning) why—why—Nobody!'—when I'd ſwear by the ghoſt of a ſhadow that I never ſaw the huſſy.)

Obadiah Primroſe is a beau: he ſtruts about big with himſelf; wears a frizzled crop, bolſter cravat, three inch veſt, ſack pantaloons, Suwarrow boots with taſſels; carries a ſix inch rattan, and viſits the ladies.

The other day, in a large circle, whilſt officiouſly preſſing a lady to take ſome lemonade, which ſhe had repeatedly declined, he turned a part of it upon her gown. A friend, who ſat near, but did not at the moment ſee the tranſaction, ſhortly after obſerving her gown ſoiled, inquired who did it? Maria, twiſting up the tip of her noſe, and glancing at Obadiah, replied with burleſque ſolemnity, 'Alas! *Nobody*;" What an inſult to my name!

A young woman makes a falſe ſtep; it

leaks out, all the world whiſpers, 'Whoſe is it; whoſe is it? and the ſame world maliciouſly anſwers, '*Nobody knows!*'' Scoundrels! when I know nothing at all about it.

TO CERTAIN LADIES OF W———,

and its vicinity, the petition of the word

"SHOULD,"

HUMBLY SHEWETH

That your petitioner has, from time immemorial, by the united ſuffrage of all the Lexicographers, Dictionary-makers, Grammarians, and other word mongers, who have exerciſed juriſdiction over the Engliſh language, been denominated, claſſed and arranged among the auxiliary verbs—and that all the aſſiſtance which your petitioner has been called upon to render to the principal verbs, to which he has from time to time been attached, has been in caſes, where duty was implied, doubt expreſſed, or a queſtion aſked —As, for example;

"Your ladyſhip *ſhould* ſpeak correctly."
"If your ladyſhip *ſhould* ſpeak correctly."
"*Should* your ladyſhip ſpeak correctly?"

For the verification of theſe ſtatements, your petitioner refers your ladyſhips to the works of *Lowth*, *Perry*, *Ash*, *Sheridan*, *Johnson*, *Lindley Murray*, and others.

Yet, notwithſtanding the buſineſs of your petitioner was thus definite and confined, he has of late been frequently placed in ſituations awkward and uncomfortable, and which he was never deſigned to fill. With much humility, your petitioner ventures to add, that your ladyſhips have been greatly implicated in the abuſes he has ſuſtained. Your petitioner, May it pleaſe your ladyſhips, is far from intimating, that you have thus abuſed him, with an *intent* to wrong and injure—No; he knows that you have acted by the inſtigation of a certain determined foe to all correctneſs of diction, known by the different names of *Ton, Faſhion, and modern refinement.*

Your petitioner will proceed to ſtate the particular caſe, in which he conſiders himſelf principally aggrieved. It has become faſhionable, when a remark is to be retailed *ſecond hand*, and it is needleſs to ſtate, how often *your ladyſhips* have occaſion for that mode of ſpeech—it has become toniſh in ſuch caſes to forego the old, homely, eſtabliſhed form and to introduce your poor petitioner—thus laying on him a grievous and unprecedented burden; as, *ex. gra.* inſtead of "I heard that Mr.——ſaid &c."—"I heard Mr. ——— *ſhould* ſay, &c, &c."—thus conveying an idea not that Mr.——*made* the remark, but that he *ought* to have made it. When the object is ſimply to ſtate a declaration actually made by Mrs.———, your petitioner cannot perceive the neceſſity of ſuch a mode of ſpeech as the following, "*I heard Mrs.* ——*ſhould* declare." Nay, ſo irritated is your petitioner with his perſonal injuries, and ſo anxious for the purity of that diction, of which he forms a humble member, that he does not heſitate to declare ſuch perverſions of language, groſsly ridiculous, monſtrouſly affected and abſolutely abſurd.

Your petitioner, therefore, humbly prays, that his caſe may be taken into conſideration and that your ladyſhips would be graciouſly pleaſed to correct this procedure—and,

He, as in duty bound ſhall ever pray—

TRUTH.

Truth may juſtly be defined a conformity of words with thoughts and actions. When, the queſtion is aſked, "Can you tell me the truth," every one readily anſwers in the affirmative.

The truth is ſo ſimple and eaſy to be ſpoken, that the child, the poor and illiterate, have the ſame ability in this reſpect, as the man of mature years, the affluent, and the learned.

All acknowledge the general utility of truth, and their indiſpenſible obligation to adhere to its ſacred injunctions; therefore it is no wonder it finds ſo many friends and advocates.

I will enumerate a few claſſes and profeſſions of men conſpicuous for *this virtue*, and at the ſame time, I would have others who are not particularly mentioned, conſider themſelves not leſs ſkilful in this *uſeful art*.

The farmer has live ſtock and produce to ſell The purchaſer comes, and begins his inquiries. The farmer begins to tell the *truth*. His horſes are ſound, wind and limb.

His oxen are excellent for bufinefs, gentle, eafy to manage, and never leaped over a fence two feet high. His cows are firft rate for milk, and each fills a pail. His butter was all made in autumn, and his cheefes are all new milk.

The buyer depreciates every thing, and can afford to give but fmall prices. The market, fays he, was extremely dull laft week, articles fold for almoft nothing, and, the probability is, they will continue to fall.

No fooner has the cuftomer entered the merchant's fhop, than he begins to hear the *truth*. The vender makes a fpecious introduction, mentions his fine affortment, and the good quality and cheapnefs of his goods. His gin is all Holland gin—his brandy unadulterated, all French brandy and very high proof. His rum is all Santa Croix, excellent flavour, and totally unacquainted with *New England*. His molaffes never drank any water, and his bohea tea never, by any accident, got mingled with his fouchong and hyfon. His broadcloaths are fuperfine; very cheap, and will laft forever. His calicoes, cambrics, chintzes and vefts, &c, are beautiful figures, and the neweft fafhions.

In civil controverfies, the party aggrieved haftens to the lawyer and tells the encroachment of his neighbour. Now, fays the plaintiff, hear all the circumftances, view the merits of the caufe, and give me faithful advice. He efpoufes the caufe with friendly enthufiafm, and promifes to fpeak impartially. He begins to tell the *truth.* The caſe is plain — you have been injured, your rights infringed, and the termination of the ſuit will certainly be favourable. The trial commences, and the attorney is extremely happy to ſay that the merits of the cauſe which he advocates, perfectly coincide with his private opinion. Then witneſſes advance, mount the ſtand and ſwear harmonious truths by wholeſale.

Tailors and ſhoe-makers have, generally, a wonderful knack at ſpeaking the truth.

Strolling beggars and bankrupts are famous for the truth. The honeſt beggar has lately been caſt away at ſea, or he was a faithful ſoldier in the revolutionary war, and was wounded fighting for his country.!!

The bankrupt has failed in trade He has always been induſtrious, and managed with prudence and diſcretion. He has not ſpent his money at theatres—he has not attended balls and aſſemblies—he has not frequented brothel houſes, he has not followed gambling—he has not been extravagant:—*but he has been unfortunate!* He finds his debts exceed his capital, and cloſes buſineſs. He is *willing;* nay, very particular, to ſurrender to his creditors *all* his money and effects.

And now, I have mentioned a few claſſes of men " valiant for the truth." You have been made acquainted with their merits and you know their wiſhes. You know, likewiſe, that " truth is the firſt ingredient in converſation"---a neceſſary requiſite in legal proceedings and commercial intercourſe, and the beſt friend of Rulers and people. I have dwelt on the truth and nothing but the truth, and, preſume the evidence adduced in behalf of the above characters is ſufficiently explicit, and that you are ripe for a deciſion. I now put the final queſtion whether you will give full credence to their declarations.

If it be your minds, to believe the *farmer*, *merchant*, *lawyer*, and *others*, you will pleaſe to ſay *Aye*. Gentlemen of a different opinion will ſay *No*.

TALE.

Reclin'd upon a bed of down,
(From ſome ſad debtor ruthleſs torn)
The lawyer cloſ'd his wearied eyes:
Intreating ſleep, grown coy, his reſt to crown,
That with the early ſun's upriſe
He might his wonted path purſue
Where orphans goods attract his eager view,
Whoſe ſpoils already half his houſe adorn!
And where by potent aid of pliant law
He may their little all in his deep vortex draw.

Sudden a ray of diſtant light
Invades the doubly cloſ'd receſs;
His hov'ring ſlumbers put to flight,
And with increaſing blaze, his ſight oppreſs.
His curtain opes! a form whoſe look
His guilty ſoul with horror ſhook,
Faſt by his ſide in blood-ſtain'd robes appears,
And in his quivering hand a dazzling mirror rears!

"Doſt thou not know me? ah, full ſoon
Shall we terrfic converſe hold,
Unleſs thou grant'ſt my righteous boon
And quit thy cruel thirſt of gold!"

Slowly he rais'd his drooping head,
And to the viſion, trembling, thus he ſaid,
" Who art thou! and what mighty ſacrifice
Requir'ſt my paſſport to the ſhades of peace?"

" My name is Concience! oft in vain
I ſtrove to touch your flinty heart;
But when at length acceſs I gain,
Think not too lightly I depart?
'Tis reſtitution! I demand!
May that dread word ſtill thunder in your ear,
Till it unclench your yet unſparing hand,
And of your crimes in part my records clear.

" Behold! where in this mirror true,
Yon injur'd woman fainting lies!
Her helpleſs orphans, robb'd by you,
Have ſent to Heav'n their plaintive cries!
God heard them! and commiſſion'd me
Still on your midnight vigils to attend;
Till you his high avenging arm ſhould ſee,
Or, by reſtoring, make your Judge your friend!

" See further in that gloomy jail,
Your aged victim hopeleſs pines!
Nor aught his recent plunder can avail,
While famine, ſickneſs, aid your dark deſigns!
The little your rapacious hand
Has failed to reach, your greedy eyes allure;
And Death, that little to ſecure,
Awaits, prepared to ſtrike, at your command!
Haſte then! make reſtitution! ſet him free!
Or in a louder voice you yet will hear from me."

THE CONTEST.

'Twas in a lone ſequeſter'd wood,
Cloſe by the Miſſiſſippi's ſide,
Where genial zephyrs fann'd the flood,
Or ſkimm'd the ſurface of the tide:

A Mock-Bird, 'midſt the feather'd throng,
Tun'd his glad notes to mirth and love:

The banks re-echoed to the fong,
  And fill'd with melody the grove.

When from a myrtle's branches gay,
  With beauty join'd, with fragrance bleft;
Sweet Philomela rais'd her lay,
  And thus the lift'ning gale addrefs'd:

" Now tranquil is the winding fhore,
  And ftill the daified meadows feem,
Save where the dafhing of the oar,
  Sounds on the Miffiffippi's ftream.

Or where the Mock-Bird, perch'd on high,
  With rapture fills the fhady dale;
With me let him the conteft try,
  To charm the much lov'd peaceful vale?"

Then thus began where breezes figh'd,
  Amongft the willows of the brook;
The Mock-Bird with a confcious pride,
  And the foft, daring challenge took;

MOCK-BIRD.

" See, fee, the rofe expands his bloom,
  To fcent th' ambient air around;
But foon fhall meet an haplefs doom,
  And drooping prefs the dewy ground.

Thus all muft fade and leave this grove,
  Where milder funs difplay their beams;
Where temperate pleafure loves to rove,
  And vifit oft the murm'ring ftreams."

NIGHTINGALE.

" Behold, the fun reclines his head,
  To fink beneath yon weftern hill;
The evening fky is ftreak'd with red,
  And fmoothly glides each limpid rill.

The lily's fnowy beauties fpread,
  To court awhile the vivid breeze;
Whilft bloffoms mingled odours fhed,
  Far fcenting from a thoufand trees."

MOCK-BIRD.

"But look around where fable night,
With raven wing leads on the hours?
Homeward each warbler bends his flight,
To feek repofe in leafy bow'rs.

And from the mofs clad foreft, hark!
Faint echo's diftant notes rebound;
Roam through the regions of the dark,
And foft refpond a feebler found."

NIGHTINGALE.

"Now darts the moon her filver ray,
See how it gilds yon ivied grot;
The gentle ftreamlets ling'ring ftray,
As loth to quit this lonefome fpot.

Safely now couch'd each warbler fits,
No agile pinions fkim the fky;
Save where the hateful fcreech owl fits,
And yields a tunelefs feeble cry."

Thus Philomela pour'd her note,
Melodious on the night's dull ear;
Till emulation quell'd her throat,
Scarce can the mufe withold a tear.—

Too weak fo long to urge the ftrain,
Eternal darknefs fhades her eyes;
O'er-fpent, fhe falls upon the plain,
Then faintly ftruggling, breathlefs dies.

There oft the Mock-Bird tells the tale,
And plaintively bewails her doom;
When fofter breathes the genial gale,
To cheer him in the mournful gloom.

E'er fince, he tunes his nightly fong,
Where groves and fylvan fcenes excel;
Where winds the filver ftream along;
Mourning the notes he lov'd fo well.

MODESTY.

NYMPH of the downcaſt eye,
Sweet bluſhing MODESTY,
Whoſe mien ſupplies the muſic of the tongue;
Thy charms were ſtill delay'd,
Thy beauties unpourtray'd,
Though Fancy pencil'd while the Muſes ſung!

More lovely to my ſight
Than morn's returning light,
That wakes the lowly dew-encumber'd roſe,
Or, mingling into day,
With bright and purer ray,
Its mellow luſtre o'er the landſcape throws.

O thou, the more admir'd
When ſeeming moſt retir'd—
Who far from pomp and grandeur lov'ſt to dwell;
Thou who art oft'ner ſeen
Upon the village green,
Or in the cottage, or the humble cell!

Come, ſweet nymph, and bring with thee
Thy ſiſter, dear SIMPLICITY.

Come, gentle exile of Patana's ſhore,
And draw the veil by Faſhion rent aſide;
Forbid each eye promiſc'ous to explore
Thoſe latent beauties Nature meant to hide.

Illume the cheek that recently diſplay'd
At once the lily's and the morning's glow:
E'en in thy abſence, health begins to fade;
And, ſee! the crimſon yielding to the ſnow.

And when thou com'ſt more grateful than the ſpring,
Crown'd with green garlands, after winter's reign,
With all thy bleſſings this inſtruction bring,
And let the moral echo round the plain:

" Thoſe charms ſo fair were far more lovely ſtill,
If obvious only to the mental eye:
Thoſe beauties, form'd the raviſh'd heart to thrill,
Expos'd to all, will ſoon that power deny.

"Thoſe ſmiles, ſo open to the vulgar ſight,
Were ſoon unheeded as the mid-day beam:
That boſom gives more exquiſite delight
Conceal'd, and throbbing but in fancy's dream.

"Arabia's perfumes, laviſh'd on the breeze,
Soon grow familiar to the fated ſenſe;
And each attempt that Beauty makes to pleaſe,
Devoid of modeſty, but gives offence.

"The lofty fruit, that toil to reach demands,
Acquir'd, a richer recompence beſtows;
And the rude thorn, that guards from vulgar hands,
But gives a higher value to the roſe."

THE PERPETUAL COMPLAINT.

BEING among the number of thoſe with whom mankind are continually diſſatisfied, I beg leave to ſubjoin my complaints to thoſe that have occaſionally introduced them to the public. When I tell you I am as old as Time herſelf, you will allow, that on the ſcore of longevity I ought to be reſpected; and when I add that I am venerable in my appearance and temperature, as mortals themſelves, you will alſo be diſpoſed to grant that I am not to be reprobated on the ſcore of inconſtancy. Yet ſo it is, that though I ſeemingly take pains to accommodate my variable diſpoſitions to the variable diſpoſitions of mankind, this circumſtance produces no ſympathetic congeniality between us; and my inconſtancy is rendered proverbial, while their own propenſity to fickleneſs never occurs to their recollection. I have no quarrel with the world on the ſubjects of indifference, neglect, or diſregard; for I muſt confefs, every body pays me due attention; I am inquired after every night and every morning, and am fo much the topic of converfation, and fo regularly introduced after the cuftomary greetings of ceremonial intercourfe, that I may be faid to be a kind of neceffary affiftant to converfation: for when people are barren of ideas, I am always at hand to fupply the vacuity of their minds; yet I am fcarcely mentioned in any other light than as the fource of complaint and diffatisfaction, and without having fome opprobrious epithet attached to my name. Sometimes I am accufed of being too warm in my behaviour, fometimes too cold. If I fmile unexpectedly, I am fufpected of harbouring treacherous defigns; and men fay to one another farcaftically, "We fhall pay for this!" If I continue my placid deportment, and am mild, fweet, and amiable, for any length of time, I am faid to be good humoured even to fatiety. Some wifh me to weep when I am difpofed to be merry, and fome to be gay when I am inclined to be fad. Thick, heavy, dull, nafty, are epithets commonly applied to me. If I am ftill, I am faid to be vapourifh—if loud, boifterous and rude.—Aches, pains, rheumatifms, and fhooting-corns, are often attributed to my influence. In fhort, I am fo wretched, fo cenfured, fo abufed, every day, that it would feem as if I were a ftranger upon earth, and born but yefterday, rather than an inhabitant of Paradife, known to Adam and Eve, and one who was present at the Creation.—But I will not detain you any longer, for I see you are looking at me through the window, and meditating an interview with your very old acquaintance THE WEATHER.

BEGIN IN TIME.

Albert possessed, at the death of his father, a wide domain; he planned vast improvements; and intended to meliorate the condition of his tenants. He daily contemplated this object; and resolved to set about it quickly. He thought of it in the morning and in the evening: but the follies and fashions of the times engrossed him for the remainder of the day; still he would do it; he was determined on it. Thus he continued until he had arrived at the age of forty, when he set about it in good earnest: But e'er he could complete his project, he died. He did not *begin in time.*

Clarissa was an enchanting girl; handsome, but not accomplished. She wished to be pious and godly; but she was *so* young; and had *so* many admirers—and, it would do when she grew older. She fell sick; Death hovered about her; then she wanted Religion; it was then she would begin; it was too late: she died in a phrenzied state. She did not *begin in time.*

Tom Dashall had a habit of swearing. He would fain mend it; he resolved on doing it; and he would begin soon. He kept on, however, till the age of fifty, and was then a difgufting object of profanity. He began to mend; but next year he departed this world. He did not *begin in time.*

Sam Thirfty was fond of ftrong drink. His friends told him if he perfifted it would kill him. Sam laughed, thinking he could leave it off when he pleafed. He grew old and grew worthlefs. Then he ftrove againft it; but it was all in vain: He did not *begin in time.*

Timothy Giddy chofe to be a lawyer. He would ftudy hard, that he would. He frolicked with the men and coquetted with the girls: Yet, he would begin, he faid, to apply himfelf clofely very foon. He went on in the old way, frolicking, coquetting and refolving, till the time came for him to appear at the bar. He knew nothing of law; he had every thing to learn: He was laughed at, and fcorned. He did not *begin in time.*

So it is with all things in life. Whatfoever you have to perform, therefore, do it prefently, left you die and the work fhould be left unfinifhed. Whether it be the improvement of the heart, of the mind, or of your eftate, *begin in time.*

TOWN DRESS.

I am the only fon of a farmer who has lived within twenty miles of your town for fix years, and I have never yet been to fee it; but father has promifed fifter Nance and I, that as foon as haying and harvefting are over, we fhall go to Marietta; fo you may conclude we are in a great "flufteration" about it,

Farmer Winrow's ſon was in your town laſt week, and tells ſuch ſtrange ſtories about the dreſs of the young men and women, that Nance and I are afraid to go there till we have heard more about it: he ſays as how the young men wear great trowſers as big as meal-bags with pockets at each ſide, into which they thruſt their hands up to their elbows; and he ſays too as how they come up cloſe under their arms—well, ſays I, then I ſuppoſe they dont wear any jackets? jackets, ſays he! why Tom they are not longer than a raketooth—ſo ſays I, and how is it then about their jacket pockets? pockets, ſays Ned Winrow! why they have cut off their old jackets above their pockets, ſo as to make new jackets, and new faſhions of them; that's a good plan, ſays I, ſo away I goes, and gets mine cut the ſame way. Well; laſt Sunday when I went to dreſs me for meeting—fegs! the firſt I knew was that my jacket and trowſers would not meet by nine inches! ſo I had to give over going to meeting for that day, and father will not buy me any others, ſo I muſt ſtay at home and wear the old frock and trowſers, unleſs you think it will anſwer, to have my meeting ones lengthened up with wide waiſtbands and forepieces of another colour.

Now Ned Winrow tells ſiſter Nance ſtrange things about the way the girls muſt dreſs and talk if they mean to have folks take notice of them—he ſays they muſt firſt have a new bonnet from Mr. what do you call him's new ſtore; and then they muſt go with their arms naked up to their ſhoulders: they muſt cut away the fore part of their gown down to within one inch of the Belt-Ribbon; and muſt then draw over the open part of the neck, &c. a thin piece of gauze or Paris net juſt to keep the flies from being troubleſome. Now, ſays Nance, Ned, I do not believe that: O yes, ſays Ned, it is certainly true.—And then, ſays Ned, you muſt not call any of the male creation by their proper name, except a man, or they will turn up their little noſes, cover up their faces, and bluſh.—And Ned further tells us as how he heard that you had alarmed ſome of the ladies ſo, they are almoſt afraid to look into your paper by publiſhing ſomething that had Obs—Obs, *Obſcurity* in it, I think they called it.—

Now I wiſh you to let me know how it is about piecing up the trowſers as ſoon as poſſible—alſo how you think it is beſt for Nance to dreſs when ſhe goes to town.

STYLE.

CARE ought to be taken that our newſpapers do not ſpoil our Engliſh. Every body reads them, and of courſe every body will be either diſguſted with their faults, or adopt them for authorities.

If it be not incorrect, is it not affected to ſay, Mr. J. arrived paſſenger *on* the ſhip Florida? As a large ſhip will contain ſeveral hundred men, I ſhould think one man might be ſuppoſed to go in the ſhip and cabin too, and not like a barnacle ſtick upon the bottom, or like lumber be expoſed to the weather on the deck. Let affectation, which always looks a good deal like meanneſs, vanity and hypocriſy, let affectation be diſcarded, and in future let paſſengers arrive as formerly, ſnug and ſheltered *in* a ſhip.

A writer *over* the ſignature of Zanga, is another buckram expreſſion. Cuſtom juſtifies, and therefore requires us to ſay, a writer *under* ſuch a ſignature. The Connecticut papers are remarkable for telling us that a number of great *characters* came to town in the ſtage-coach. A man not unfrequently finds when he travels, that his character goes before him, and ſometimes an unfortunate traveller leaves his character behind him. Now, this being permitted, it is quite clear that the aforeſaid *characters* in the ſtage did not arrive alone without their lawful owner.

If a houſe burn down, which you know is generally occaſioned by fire, our Gazettes inform us that the edifice fell a prey to the *devouring element*. Is not this high flown nonſenſe?

An *Obituary Notice*, tranſlated into our mother tongue, means that ſomebody died. But as death kills ſome one or another every day, an obituary notice gives a ſort of epick grandeur to the event. The French are very Homerick in their accounts of the ſlain in battle. They make every dead man bite the duſt. Inſtead of all Greek and Latin words, hard for common readers to underſtand, would it not be well to lay aſide, in future, our *Obituary Notice*, and our *Necrology*, &c. and head the liſt of deaths with *Bite the duſt?*

Common events cannot be related too ſimply and plainly, and too much vigilance cannot be uſed to prevent thoſe corruptions and provincialiſms which we have reaſon to fear will make our language as it is now written and ſpoken, unintelligible to our poſterity.

CANTING.

THOUGH moſt men are different, yet ſearch mankind through,
And *all* have a *Cant*, in whatever they do—
" *Mam*, examine that muſlin," the *Shopkeeper* ſays,
Who has retail'd in Corn-hill, ſuch things all his days,
" 'Tis as fine as a *hair*, and as thick as a *board*,
And more money, in London coſt, *Mam*,—on my word."
Thus praiſing their goods, they *all* lie and rant,
But never believe them—for 'tis but their *cant*.

Call the *Doctor*, and lo! he puts on a grave face,
" Hem, Sir, I aſſure you, a very bad caſe;
I ſhould have been ſent for before; but no doubt
My ſkill and my pills the diſeaſe can drive out."
Of his wonderful cures too, much he will vaunt,
Perhaps true, perhaps not, 'tis only his *cant*.

Apply to the *Lawyer*, behold he will quote
What my Lord *Coke* has ſtated, or *Littleton* wrote!
He will prate of replevins, demurrers and coſt,
" And an action ſo manag'd can never be loſt."
The continuations and proof he will want,
And will *pocket his fee*—for that is his *cant*.

The *Soldier* will tell you the perils he's ſeen,
The ſieges and battles in which he has been ;
Of the wounds he receiv'd and the feats he has done,
And no muſic to him's like the roar of a gun.
A part of his ſtory moſt fully we grant;
For the reſt—a ſoldier ſometimes has his *cant*.

The *Critic* will ſnarl—" that line is too long,
And the ſubject of this is too grave for a ſong."
Then the ſtyle—" oh 'tis flat"—the metre—" oh worſe ;"
" But we may put *any thing* now into verſe."
To ſeek out a blunder or fault he will pant,
And cavil for words—for 'tis but his *cant*.

The *Author* exclaims, " 'tis loſing one's time,
To employ it in proſe, or in *faſhioning* rhyme :
If good, or if bad, yet ſtill 'tis in vain,
For the author no money nor praiſe can obtain ;
No judges of merit or taſte are extant,
Are not all poets poor ?"—and that is his *cant*.

The *coquet* too will ſay, " I pray you be gone
I ne'er was before with a man all alone ;
O ! what will the world ſay ; I hate you, ſo go ;
Nay, don't be affronted—I did not mean ſo."
About *virtue* and *honour* too, much ſhe will rant,
You all muſt allow a coquet has her *cant*.

The *Buck* he will yawn and cry what a bore,
" I ne'er ſaw the town half ſo ſtupid before ;
I ha'nt had a row for at leaſt now *four* days,
And then ſo *fatiguing* are all our dull plays,
Then the girls—my dear Jack, not a ſmile will now grant,
'Tis ſo curſed provoking"—and that's a Buck's *cant*.

If you ſpeak but of London, or any thing in't,
The freſh return'd *Traveller* quick takes the hint.
" Excuſe me—tis not ſo—I hope you'll allow
My right—for I've been there, and therefore *muſt know*."
Of the wonders he has ſeen too, much will he vaunt,
And moſt tireſome of all is the *traveller's cant*.

The *Editor* ſays, " lines to S." are on file,
" On ſleep" is in rather too ſleepy a ſtyle.
With perſonalities we never concern us,
And muſt therefore refuſe the eſſay of " Alvernus ;"
Of dullneſs like " R. T." we're never in want,"
And much more he ſays—for 'tis but his *cant*.

PUNCTUALITY THE LIFE OF BUSINESS.

EVERY *man of buſineſs* will readily confeſs the truth of my text; and yet not one in a hundred, perhaps, is governed by it.

You are in great want of a pair of ſhoes—your ſhoemaker meaſures you for them—he will have them done ſuch a day for certain—you call and ſend and ſend and call, and have good luck if as much as a thickneſs of ſoal leather be not worn out in running for them before you get them—while you are ſuffering in your health, and endangering your life by tramping about in leaky ſhoes.

The Taylor meaſures you for a ſuit of clothes—you have put off getting them as long as you could do without, and are now in a great hurry for them—he is liberal in promiſes, for promiſes coſt nothing—but a violation of truth !—You are ſurely to have them on a ſet day—you fix your heart upon them—They are not done, but will be to-morrow—and may be this ſame ſtory may be repeated till it is as thread bare as your old clothes, and your many diſappointments devour more than half your pleaſure in your new ones.

You take a piece to the weaver—you or your children are almoſt ſuffering for it.

"It ſhall be done in a few days." A few weeks elapſe—ſometimes months, and even years, before you get your piece woven—and if it be not injured by mice or moths, you have to thank their forbearance for it.

The miller promiſes you your griſt the next morning—Morning comes, and not a grain of it is ground. Several days roll round, your corn is ſtill in the bag; and not unfrequently remains there till your hungry belly-ache makes you roar loud enough to frighten it into the hopper.

You want your graſs cut, your harveſt in, your grain threſhed out—You engage a perſon to aſſiſt you—You may depend upon it he will not diſappoint you—But if your hay and harveſt rot on the field, or the rats devour your grain, before your labourer arrives, you may conſole yourſelf with the reflection that you are not the firſt perſon that has been ſerved ſo.

It is not merely theſe deſcriptions of perſons who forget to remember that "punctuality is the life of buſineſs;" the ſame forgetfulneſs infeſts all claſſes of mankind.

The *employer* is often as far from punctuality as the *employed*.

Have not you ſuffered your taylor, your ſhoemaker, your weaver, or other workmen, to call again and again before you paid them their juſt dues?—Is not this a kind of robbery?- Beſides robbing them of their money for a ſeaſon, you rob them of their time in coming or ſending for it—and "time is money." If "the labourer be worthy of his hire," ought it not to be paid him when his labour is finiſhed ?

You, Mr. ——, have owed your doctor a great while. He perhaps ſaved you from a ſpeedy conſignment to the "houſe appointed for all living"—and now you requite his ſervices by refuſing to pay his honeſt demand. Ingratitude is the vileſt of vices—for all others there may be ſome apology—for this, none.

You, Mr. ——, have a long bill due at Mr. ——'s ſtore. Punctuality is in a ſpecial degree the life of his buſineſs—without money he can get no goods—and without it, he had better ſell none. Yet you detain his money from him, and perhaps lay it out for other objects not half ſo juſt or honourable. Theſe things ought not ſo to be.

The Parſon, among other good men, feels frequently, too ſenſibly feels, your want of punctuality. In this free country, no one is obliged to ſubſcribe to the ſupport of any Miniſter; ſo much the more ought you to be punctual in paying the ſmall pittance which you have promiſed "the man of God." While he is toiling to furniſh food for your immortal ſouls, ſurely you ſhould provide him with ſuſtenance for his mortal body—While he is ſeeking to make your death-bed eaſy, you cannot refuſe your aid to render his life comfortable. Remember who has ſaid, "The labourer is worthy of his hire."

Perhaps it may not be amiſs to remember the Printer in my diſcourſe. He is in a very difficult and diſagreeable ſituation. He truſts every body, he knows not who; his money is ſcattered every where, he hardly knows where to look for it. His paper, his ink, his preſſes and his types, his labour and his living, all muſt punctually be paid for. You, Mr. ——, and Mr. ——, and Mr. ——, Mr. and Mr. ——, and an hundred others that I could name, have taken Meſſrs. ——'s paper a great while—You and your wives, and your children, and your neighbours, have been amuſed and informed, and I hope improved by it—if you miſs one paper you think very hard of the printer or poſt for it, for you had rather go without your beſt meal than without your paper—have you ever complied with the condition of ſubſcription? Have you taken as much pains to furniſh the printer with his money as he has to furniſh you with your paper? Have you contributed your mite to repay him for his ink, his paper, his types, his preſſes, his hand-work, and head-work? If you have not—go—pay him off, "and ſin no more."

Verily, brethren, this want of punctuality is "a ſore evil under the ſun"—an evil which is felt by all claſſes and conditions of life, and which all ought to unite to ſcout out of ſociety. The ſcripture moveth us in ſundry places to render unto every one his due, and to "owe no man any thing;" and experience teacheth us that without punctuality there is neither profit nor pleaſure in buſineſs. But were it otherwiſe, promiſes ought not to be broken—" for what ſhall it profit a man to gain the whole world and loſe his own ſoul?"

ADVERTISEMENT.

DOCTOR LOGGERHEAD,

Has the pleaſure of informing his friends, and the public, that his celebrated " Omnipotent and Antimortuous Grindſtones," have proved to be an undoubted *remedy for the whole catalogue of human maladies.* The whole fruits of his reſearches are united, in a wonderful manner, in theſe invaluable grindſtones, and none have witneſſed their effects, without aſtoniſhment the moſt profound. Having devoted a long and laborious life, ſolely to the inveſtigation of thoſe arcana in medicine, which have hitherto been hid from the Hippocrates' and Galens, both of ancient and modern times, Dr. LOGGERHEAD would deem it but affected modeſty to deny, that he is a perfect maſter of his profeſſion. He is ſenſible that many impoſitions have been practiſed on the public by illiterate and deſigning pretenders to diſcoveries in this ſcience; and, although a few of thoſe diſcoveries have been highly honourable to their authors, and uſeful to the community, yet not a ſingle medicine has hitherto been known, whoſe power has not been baffled by ſome one of the diſeaſes incident to man. Obſerving this grand difficulty, and irreſiſtibly impelled, by motives of humanity, to attempt its removal, Doctor

LOGGERHEAD conceived, and has proved, the poſſibility of a general antidote. Uniting, in a ſingle article, the virtues of all medicines, he has rendered the means of health perfectly efficacious and ſimple. So ſtrong is the Doctor's conviction of the univerſality of the grindſtone's applicability, that he heſitates not to riſk his reputation as a man of truth, *and even as a phyſician*, in pronouncing his Grindſtones a *certain, ſafe, and ſpeedy cure for any diſeaſe whatever.*

Directions. The Grindſtones muſt be taken, morning and evening, in doſes of one to ſix dozens, according to the age, and conſtitution of the patient. To infants, they muſt be given in leſs quantities, and without the cranks. They may be maſticated, or ſwallowed whole as is moſt agreeable, or convenient; for, in trifling matters, it is beſt to indulge the fancy of the patient. Should they create a nauſea, the doſe muſt be repeated; and in caſe of indigeſtion, a ſaw-mill, while in motion, muſt be adminiſtered; or, if the patient will ſubmit to it, about 3 8ths of a grain of Eſſ Giz Jac, or the eſſence of the common Jacobin's Gizzard

Doctor LOGGERHEAD has often been himſelf diſguſted by certificates of cures offered to the public—yet ſo reſpectable are the ſources of the following, that he cannot, in juſtice to himſelf, and the public, refuſe them publicity.

I hereby certify, that being for many years ſubject to ten thouſand diſorders, I uſed very plentifully of Doctor *Loggerhead's* omnipotent and antimortuous grindftones, and was inftantly reftored to perfect health.

TIMOTHY TUFFER.

I hereby certify, that I was formerly very much addicted to the hippo; being ery furly and fullen, and frequently falling into mad fits; in one of which I very fpitefully devoured all the patent Grindftones I could find, and have been hopping up and laughing ever fince.

JEMMY JUMPS.

I hereby certify, that I unfortunately fell down in a mud puddle, and was unable to get up, until Doctor *Loggerhead* very humanely unloaded upon me a cart full of his omnipotent Grindftones; fince which time I have never feen a mud puddle, nor have felt any inclination to approach one.

MARY PRIM.

This may certify that I have ever been taken for a natural fool, but Doctor *Loggerhead* fays I am a very refpectable man.

STULTUS SUMVELFUI.

Indeed it is very certain that I have been very fick all the days of my life; but Doctor *Loggerhead* has made me very well ever fince.

PADDY O'BRIEN.

Middlesex ss.—August 26, 1805.

Then personally appeared the subscribers to the above certificates and made solemn oath that they are all true according to the best of their knowledge and belief.

VARNEY VERITAS, *Jus. P.*

N. B.—To prevent impositions, the public are informed that the *genuine* omnipotent and antimortuous Grindstones are round and flat; and are moreover accompanied with the seal and signature of the patentee.

SPECTACLES-MAGICAL.

THE custom of wearing spectacles, which I have observed has lately become so predominant among young men, has suggested to me many curious speculations. As glasses were formerly worn by aged persons to aid the imperfections of their visual organs, and seldom by any other persons, or for any other purpose, I became somewhat alarmed at seeing so large a portion of the young men suddenly accoutred with this badge of optical imperfection:—and being yet in my juvenile days, I was led to investigate the cause of so sudden and general a revolution in the optical system, under an apprehension of my own liability to so great a malady. That this grievous affliction should be peculiar to the male sex was what also much alarmed me, and led me into many curious and elaborate investigations of the structure of the different sexes, and particularly of the head.

But all my reſearches in philoſophical as well as anatomical writings were in vain—I was ſtill in the dark—ſtill in jeopardy.

I have alſo for a long time laboured under grievous apprehenſions from another conſideration. Being ſomewhat inclined to ſtudy and deep thinking, I imagined that whenever my eyes failed ſo much as to need the aſſiſtance of glaſſes, I ſhould be wholly deprived of the power, pleaſure, and utility of thinking. You may, perhaps, think this very odd, but as the *root* of the noſe is ſaid to be the ſeat of thought, I readily ſuppoſed that the iron legs which are placed aſtride that part of the noſe, would by their preſſure preclude the poſſibility of thinking. I accordingly made the experiment; and truly, I found all my cogitative powers immediately benumbed; and I could do nothing but ſtare through the glaſſes at objects which were preſented to my eyes. All power of reflection was loſt. Hence I concluded glaſſes were an index of ſtupidity as well as defective eyes, particularly in *young* men.

But how rejoiced was I, when I diſcovered that the cuſtom did not originate in any male-natural-optical-imperfection; but on account of a truly magical power which they are ſaid to poſſeſs, the wonderful effects of which are diſcovered in the female ſex only.

In juſtice, however, to ſome of the fair ſex, I am conſcious that there are thoſe in whom theſe effects are not found. A young man of my acquaintance had the misfortune to poſſeſs a pair of large white eyes, which were ſo forbidding to the ladies, that he deſpaired of any ſucceſs in gallantry; but no ſooner had he caſed them with a pair of glaſſes, than all the ladies in town were proclaiming his elegant and reſpectable appearance. He found that he had undergone, in their eyes, a complete transformation. Every thing which he did was admired—every motion which he made was graceful and elegant. He was captivating—he was charming. Another young lad, who being by profeſſion a Cobler, and by the bye not the pureſt character in the world, having diſcovered the magical power of ſpectacles, determined on trying what effect they would have in purifying *his character*, and how far they would operate in transforming him into a reſpectable gallant. Accordingly he put on his Sunday dreſs, and ſaddled his noſe with a new pair of daſhing ſpectacles-magical, and went into the next town, where he was wholly unknown; and in leſs than three days, if you will believe me, he was introduced into all the polite female circles of the town. He was careſſed, flattered, and admired. His very impudence and ruſticity were called originalities and faſhionable accompliſhments. In ſhort, to ſpeak in the ſtyle of his admirers, he was all *the go*—all *the rage*.

Another young beau, who had the misfortune to be the ſubject of frequent burleſque among the ladies, on account of the crookedneſs of his legs and roundneſs of his ſhoulders, and ſeveral other natural deformities, beſides a natural imbecility of intellect—having ſeen the ſurpriſing effect of ſpectacles-magical, clapped on a pair, and immediately found himſelf cried up by the ladies as one of the moſt elegant and ſenſible young men in the town.

Another, whoſe thorough libertiniſm and debaucheries had fixed upon his character, as he ſuppoſed, an indelible ſtigma among the fair ſex, by the aid of a pair of ſpectacles-magical, immediately wiped away all ſtain, and found himſelf as unſpotted and chaſte as Diana.

Thus, I am extremely happy to find that we are not all about to be troubled with ſo great an evil as I at firſt imagined; and I am ſtill more happy, yea, "*terque quaterque beatus*," to find that our perſons and characters can be transformed and purified with ſuch eaſe, that fools can become men of ſenſe and underſtanding, as it were, "in the twinkling of an eye." Who then is ſo great a fool, as that he would not wear ſpectacles to become a favourite of the ladies, even at the riſk of ruining a good pair of eyes?

HONESTY THE BEST POLICY.

MOSES TRUEMAN and James Sharper had been ſchool-fellows. Trueman had a plain plodding mind; he was orderly and diligent, but diſcovered no marks of uncommon ingenuity. Sharper was quick to learn, had ready wit, and was diſtinguiſhed for craft and ſtratagem. He was eſteemed the brighteſt boy in the ſchool; and his doating parents fondly anticipated his future greatneſs. Their education finiſhed, it happened that thoſe two young men went into buſineſs about the ſame time, and under nearly equal circumſtances.

Trueman was diligent, frugal, careful, and contented himſelf with the gain of honeſt induſtry. His promiſe he ever held ſacred, and his word was as good as his bond. There appeared no kind of art or myſtery about him; no diſpoſition to take advantage of the ignorant or inexperienced; but he walked on in the plain path of downright honeſty, meting out an equal meaſure to every perſon with whom he had dealings. Thus his character for prudence and ſtrict integrity ſoon became eſtabliſhed. His credit was ſuch, that he was able at any time, on the ſtrength of it, to obtain ſupplies of goods or caſh: yet he made a frugal uſe of even his own credit, generally declining to extend it as far as it might go; for he prudently conſidered that he had better forego ſome preſent advantages in buſineſs, than to diſappoint creditors, and at the ſame time put to hazard his own character for punctuality. No perſon ever heard Trueman ſay a witty thing. Though his judgment was ſound, he was never thought a man of bright parts; but, what was much better, he was univerſally eſteemed a man of ſolid worth. His induſtry, frugality, and careful management, gained him a handſome eſtate; and his ſtrict honeſty acquired him the reſpect of all his acquaintance.

Sharper heartily deſpiſed Trueman's plodding method of life, and was determined to be a daſhing fellow, and to grow rich by cunning and artifice. He knew that he was able to lay a hundred plans to deceive and take in ſimple people; and he had no doubt but he could make his fortune by it. At firſt he had ſome ſcruples of conſcience; but he flattered himſelf, that when he ſhould become rich, he ſhould make ſuch a liberal uſe of his riches as would atone for his knavery in getting them. He conſtantly buſied his brain in ſpreading ſnares for plain, unſuſpecting people; and he ſoon found that his craft and his gains exceeded even his expectations. Sometimes he would gain more on a ſingle day, than Trueman did in three or four months. At one ſtroke, he ſwindled Timothy Goſlin out of the whole of a ſnug eſtate: and he did it ſo cunningly, that no human law could touch him for it. Sharper's heart ſmote him a little, at the thought that he had brought Goſlin and his family to ruin; but meanwhile, it tickled his vanity that he had performed the trick more artfully than almoſt any other perſon could have done it. Poor Goſlin was not the only man that fell a prey to Sharper's craft—he utterly ruined ſeveral induſtrious, thrifty families; and there were ſcores, and even hundreds, that he had cheated, more or leſs.

After all, Sharper is not worth a groat—nay, he is many degrees below *cypher*. All this may be eaſily accounted for. In the firſt place, it was a fixed principle with him, never to pay a debt until he was forced to it; and therefore, with the coſts of court and the ſheriff's fees, he often had to pay almoſt double. A few times, alſo, he met with ſharpers who "bit the biter," and even outwitted him in his own way; and notwithſtanding his crafty art, he ſometimes was detected in his roguery, and had to pay dear for it. His credit loſt, and his character blaſted, every man's hand was againſt him: every man felt an intereſt in hunting him down, as if he was a beaſt of prey. If he happened to have a good cauſe in a court of juſtice, he was almoſt ſure to loſe it; by reaſon that the jury, knowing him to be a villain in his general character, could not eaſily be made to believe that he had acted honeſtly in any particular inſtance. Sharper has lived a life of induſtry and extreme diſquietude. His mind has been continually on the rack, either painfully buſied in deviſing means to enſnare others, or agitated with fearful apprehenſions of detection, or haunted and mangled with the whips and ſtings of remorſe and ſhame. Oft has he heard himſelf reproached and curſed—oft has he beheld the finger of ſcorn pointed at him—oft has he had to hide himſelf from the officers of justice. Sharper is wretched, and nobody pities him; nobody is disposed to assist him. The same talents and the same portion of industry bestowed honestly on useful business, which he has employed in knavery, would have insured him a good estate, and rendered him respectable in society.

TALE.

There was a man of Adam's race,
A man was he, indeed, sir,
Who tumbled down upon his face,
Which caus'd his nose to bleed, sir.

His nose it bled—it bled full sore,
It bled an hour or two, sir,
It bled an hour or two, or more;
Upon my word, 'tis true, sir.

Mean-while his friends and neighbours dear,
Post-haste for surgeons sent, sir,
They sent for surgeons, far and near,
To stop the bloody vent, sir.

The surgeons came with look demure,
Each panting hard for breath, sir,
Each panting hard they came to cure,
This *case* of *life* or *death*, sir.

Doctor Grimalkus first came in,
With magic Tractors arm'd, sir,
He view'd the patient—gave a grin,
Which might have death disarm'd, sir.

He strok'd his nose full oft, full well,
Still dropp'd full many a drop, sir,
He strok'd his nose—but sad to tell,
The blood he could not stop, sir.

With *zine and silver*, next approach'd,
Galvin, the blood to still, sir;
Doctor Grimalkus, he reproach'd,
Reproach'd, for want of *skill*, sir.

With much parade—parade—and show,
He shock'd the bleeding man, sir—
But still the fluent blood did flow,
The fluent blood still ran, sir.

Next came a host of *patent* quacks—
Of *patent* quacks a host, sir,
Of *patent* nostrums, on their backs,
They proudly made their boast, sir.

Each *patentee*, with hopes elate,
His sovereign cures did try, sir,
But each, alas! was "*call'd too late*,"
"*The man must surely die, sir.*"

* * * * * * * * * * * *

Upon his back cold keys were laid—
Cold keys upon his back, sir;
Until at length, the blood was stay'd—
The blood, at length, did slack, sir.

YANKEE PHRASES.

AS sound as a nut o'er the plain,
I of late whistled chuck full of glee:
A stranger to sorrow and pain,
As happy as happy could be.

As plump as a partridge I grew,
My heart being lighter than cork:
My slumbers were calmer than dew!
My body was fatter than pork!

Thus happy I hop'd I should pass,
Sleek as grease down the current of time;
But pleasures are brittle as glass,
Although as a fiddle they're fine.

Jemima, the pride of the vale,
  Like a top nimbly danc'd o'er our plains:
With envy the lasses were pale--
  With wonder stood gaping the swains.

She smil'd like a basket of chips—
  As tall as a hay-pole her size—
As sweet as molasses her lips—
  As bright as a button her eyes.

Admiring I gaz'd on each charm,
  My peace that would trouble so soon,
And thought not of danger, nor harm,
  Any more than the man in the moon.

But now to my sorrow I find,
  Her heart is as hard as a brick:
To my passion forever unkind,
  Though of love I am full as a tick.

I sought her affection to win,
  In hope of obtaining relief,
Till, I, like a hatchet, grew thin,
  And she, like a haddock, grew deaf.

I late was as fat as a doe,
  And playful and spry as a cat:
But now I am dull as a hoe,
  And as lean and weak as a rat.

Unless the unpitying fates
  With passion as ardent shall cram her,
As certain as death or as fates,
  I soon shall be dead as a hammer.

A TALE OF WONDER.

"NOW the laugh shakes the hall, and the ruddy
    wine flows;
  Who, who is so merry and gay?
Lemona is happy, for little she knows
Of the monster so grim, that lay hush'd in repose,
  Expecting his evening prey.

While the music play'd sweet, and, with tripping so
light,
Bruno danc'd through the maze of the hall;
Lemona retir'd, and her maidens, in white,
Led her up to her chamber, and bid her good night—
Then went down again to the hall.

The monster of blood now extended his claws,
And from under the bed did he creep;
With blood all besmear'd he now stretch'd out his
paws—
With blood all besmear'd, he now stretch'd out his
jaws,
To feed on the angel asleep.

He seiz'd on a vein, and gave such a bite,
And he gave with his fangs such a tug—
She shriek'd! Bruno ran up the stairs in a fright,
The guests follow'd after—when, brought to the light,
O have mercy! they cried, what a *BUG!*"

"STOOP! STOOP!"

THERE do at times very many advantages arise from stooping, which I shall not now attempt to enumerate. It is a hard matter to get along through this up-and-down life without stooping now and then—and in default thereof evil consequences do sometimes arise; witness what follows. In the particular incident, which gave rise to my motto, this idea is illustrated. Dr. Franklin was walking heedlessly along, and Mr. Mather vented the pathetic ejaculation. "I did not understand him," says the Doctor, "until I felt my head hit against the beam."

The analogy between Dr. Franklin's case and mine, has, from mere vanity at so near a connection with the inventor of lightning-poles, more than half reconciled me to my misfortune.

Going into my room the other night, being a remarkably large man having neglected Mr. Mather's precaution, I bruised my nose most woundily. My hostess, who is well skilled in herbs, and has read Doctor Stearns's Materia Medica, applied catnip and vinegar. One of the Quinsigamond doctors was called, and he ordered it to be wrapped in green baize and to be very gently exercised; to avoid sneezing, in consequence of which my hostess and the family are to abstain from tobacco, and snuff, for the space of ten days; and after applying a triangular plaister, of twelve inches round, he gave me hopes of its speedy renovation.

"*Tedious the task, to paint the numerous ills,*"
Which do attend big noses.

This event has put me in the way of studying into the anatomy of noses. I have made no great progress as yet, but am fully convinced, that far from giving one any more distinct ideas of flavour, they are cumbersome and offensive only to the possessor; and I have wondered by what means this fact escaped the observation of Dr. Darwin, and other physical philosophers.

I have been pondering with myself whether it would not be an useful improvement in the human physiognomy to have two noses, and have them change places with the ears. Overflowing with this idea, I bartered with the barber down the lane for a block, whereon to make experiments. With the help of a gouge and chisel, I have been enabled to form a tolerably correct idea of the appearance of one's face under such circumstances; and am fully convinced, that a nose on each side of the head, and two pretty ears in front, would make a very handsome appearance. I could give information of sundry advantages, which would accrue from such a disposition of the organs of smelling and hearing; as, for instance, the taking of snuff would be far less obnoxious to *me*, than at present it is.

I have too much modesty attached to my natural bias, to suggest it myself to the honourable legislature, to take this matter into consideration; but I think, that in case of war, it would give our militia more rational hopes of victory in some instances, than they could otherwise reasonably entertain.

Two such *momentous inventions* coming together, as Charles Packard's wings and my new fashioned head, is a very rare thing, and a striking evidence of the progressive state of the arts. All that is now left for mankind to practise their ingenuity upon, is, as I am informed, the *perpetual motion*. This I intend to discover sometime in the autumn of the present year.

The wooden block, on which I have been working, may be seen at my lodgings every day, Sundays excepted, until the 31ſt inſtant, when I ſhall forward it to the American Academy of Arts and Sciences.

MEDICAL CONSULTATION.

A drunken Jockey having fallen from his horſe at a public review, was taken up ſenſeleſs, and extended upon the long table of the tavern. He ſoon recovered his breath, and groaned moſt piteouſly. As his head ſtruck the ground firſt, it was apprehended, by ſome unacquainted with its ſolidity, that he had fractured his ſkull. The faculty haſtened, from all quarters, to his aſſiſtance. The learned, ſcrupulous phyſician, after requeſting that the doors and windows might be ſhut, approached the patient, and with a ſtately air, declined giving his opinion, as he had, unfortunately left at home, his Pringle on Contuſions.

The cheap Doctor immediately pronounced the wound a compound fracture, preſcribed half a doſe of crude opium, and called for the trepanning inſtruments. The ſafe Doctor propoſed brown paper, dipped in rum, and cobwebs to ſtaunch the blood. The popular Phyſician, or Muſical Doctor, told a jovial ſtory, and then relaxing his features, obſerved, that he viewed the groaning wretch as a monument of juſtice, that he who ſpent his days in tormenting horſes ſhould now, by the agency of the ſame animal, be brought to death's door. The Literary Quack, preſſing through the crowd, begged that he might ſtate the caſe to the company; and with an audible voice thus began—The learned doctor *Nominativ-ohoc-Caput*, in his Treatiſe on Brains, obſerves, that the ſeat of the ſoul may be known from the affections of the man—The reſidence of a wiſe man's ſoul is in his ears; a glutton's, in his palate; a gallant's, in his lips; an old maid's, in her tongue; a dancer's, in his toes; a drunkard's, in his throat. "By the way, landlord, give us a button of fling." When we learned wiſh to know if a wound endangers life, we firſt inquire into the affections of the patient, and ſee if the wound injures the ſoul: if that eſcape, however deep and ghaſtly the wound, we pronounce life in no danger. A horſe-jockey's ſoul, gentlemen—I wiſh your healths—is in his heel, under the left ſpur. When I was purſuing my ſtudies in the hoſpital, in England, I once ſaw ſeventeen horſe-jockies, ſome of whom were noblemen, killed by the fall of a ſcaffold, in Newmarket, and all wounded in the heel. Twenty others, with their arms, backs, and necks broken, ſurvived. I ſaw one noble jockey, with his *nominativo caret*, which is Latin for a nobleman's head, ſplit entirely open. His brains ran down his face, like the white of a broken egg; but, as his heel was unhurt, he ſurvived, and his judgment in horſes is ſaid not to be the leaſt impaired. Come—pull off the patient's boot, while I drink his better health. Charmed with the harangue, ſome of the ſpectators were about following his directions; when the other doctors interfered.—They had heard him with disdainful impatience; and now each raised his voice to support his particular opinion, backed by his adherents. Bring the brown paper—compound fracture—cobwebs. I say—hand the trepanning instruments—give us some toddy, and pull off his boot, echoed from all quarters. The Landlord forbade quarrelling in his house. The whole company rushed out to form a ring in the green for the medical professors, where they had a consultation of fistycuffs.

The practitioner in sheep, horses, and cattle, poured a dose of urine and molasses down the patient's throat, who soon so happily recovered as to pursue his vocation, swap horses three times, play twenty rubbers of all-fours, and get dead drunk again before sun-set.

QUARRELLING.

QUARRELLING!—But you think it a mean and vulgar vice, through the prejudice of education. It had never fallen under that foul odium, had mankind generally been possessed of sufficient expansion of intellect, to consider this globe as a vast *arena*, inclosed and sanded for the combats of men with men; where cudgels crash, stones and brickbats fly, spears shiver, cannons roar; while blood flows, and groans of death and yells of conqueſt rend the heavens. Is not this the world we ſee, and quarrelling a conſtant part of the great whole?

In the golden age, anterior to the reſtraints of law, and the tyranny of government, men wandered uncontrouled. With dominion for their object, and war for their trade, each was armed with his cudgel, and it was almoſt as common to knock a man down as to meet him. Once on a time, two of theſe lords of creation, after a hard fought battle, conceived the idea of uniting for the ſubjugation of others. But as implicit confidence was unſafe, each ſeized the cudgel-hand, that is, the right hand of the other, and ſo made a league. Hence the cuſtom of ſhaking, and hence the plighted right hand has in all ages and countries been a token of friendſhip, and the phraſe a term of art for a treaty. Thus quarrelling laid the baſis of ſociety in the ſocial compact; a matter of ſuch infinite moment that a great nation, during the laſt century, found it neceſſary to decree, that among thirty millions of human beings there was neither parent nor child, huſband nor wife, but all as perfectly unconnected as if they had been rained from the clouds. And agreeable to our hypotheſis, it took an immenſe deal of cudgelling to bring them together again. This I think a more rational account of the origin of ſociety, government, laws, and letters, than to ſuppoſe that men caught all theſe in the chaſe of wild beaſts, or fiſhed them out of the ſea, or ploughed them out of the ground, as certain grave philosophers have asserted.

Be so kind as to imagine that while the society mentioned, was forming, numerous others were going on in the same way. And there we shall have the whole population of our globe separated into compact and organized societies; and nothing remains but to rule them. As this was impossible while all retained cudgels; the strongest disarmed the rest, reserved a tremendous cudgel for himself and became their governor. This was the state of things at the siege of Troy.—Hence Homer never suffers an officer to appear on parade without his cudgel, and introduces king Ulysses, whose eloquence, he tells us, descended like falling snow, answering a seditious harangue of Thyrsites by a terrible mauling with his cudgel, or sceptre. The illiterate have, I know not what sublimated idea of the thing called a sceptre, but men of letters know that it is a cudgel only in Greek. And I would suggest whether for the avoiding of pedantry "The sceptre-bearers of mankind" ought not to be translated "the cudgellers of mankind." It would throw vast light on the science of government.

In ancient times, the judiciary department of government was administered by the cudgel. This is no flight of fancy. I defy all the antiquarians and literati of the age to show how it was possible to imprison men before the erection of houses, or fine them when there was no money, or hang them before the invention of ropes. And who, that beholds the corps of conſtables, with their tremendous tipſtaffs, drawn up around the tribunals, but muſt recognize in this precious relick of antiquity, a proof of our theory. In thoſe happy times execution followed the ſentence like a clap of thunder. — Treaſon would naturally be puniſhed by knocking out the culprit's brains, high crimes and miſdemeanours by knocking him down; and contempt of court by breaking his legs.

So ſacred was the cudgel of old, that church diſcipline was exerciſed by no other weapon. Thus Homer introduces the prieſt of Apollo to Agamemnon with a crown in one hand, and a cudgel in the other; the monarch imprudently profaned the latter; but he and his army ſoon got ſuch broken bones, that he was forced to revoke his imperious choice. You may be ſure the church militant has too much grace to forget the precedent. In ſhort, the eccleſiaſtical cudgel has knocked on the head thouſands of kings and emperors. It is true, the wood of which this holy cudgel was formed ſeems not to grow in this country, and there is a ſevere law againſt its importation, but what vigilance can wholly prevent ſmuggling?

But I cover my wing, and deſcending from kings, prieſts, and lawyers, pounce down on the rabble, that is, the mob. I mean the people themſelves—Pugh! how imperfect is language. You know what I mean. I mean the quarrellers who are not kings nor lawyers, nor priests; for we call these quarrels, battles, &c.

A quarreller is the glory of human nature. View him. He is a microcosm. He is the quintessence of creation, uniting in himself every great quality. He possesses the fierceness of a tyger, the courage of the cock, the pertinacity of the bulldog. He enters an assembly; every eye is fixed on him alone; his eye flashes; his brow thunders; every feature threatens. He insults ladies, and contradicts men: in a word, he is up to every thing. He cannot open his mouth, but liar, scoundrel, coward, leap out together. And then it is but a word and a blow. And for buffeting, clenching, kicking, biting, gouging, nothing can equal him. He minds neither blows nor bruises.

He rises into distinction surprisingly. In his own circle, and the earth has but its circle, he is hailed as a redoubted champion. Big Ben was as celebrated a personage in London as his sovereign; and Mendoza was at once the pride of one sect, and the envy of another. Bill the buffer, and Dick the dasher, are extolled to the skies; where the hero of Macedon is not once mentioned.

Celebrate, ye historians, your Alexanders, your Cæsars, and your Bonapartes; who shed blood by the hogshead; but commend me to the champion of the fist, or cudgel, before them all. Who can behold one of these godlike men, with his nose demolished, spitting out mouthsfull of clotted blood and broken teeth without adoring the dignity of human nature? It was such a sight that made the philosophick Plutarch exclaim, "A brave man battered on all sides with blows, is an object on which Lords may look with envy." And I submit to the physico-theologists, whether it was not for the contingencies of the quarrel, that the creator furnished man with a spare eye.

States recognize and reward the quarreller's merit; in his case republics cease to be ungrateful. Legislators exhaust their wisdom in consulting for his interest; build him impregnable castles; appoint and pay his porter, cooks, and valets. Secluded from the gaping stare of vulgar curiosity, he pursues in solitude and silence the sublime projects of his mighty mind. And it is no small favour if the lord in waiting permits you to glance at his sacred majesty through the keyhole. On levee-days, when he meets his court, files of armed men protect his sublimity from insult. The gravest judges are his privy counsellors; the most eloquent lawyers eulogize his merits; the news-writers, volunteering in the cause of virtue, give wings to his fame. In a word, who but he, and all the world must know him. By this single virtue, many a man, whom cruel fate seemed to have buried in the obſcurity of his own alley, has ariſen, towered, and ſoared into public notice.

O my country, how far art thou behind in the career of glory! In Europe, where ſcience has ſeized the ſummit of Parnaſſus, every college can boaſt of a profeſſor of quarrelling; while we, with mean parſimony, refuſe ſuch endowments, and our riſing hopes are neceſſitated to pick up a ſmattering of the art, on holidays and in taverns. Unleſs ſomething can be done by lottery, I ſee no means of promoting this ſublime art, except making it a branch of domeſtic education. And as we have already anticipated the pernicious effects of religious prejudice, by excluding the Bible from our ſchools, it is hoped that our ſcience may, in the family, ſupplant the catechiſm. There are probably not a few heads of families, better qualified to teach it, than the abſtruſe doctrines of chriſtianity. "I will let you know, ſir," ſaid the dear creature, ſhaking the fiſt at her huſband's noſe, "I will let you know, ſir, that I am your wife." "And I will teach you madam," exclaimed he, brandiſhing a maſſy cudgel, "that I am your huſband." *Fortes creantur fortibus et bonis.* The children of ſuch parents are deſtined to high things.

I muſt remark, however, that there is a rank among virtues as well as among men. Quarrelling is a maſculine virtue, requiring ſuch bone, ſinew, nerve, toughneſs of integument and ſolidity of brain-pan, that young men who have been nurſed in nightcaps, and have ſlept in beds of down, eſpecially if they have enfeebled their native virtues, by the ſtudy of claſſical and polite literature, cannot hope to attain to the true ſublime of this practice. But I conjure them in the name of Patriotiſm, to acquire at leaſt a moderate proficiency, as their country may demand the exerciſe of their talents in its high legiſlative aſſemblies. And there

When the fix'd parties, dumb and ſullen ſit,
Unmov'd by truth, and eloquence, and wit,
To rouſe their feelings, ſmite them on the noſe,
And on their ears pour ſyllogiſtic blows.

THE WOODMAN.

YOU aſk, who lives in yonder cot,
  Remote, where ſtrangers ſeldom tread?
A woodman there enjoys his lot,
  Who labours for his daily bread.
In this lone foreſt wild and rude,
He earns his meal by—cutting wood.

No wife has he to whom confin'd,
  No child to bring perpetual care;
No ſervant to perplex his mind,
  No friend his frugal meal to ſhare;
Alone, and in a cheerful mood,
He earns his bread by—cutting wood.

From wealth and power he lives ſecure,
  Unknown beneath his humble roof,
Untaught, yet bleſt—content, though poor;
  While every care he keeps aloof;
Thus having naught o'er which to brood,
He ſpends his day in—cutting wood.

Soon as he views the riſing ſun,
  He eats his cruſt of coarſe brown bread,

Shoulders his hatchet and his gun,
  And thus, by conſtant habit led,
In that receſs where oft he's ſtood,
He ſtill continues—cutting wood.

To him indifferent, ſeaſons roll,
  He values not the lapſe of time;
He only ſeeks to mould his ſoul,
  And fit it for a happier clime,
Where pain and ſorrow ne'er intrude,
Where ſoon he'll ceaſe from—cutting wood.

Does not this peaſant happier live,
  Than thoſe who "follow wealth and fame?"
Can theſe beſtow what peace can give,
  Or raiſe to health the ſickly frame?
He's bleſt, indeed, who poor and good,
Earns his brown loaf by—cutting wood.

MY FATHER.

WHO took me from my mother's arms,
And, ſmiling at her ſoft alarms,
Show'd me the world and nature's charms?
My Father.

Who made me feel and underſtand,
The wonders of the ſea and land,
And mark through all the Maker's hand?
My Father.

Who climb'd with me the mountain's height,
And watch'd my look of dread delight,
While roſe the glorious orb of light?
My Father.

Who, from each flow'r, and verdant ſtalk,
Gather'd a honied ſtore of talk,
To fill the long, delightful walk?
My Father.

Not on an inſect would he tread,
Nor ſtrike the ſtinging nettle dead—
Who taught at once my heart and head?
My Father.

Who wrote upon that heart the line
Pardeia grav'd on Virtue's ſhrine,
To make the human race divine ?
My Father.

Who fir'd my breaſt with Homer's fame,
And taught the high, heroic theme,
That nightly flaſh'd upon my dream ?
My Father.

Who ſmil'd at my ſupreme deſire,
To ſee "the curling ſmoke" aſpire,
From Ithaca's domeſtic fire ?
My Father.

Upon the raft, amidſt the foam,
Who, with Ulyſſes, ſaw the roam,
His head ſtill rais'd to look for home ?
My Father.

" What made a barren rock ſo dear !"
" My boy ! he had a country there,"
And who, then, dropt a preſcient tear ?
My Father.

Who, now, in pale and placid light
Of mem'ry gleams upon my ſight,
Burſting the ſepulchre of night ?
My Father.

O teach me ſtill thy Chriſtian plan,
Thy practice with thy precept ran—
Nor yet deſert me—now a man,
My Father.

Still let thy ſcholar's heart rejoice,
With charm of thy angelic voice—
Still prompt the motive and the choice,
My Father.

For yet remains a little ſpace,
Till I ſhall meet thee, face to face,
And not, as now, in vain embrace,
My Father.

THE BIRTH OF FRIENDSHIP.

WHEN CUPID firſt receiv'd his dart,
The boy exulting cried;
" Now mortals, dread its potent ſmart,
It ſurely ſhall be tried."

Beneath his feet all proſtrate lay,
A hoſt of nymphs and ſwains,
The vengeful urchin deem'd it play;
And laugh'd to ſcorn, their pains.

His mother ſaw his wanton ſport,
And chid th' ungracious boy,
Who taunting, gave her this retort;
" You gave—and I deſtroy."

" Since then," ſhe cried, " that gift's abus'd,
By your relentleſs rage;
Another pow'r ſhall be transfus'd,
And thoſe dire wounds aſſuage."

At that bleſt hour her teeming thought,
For gods create at will;
To life a fair perfection brought,
As e'er grac'd Ida's hill.

This bantling, placid and ſerene,
The mother, FRIENDSHIP nam'd;
And bade her hie with pleaſing mien,
Where tyrant CUPID reign'd.

She, ever faithful to the charge,
Her ſoothing pow'rs diſplay'd;
And pour'd balſamic gifts at large,
O'er wounds his dart had made.

He, weeping that her art indu'd,
With pow'r to balk his arms;
Awhile transfix'd, with wonder view'd,
HIS RIVAL SISTER'S CHARMS.

" Oh then," he cried, " ſince 'tis decreed,
Your ſkill ſhall equal mine;

Let peace emblazon ev'ry deed,
And LOVE our hearts entwine."

The lovely maid, who knew not hate,
Her yielding heart resign'd ;
Till then we trace the happy date,
When LOVE and FRIENDSHIP join'd.

And should the boy still pierce a heart,
Or cause one tear to flow ;
Lo, FRIENDSHIP shall her balm impart,
And sooth each child of woe.

DUELLING.

I address you on the ancient and honourable practice of duelling. Had I no higher object than to amuse you with description, or to kindle the flash of feeling, I would call the *duel* the crest of human glory, the cheap defence of *honour*, the Corinthian pillar of polished society. But such pompous encomiums would be as offensive to correct taste, as the tremendous declamations of the enemies of *duelling*, who, by daubing it over with horrid colours of malice and murder, have exposed it in such a shocking appearance, that one would think it fitter for the infernal spirits, than for the polite class of mankind. Avoiding equally the partiality which drives praise to extravagance, and the moroseness which delights in aggravating the atrociousness of what it would calumniate, let us calmly inquire into the good and evil effects of *duelling* and carry candour along with us.

Let it be admitted that the *duel* partakes

of the imperfection of human things, producing, when it falls into improper hands, partial evil; though its natural tendency be towards general good. After this large concession is made, still it can be asserted that the *duel* has been practised, from time immemorial, in all civilized states; that it has never degenerated from its original principles and tendency; that it has been adored by those who have experienced its beneficial consequences; and reprobated by such only as have had no practical acquaintance with it; that when properly managed it has never failed to remove controversy, and its *cause* out of society; and in no single instance has the loser, who is always apt to complain, carried an appeal from a definitive sentence to any human tribunal. Can the pulpit or the bar, say so much for any one of their institutions?

The enemies of *duelling* fight with a shadow. What a horrid crime they cry for one christian to shed the blood of another in a duel! who ever doubted it? but whoever heard of such a thing? These gentlemen, when they prove that certain classes of mankind ought not to fight *duels*, sophistically conclude that the duel is universally unlawful. No, the advocates for *duelling*, unequivocally declare that the *duel* would be debased by rendering it universal; they maintain that not one in ten thousand of the human race, is entitled to the honour of leaving the world in this manner. The ladies are excluded in a mafs; becaufe it appears to have been the intention of the Creator,—that they fhould cherifh, not deftroy human life. Their virtues are of a very different nature from thofe difplayed on the *duelling-ground;* befides as ladies never give the *lie*, the caufe of the *duel* does not exift among them. Among men, that large clafs denominated chriftians, are prohibited by this law, and reftrained by their temper from *fhedding blood* in *fingle combat;* humility is *their* honour, and forgivenefs *their* piftol. Lawyers fettle their difputes by the *ftatute* book; the merchant appeals to the *ledger;* and the labouring clafs of mankind are fo little accuftomed to think, that they are incapable of forming that extremely abftrufe and refined idea of *honour*, which makes it a man's duty to fhoot his friend; and hence they univerfally confound the *duel* with *murder.*

There remains then one fmall clafs only who have the leaft pretenfions to the *duel:* I mean *the gentlemen*, or *men of honour*, fo called, becaufe honour ferves them for bible, God, and confcience; they live, fwear and die, by honour. In a word they are fubject to the law of honour! Were it the law of God, the law of the land, or the law of nations, modefty would feal my lips in the prefence of this learned affembly—But as there may be a man of honour prefent, I fhall anfwer the query in the exquifite words of Paley.

"The law of honour," ſays that great philoſopher, "omits all ſuch duties as belong to the ſupreme Being, as well as thoſe which we owe to our ſuperiors, for which reaſon, profaneneſs, neglect of public worſhip, or private devotion, cruelty towards ſervants, injurious treatment of tenants or dependents, want of charity to the poor, injuries done to tradeſmen by inſolvency or delay of payment, with numberleſs other inſtances of the ſame kind, are accounted no breaches of honour, becauſe a man is not the leſs an agreeable companion for theſe vices, nor the worſe to deal with in thoſe concerns which are uſually tranſacted between one gentleman and another."——He adds:

"The law of honour being conſtituted by men occupied in the purſuits of pleaſure, and for the mutual conveniency of ſuch, will be found, as might be expected, from the character and deſign of the law-makers, to be, in moſt inſtances, favourable to the licentious indulgence of the natural paſſions." And concludes with theſe words, which ſhould be engraven on the hearts of *gentlemen*. "Thus it allows of fornication, adultery, drunkenneſs, prodigality, duelling, and of revenge in the extreme, and lays no ſtreſs upon the virtues oppoſite to theſe."

The greateſt advocate for *duelling* never extended the privilege beyond theſe honourable men. It is their *right* as *gentlemen*, their elective franchiſe, their jury trial, their coat of arms: in ſhort, they could do no more without it, than a philoſopher without cockle-ſhells and butterflies; aboliſh *duels*, and they ceaſe to be accountable creatures: how could they be governed or ſettle their controverſies without it? How often, for inſtance, does it become neceſſary to aſcertain which of two gentlemen is a *liar*, or which of them is better beloved by their common female friend? Theſe and a thouſand other equally difficult and important ſubjects admit of no other mode of deciſion. I hope a great and magnanimous nation will never rob gentlemen of a privilege without which the aſſociation of honour would crumble into atoms. And when it is conſidered that the principle of accommodation is interwoven with the whole texture of our conſtitution and laws, that it has been carried ſo far as to allow a large claſs of the community to ſpeak the truth without ſwearing, I hope it will not be refuſed to men of honour to ſettle their diſputes in their own way.

More might be ſaid if one dared. Our conſtitution, after all the fine things that have been ſaid of its merits, which indeed are great—is groſsly wrong in the articles which forbid nobility and titles of *honour*. It ſhould be amended ſo as to admit the conſecration of nobility of merit, without remainder however. Into this legion of honour ſhould be admitted all ſuch as could prove themſelves ſubjects of the law of honour, in all its poſitive and negative clauſes, which proof would be an eaſy matter, as their conduct is *notorious*. The title ſhould continue for life, unleſs forfeited by ſome diſhonourable crime, ſuch as *repentance*. The inſignia of the order ſhould be a *dagger*, worn at the belt; and to diſtinguiſh them from the induſtrious claſs of citizens, a *cap* ſhould be added, ſurmounted with a large *pair of piſtols*.

The advantages of ſuch an order would be incalculable; for, firſt, common citizens could then avoid their company—and ſecondly, when foreign men of honour ſhould viſit our cities, they could at once find a gentleman to conduct them to places of genteel reſort, and diſplay our virtues and manners to them in the moſt advantageous light; while our illuſtrious gueſts would be ſpared thoſe awkward embarraſſments into which they are ſo apt to fall, upon their firſt mixing with our ſimple and unpoliſhed citizens; *duels* among ſuch ſhould be transferred from the claſs of *crimes* to that of *virtues*.

This matter is perfectly practicable. For if it be a correct principle that the *materials of legiſlation* ſhould be ſought for in the tacit maxims and habits of ſociety, no time can be more ſuitable for ſuch a law, than the preſent, as public ſentiment has anticipated the law. Death by duel is not at all conſidered as *murder*.

Should one drunken porter in a rage knock out the brains of another, with a billet of wood, or paving-ſtone; or a negro in the kitchen run a fellow-ſervant through the body with a ſpit, the city would be thrown into univerſal uproar, the union would ring with proclamations and rewards for his apprehenſion: nought but his blood could appeaſe the incenſed vengeance of the community; becauſe ſuch perſons are conſidered as ſubjects of moral government. But a man of *honour* ſteps out in the morning with his ſecond and ſurgeon, blows out his friend's brains, or whips him genteelly through the heart with a ſmall-ſword; returns home, dines with his friends, and appears at the theatre in the evening perfectly diſembarraſſed; were it not for the licentiouſneſs of the *preſs*, nobody would hear a whiſper of the matter. No perſon conſiders it as *murder*. *Homicide* it cannot be in any ſenſe of the word; it is only the *extinction* of a *gentleman*.

The objections I have heard againſt *duelling*, are, in my opinion, and I hope you will think ſo too, unworthy of a ſerious anſwer. To the pathetic deſcriptions of *weeping mothers* and *ſobbing ſiſters*, and *widows* diſſolved in tears, I anſwer in the words of the poet—that

> Heaven is pleaſed to make diſtreſs become them,
> And clotheth them moſt amiable in tears.

You point me to the orphans of the deceaſed—I point you to the children of the ſurvivor, and aſk, are they in a preferable condition? You exclaim it was a violation of the laws of the land—I anſwer, that is the law's fault; repeal it, and the offence ceaſes. But the man deſerted his poſt—No, he fell at it: he left a blank however in ſociety! Grant at leaſt that ſociety has been ſaved the trouble of making the eraſure.

But of all other things, I am ſurpriſed that it ſhould be made an objection to duelling, that it excludes from the kingdom of Heaven. The objection would be inſuperable if any man of honour ever propoſed, or wiſhed to remove to that country; but its laws, maxims, habits and enjoyments, are ſo entirely at war with all the ſouls of men of *honour*, that if they were caſt on its ſhore by ſhipwreck, they would leave it the firſt fair wind. I have read ſomewhere that the *devil* left it as ſoon as he got a ſpark of *honour* in him, and I preſume *men* of *honour* would follow the example. The only diſhonourable circumſtance attending the death by *duel*, for which I owe the mortification of an apology, is, that when men have not had the happineſs of being *killed* dead on the ſpot, they have been known in a few rare inſtances to *pray!* and, what is ſtill more rare, clergymen have been ſent for. But when it is conſidered how much mental energy is impaired by a large effuſion of blood, a candid mind will attribute ſuch ſeeming defection to debility of reaſon, or the recurrence of childiſh habits. Beſides, theſe occurrences are extremely rare.

In a word, if *duelling* were confined to its proper objects, men of honour, there is no reaſon why the laws ſhould prohibit it: no cauſe why we ſhould be diſturbed with abſurd lamentations about the irreparable injury which it does to ſociety.

And if once in a century a moral agent ſhould, without paſſing through the lower grades of promotion, aſpire at once to the honour of *fighting a duel*, men of honour ſhew their liberality by admitting him into their corps without further ceremony. And ſurely it betrays little dignity on the part of thoſe whom he forſook, to weep inceſſantly over the loſs of a man, who would rather be *damned* than keep their company.

THE DYING DAUGHTER TO HER MOTHER.

MY Mother! when theſe unſteady lines
Thy long averted eyes ſhall ſee,
This hand that writes, this heart that pines,
Will cold, quite cold, and tranquil be.

That guilty child, ſo long diſown'd,
Can then, bleſt thought! no more offend;
And ſhould'ſt thou deem my crimes aton'd,
O deign my Orphan to befriend:—

That Orphan, who with trembling hand,
To thee will give my dying prayer—
Can'ſt thou my *dying* prayer withſtand,
And from my Child withhold thy care?

O raiſe the veil which hides her cheek,
Nor ſtart her mother's face to ſee,

But let her look thy love beſpeak—
For once that face was dear to thee.

Gaze on—and thou'lt perchance forget
The long, the mournful lapſe of years,
Thy couch with tears of anguiſh wet,
And e'en the guilt which caus'd thoſe tears.

And in my pure and artleſs child
Thou'lt think her mother meets thy view;
Such as ſhe was when life firſt ſmil'd,
And guilt by name alone ſhe knew.

Ah! then I ſee thee o'er her charms
A look of fond affection caſt;
I ſee thee claſp her in thine arms,
And in the preſent loſe the paſt.

But ſoon the dear illuſion flies;
The ſad reality returns;
My crimes again in mem'ry riſe,
And ah! in vain my orphan mourns;

Till ſuddenly ſome keen remorſe,
Some deep regret her claims ſhall aid,
Nor wrath that held too long its courſe,
For words of peace too long delay'd.

For pardon, moſt, alas! denied
When pardon might have ſnatch'd from ſhame,
And kindneſs, had'ſt thou kindneſs tried,
And check'd my guilt, and ſav'd my fame.

And then thou'lt wiſh as I do now,
Thy hand my humble bed had ſmooth'd,
Wip'd the chill moiſture off my brow,
And all the wants of ſickneſs ſooth'd.

For, oh! the means to ſooth my pain,
My poverty has ſtill denied;
And thou wilt wiſh, and ſigh in vain,
Thy riches had thoſe means ſupplied.

Thou'lt wiſh, with keen repentance wrung,
I'd clos'd my eyes upon thy breaſt,

Expiring while the fault'ring tongue
  Pardon in kindeſt tones expreſs'd.

O ſounds which I muſt never hear!
  Through years of woe my fond deſire;
O mother, ſpite of all, moſt dear!
  Muſt I unbleſs'd by thee expire?

Thy love alone I call to mind,
  And all thy paſt diſdain forget—
Each keen reproach, each frown unkind,
  That cruſh'd my hopes when laſt we met.

But when I ſaw that angry brow,
  Both health and youth were ſtill my own;
O mother! could'ſt thou ſee me now,
  Thou would'ſt not have the heart to frown.

But ſee! my Orphan's cheek diſplays
  Both youth and health's carnation's die,
Such as on mine in happier days,
  So fondly charm'd thy partial eye.

Grief o'er her bloom a veil now draws,
  Grief her lov'd parent's pangs to ſee;
And when thou think'ſt upon the cauſe,
  That paleneſs will have charms for thee:

And thou wilt fondly preſs that cheek,
  Bid happineſs its bloom reſtore;
And thus in tend'reſt accents ſpeak,
  "Sweet Orphan, thou ſhalt mourn no more."

But wilt thou thus indulgent be?
O! am I not by hope beguil'd?
  The long, long anger ſhewn to me,
Say, will it not purſue my child?

And muſt ſhe ſuffer for my crime?
  Ah, no! forbid it, gracious Heav'n!
And grant, O grant, in thy good time,
  That ſhe be lov'd, and I forgiv'n!

FLEE YOUTHFUL LUSTS.

TO a perſon of reflection and ſenſibility, there cannot be a ſubject of more painful thought, than that which the morals of our youth preſent. In many of them, we obſerve the brighteſt colours of the human character almoſt totally eclipſed by the fouleſt immoralities. We ſee them triumphing in vice as a proof of diſtinguiſhed ſpirit and refinement, and permitting their paſſions to ſhoot wild in all the dreadful luxuriance of folly and guilt. Amidſt this wide-extended ravage of talents and virtue, it becomes not the man of benevolence to ſit idle. Silence would be treaſon againſt ſociety. Let us unite then, in the arduous, yet delightful taſk, of guiding the ſteps of inexperienced youth. Let us point their paſſions to heaven, and teach them to burn with a holy love. Let us teach them, that the happineſs of this earth, conſiſts not in brutal enjoyments, and in the debaſement of their faculties; but that to be truly happy, it is neceſſary that their affections be pure, their objects innocent, their minds clean, ſerene and ſteady; and that the feebleſt pulſe of conſcious virtue, diſtributes more genuine bliſs through the ſyſtem, than all the ſpaſms and convulſions of libertine purſuits.

It has been remarked of virtue and vice, that in order to render the latter diſguſtfully repulſive, and the former irreſiſtibly attractive, nothing more would be neceſſary than to perſonify them, to make them the objects of human ſight—to diſplay them naked to the eye, inſtead of deſcribing them to the mind of man. I know not what effect ſuch an exhibition might have on the frigid hearts and inveterate habits of advanced age—but on a youthful mind I am perſuaded the impreſſion would be deep and ſtrong. In vain would vice beckon them to her embrace, while her frenzied face, her gorgon locks, her diſtempered geſture, would drive back the current of blood upon their hearts, and chill it all with horror.——Virtue, on the other hand, with placid mien and ſweeteſt ſmile, would wake into life each generous affection—touch their ſouls with rapture; and ſtretching forth her arm of ſnow, would only have to bid them come, to be obeyed. Thus would the *pencil* delineate them. Ours is a more difficult taſk. We ſpeak not to the eye, through which the vivid communication is ſo direct, ſo rapid, ſo reſiſtleſs; we addreſs a ſlower organ, and muſt ſolicit patience.

The words of our motto preſent an immenſe ſubject. They might lead us to deſcant on the luſt of pride, the great as well as little paſſions of miſguided youth. Let us limit our remarks within a narrow ſphere, and ſelect from the cluſter of youthful luſts, one which is more faſhionable and perhaps more detrimental to them, in every point of view, than any other with which the preſent age is ſcourged: I mean the illicit indulgence of that paſſion which was given to us for the preſervation of the human ſpecies. Conſidered merely with reference to this life, I know not a more deadly antidote to bliſs than this lawleſs tyrant over man. How often does it dig the grave for genius and character! How are all the energies of the mind unſtrung by its exceſs; all the affections of the heart deadened or empoiſoned; every virtuous propenſity put to flight, and all the charms of chaſte ſociety loſt and forgotten. Mark that youth to-day! See his cheeks crimſoned with a ſtream of health; his eyes beaming intelligence; his ſmiling lip pourtraying the peace which preſides over his breaſt; and his ſtep, how firm, elaſtic and ſprightly. Attend to his converſation. Hear the depth of remark; the nice diſcrimination; the flaſh of fancy; the affecting ſentiment of virtue; and the tone of eloquence. Every object lends a ſpring to his feelings or his reflections. He looks abroad upon the ſcenery of nature, and his heart beats with the ſweeteſt agitation. He ſurveys the courſe of the planets—"*Wheeling, unſhaken, through the void immenſe*," and his ſoul kindles with religious fervour. He traces on the page of hiſtory the revolutions of the earth, and experiences every change of emotion and ſentiment: he applies the incidents of other nations to his own, and by the fate of one foretells that of the other. Glowing in the purſuit of knowledge, he watches the operations of his own mind's feelings; he ſcrutinizes thoſe of others—he obſerves the human character in all its grave as well as eccentrick movements. In ſhort, he is alive to all around him; and preſents to an admiring world, the intereſting ſpectacle of a youth, combining the moſt ſublime faculties, the moſt vigilant obſervations, and the warmeſt virtues. Mark the ſame youth a few months hence, after his reſurrection from the bed of ſin. Gracious heaven! can this be the ſame? Where is the vigorous geſture, the eye of fire, the firm and manly voice, and the roſeate bloom of health? See how feeble his emaciated form totters along! Fled are the roſes from his cheek; dim the luſtre of his eye;—and his voice, once all melody, is now nothing more than tremulous diſcord. Or grant that his health may yet remain, his ſoul the breath of heaven, is ſullied. No more are we enlightened by the profound remark; no more are we aſtoniſhed at the brilliant flight of imagin tion; no more are we attracted by the amiable ſentiment of virtue. His mind once ſo active, ſo extenſive, ſo towering, now grovels and ſlumbers in the duſt! All its gay and rich creation of ideas has vaniſhed like a viſion of enchantment, and all its glory is extinguiſhed! His heart too, that once beat reſponſive to every call of virtue, that melted over the tale of pity, glowed indignant at the picture of cruelty, and roſe into ecſtacy at actions of generoſity and magnanimity—

whither have all its delicate ſenſibilities fled? Scattered and hurled to ruin, before the black ſtorm of vice. Melancholy reverſe!—See with what grim diſcontent he ſcowls on that creation, the view of which once gave him pleaſure!—The ſtars, that lately beamed light to him, now become his accuſers, and prate of his midnight exceſſes! and, what of all others is the moſt heart-affecting change, that hand which but a few months ago was ſtretched forth in friendſhip and reſpect to greet him, now points at him "the ſlow, unmoving finger of ſcorn!"—Whither ſhall he look for happineſs? For *happineſs*, do I ſay? Whither ſhall he fly for *refuge?* The frightful phantoms of his ruined hopes ſtart in gloomy array before his imagination, and haunt him to madneſs! Deſpair, diſtraction in every feature, he is reduced to the bitter alternative of pondering in ſolitude on the wreck of his name, or of aſſuaging for a moment the burning ſtings of conſcience by a repetition of his crime. Miſerable remedy! —as if every new tranſgreſſion did not lend an additional thong to the envenomed ſcourge of reflection.

Is this fancy, or is it fact? Let me appeal to the man who has made a progreſs in this crime, whether bliſs be not a ſtranger to his breaſt?—nay, whether it be not the principal employment of his life to fly from the tormenting alarms of thought? Whether the clouds of ignominy and contempt which ſurround him, do not aſſume a darkneſs infinitely more dismal, when he remembers the splendour with which the sun of his youth arose? Whether he does not sigh with regret for the chaste society which he has forfeited? and whether, in the paroxysms of his anguish, he does not even pray for annihilation?

Well may he pray for it: for if the displeasure of this world be so intolerable, what will the displeasure of Heaven be—when his soul, divested of its earthly tenement, and with it of all the artifices with which he was wont to drown the clamours of conscience, shall have no other employment than to survey its own contamination—to behold at a distance the ecstatic world of saints and angels, and to writhe under the vengeance of an offended God? With what colour of plausibility can the libertine hope for future happiness? If his vices render him an unfit companion of the more respectable part of the human race, can he be a fit companion for the immaculate purity of souls in paradise? Or, suppose he were admitted to that blessed society, what happiness could he taste? Let him appeal to his experience on earth. What is the scene of his pleasure!—the company of the virtuous? No, from such his soul shrinks back, like the bird of night from the meridian effulgence of the sun: and, he seeks his poor pleasures in a circle whose every habit and sentiment, whose every look, word and deed, is pollution and guilt. Could he hope for peace then, even if he were admitted into the bosom of Heaven? No! to him every cherubic smile would be a dagger—every hymn a draught of the deadliest poison.

If then, the libertine knows no real joys on earth, and can know none hereafter—if on the contrary, his life be a perpetual flight from an accusing conscience; if his practices tend, as they certainly do, to the degradation of his intellects, to the destruction of his character and tranquillity here, and to his perdition in that life which shall never end, I would demand of him, what object his crimes give him sufficient to balance all this havock? Is the insidious and mercenary smile of a prostitute an equivalent for temporal and eternal ruin? What pity is it, that every man's lips will answer this question in the negative, while the lives of so many give it an affirmative answer. What pity is it, that while the road to peace and character here, and to bliss in the realms of never-fading light, is so simple, so obvious, so direct, youth for ever deviate into the wilderness of vice. The time will come, when this choice shall be repented of! God grant that it be not too late, when death shall have dissolved the charm which had fettered their senses, and when repentance shall have no merit.—— This view of the subject is too painful. Let us rather indulge the hope of reformation.— The arguments in its favour are so strong, that in order to be effectual, they need only to be confidered. On the one hand temperance, health, wifdom, honour, refpectability, and peace; on the other, intemperance, difeafe, infamy, and mifery. Paufe, and weigh this ftatement:—Paufe, before diffipation fhall have fcattered abroad the bloom of youthful beauty, and configned your names to indelible difgrace:—Paufe, before the anger of Heaven fhall overtake you—when your tears of fupplication and fcreams of terror fhall be mocked—when you fhall exclaim, amid the horrors of eternal ruin, "O! that I had obeyed the injunction of St. Paul! O! that I had fled youthful lufts!"

NEW-ENGLAND COUNTRY DANCE.

HOW funny 'tis, when pretty lads and laffes
Meet all together juft to have a caper,
And the black fiddler plays you fuch a tune as
Sets you a frifking.

High bucks and ladies ftanding in a row all,
Make finer fhew than troops of continentals,
Now fee them foot it, rigadoon and chaffe,
Brimful of rapture.

Spruce our gallants are, effenc'd with pomatum:
Heads powder'd white as Killington Peak* fnow-ftorm!
Ladies, how brilliant!—fafcinating creatures!
All filk and muflin.

Thus poets tell us how one Mifter Orpheus
Led a rude foreft to a country dance, and
Play'd the brifk tune of Yankee Doodle on a
New-Holland fiddle.

* "*Killington Peak*" *is the fummit of the Green Mountains, in Vermont.*

But now behold a ſad reverſe of fortune!
Life's brighteſt ſcenes are chequer'd with diſaſter,
Clumſy Charles Clumpfoot treads on Tabby's gown, and
Tears all the tail off!

Stop, ſtop the fiddler, all away this racket—
Hartſhorn and water—ſee the lady's fainting,
Paler than primroſe, flutt'ring about like
Pigeons affrighted!

Not ſuch the turmoil when the ſturdy farmer
Sees turbid whirlwinds beat his oats and rye down,
And the rude hail-ſtones, big as piſtol-bullets,
Daſh in his windows!

Though 'twas unhappy, never ſeem to mind it,
Bid Punch and Sherry circulate the briſker,
Or in a bumper, flowing with Madeira,
Drown the misfortune.

Willy Wagnimble, dancing with Flirtilla,
Almoſt as light as air-balloon inflated,
Rigadoons round her, till the lady's heart is
Forc'd to ſurrender.

Thus have I ſeen a humble bee or hum-bird,
Hov'ring about a violet or ſun-flower,
Quaff from its bloſſoms many rich potations,
Sweeter than nectar.

Benny Bamboozle cuts the drolleſt capers,
Juſt like a camel or a hippopot'mos;
Jolly Jack Jumble makes as big a rout as
Forty Dutch horſes!

See Angelina lead the mazy dance down,
Never did fairy trip it ſo fantaſtic;
How my heart flutters while my tongue pronounces
Sweet little ſeraph.

Such are the joys which flow from country dancing,
Pure as the primal happineſs of Eden;
Wine, mirth, and muſic kindle in accordance,
Raptures extatic.

ADVERTISEMENTS.

MADAM SPITFIRE,

AT the ſign of the Furies, in Hackle-ſtreet, next door to the Cat's Paw Tavern, offers her ſervices to the public to teach the noble art of *Scolding and Quarrelling*, in good or bad humour, in love or ſpite; by the week, day, hour, minute, or ſecond; early or late; before or after meal; without regard to any perſon, in Dutch or Engliſh. She has diſcovered a new way for women to pull the hair and cap of their adverſary.—Scolding, &c. taught in the genteeleſt manner, to country women as well as town ladies. Judges and magiſtrates ſcolded in the neateſt ſtyle. She has a very peculiar mode of ſcolding, adapted to every age and circumſtance in life. Married women taught to ſcold their huſbands blind, deaf, and dumb, in ſix weeks. As a proof of her abilities in this polite acquirement, ſhe ſcolded eight huſbands to death in three years time, and the ninth is far gone. She teaches how to make grimaces or furious faces; how to look ſharp and Mary Magdalen-like: ſleepy huſbands may have their wives taught to ſcold them awake. She ſcolded the teeth out of her head the firſt year ſhe followed this noble buſineſs, which renders her incapable of teaching the art of *Biting*; but, on the other hand ſhe is not afflicted with the tooth-ache, which is a great advantage. She is well provided with needles and pins, to teach how to ſcratch faces, arms, hands, eyes, &c.—Water changed into vinegar by ſcolding. Scolding done in the neweſt and moſt approved ſtyle, in black, blue, red, or any other colour, on the ſhorteſt notice.

—

HECTOR DRAWCANSIR,

PROFESSED DUELLIST,

SOLICITOUS to convince an unbelieving public of the full extent of his very ſuperior ability, in the honourable, profitable, and *Chriſtian-like* ſcience of Duelling, begs leave to inform them, that he means to give a ſpecimen of his excellence in the Art of HONOURABLE MURDER, on Monday, the 9th inſtant.

As no doubt curioſity, or perhaps a more amiable motive, may induce a number of the Fair Sex to honour his exhibition by their preſence, he begs leave to aſſure them, they run no hazard of the laceration of their feelings, as with the moſt profound reſpect he aſſures them the deſtruction attending on this DREADFUL AFFRAY, will be confined to boots, coats, and veſts. He regrets that the preſent CROPPING ſtyle, precludes his adding the demolition of a ſide curl—*a la Yorke.*

N. B. If any gentleman curious to be initiated into the myſteries of the ſcience ſhould become deſirous of acquiring a knowledge of *polite modern* practice, he may be accommodated with a *fleſh* wound, without endangering in the ſmalleſt degree the ſafety of his perſon.

Shortly will be put to preſs the

DUELLIST'S NEW GUIDE;

BEING a correct ſtatement of the various modes at preſent in practice, with conſiderable improvements by the Author, to which will be added, the moſt conciſe and accurate mode of giving a *public* ſtatement of the valour ofthe combatants.

The whole addreſſed to the patronage of Duelliſts and their Seconds.

SOL. SHAVER & CO,

EXPECT ſhortly to receive from the mint of Faſhion,

Gentlemen's Shawls and Shoulder-Straps.

Since it has been wiſely determined by the regulators of faſhion, that gentlemen's pantaloons ſhall come up as near the neck as poſſible, it muſt be very handy to have ſhoulder-ſtraps inſtead of gallowſes—beſides *gallows* is an ugly name. And whereas the aforeſaid regulation of pantaloons renders the wearing of waiſtcoats almoſt unneceſſary, the ſaid ſhawls for gentlemen, very ingeniouſly contrived for the purpoſe, will be *vaſtly* convenient and economical.

WANTED,

BY a lady of quality, among her ſervants, a full-grown woman, of a bad temper, violent paſſions, and ungovernable rage; ſhe muſt be an adept in the art of boxing, lugging, hair-dreſſing, and ſtiff ſtarching, as ſhe is to attend her ladyſhip's perſon—ſhe muſt pen anonymous letters with the bitterneſs and acumen if the expreſſion may be allowed of the devil—ſhe muſt have ſtudied the "Art of Tormenting" to refinement—her countenance and conduct muſt either be marked by conſummate hypocriſy, or overbearing pride as occaſion may ſerve; the ſmall pox, large maſculine features, and blue eyes—in ſhort, an ugly expreſſive face would be preferred; ſtrong nails and ſharp teeth are excellent weapons of female defence—ſhe muſt have no deficiency in her ſpeech, but great volubility of tongue in caſe of violent ruptures—to conclude, ſhe muſt be by nature and by art a PERFECT VIRAGO.

N. B. No perſons ſubject to ſudden ſqualls need apply, for her ladyſhip being now advanced in life, finds the taſk too much for her nerves, and wiſhes to ſee the economy of the houſe ſtill ſupported, as when ſhe was in the zenith of her power.

THE FIRE FLY.

LITTLE rambler of the night,
Where and whence thy glowing light?
Is it form'd of ev'ning dew?
Where and whence thy brilliant hue?
Hark! methinks a voice replies,
He that form'd the azure ſkies,
Great in leaſt, and good to all,
Lord of man, and inſect ſmall,
He it was, that made this veſt,
Search, adore, nor know the reſt.

Little rambler of the night,
Bleſſed be this voice of thine!

He that cloth'd thy form in light,
Is the God of me and mine.

Go enjoy in verdant fields,
What his royal bounty yields,
Nip the leaf, or taste the flower;
Sip in nature's roseate bower;
Filling full the span that's given,
With the boons of gracious Heaven.

FRAGMENT.

MONITOR.

BUT man was formed for social intercourse,
For humbler walks, and pleasures less refined.
Regarding Fancy's fascinating voice,
The mind becomes enamoured of the sound,
Accompanies the sprite through pleasant fields,
Of bland enchantment, where propitious suns,
By lucid tempests unobscured, effuse
The lustre of perpetual joy; where love
And innocence, and peace predominate.
Delighted with the visionary land,
She cherishes a hope of dwelling there,
Of tasting undisturb'd ambrosial sweets;
But soon a voice of stern authority
Remands the wanderer home. Appall'd and sad,
She journeys back, and mournfully surveys
The joyless prospect of reality;
Vanish'd the bright illusions of the brain,
Vanish'd the few felicities of life
And thrice-embittered unimportant woes.

AUTHOR.

Extremes should be avoided. Virtue's charms,
Arrayed in superstition's garb, disgust;
And Beauty's roseate smile, to vice resigned,
May hide a Milwood's heart. But who disowns
Their real, uncontaminated worth
For any adventitious injury?

MONITOR.

When Fiction's blandishments ensnare the mind,
Farewell to study's laudable endeavours;

Improvement, ardour, emulation ceaſe.
No more the glow of warm enthuſiaſm
Diffuſes rapture o'er th'awakened ſoul ;
The laurel-wreath no more inſpires the breaſt,
Reanimates no more to bold acquirements ;
But hating every maſculine purſuit,
Romance's votaries devour the page,
Where foreſts, caſtles, hippogrieffs and ghoſts,
Where moonlight, muſic, thunder, ſhrieks and groans
Diverſify the ſcene with ſweet confuſion.
The lamp burns blue, the dreadful curtain waves,
And dim-ſeen ſpectres flit along the gloom ,
Imagination ſhudders at the ſight,
And half-recoiling, eyes the ſhades aſkance ;
Emboldened ſoon the legend ſhe purſues,
Purſues with ſelf-deluſion terror's call,
Experiencing a not unpleaſant horror.
Thus paſs the hours of miſconceiving youth,
Thoſe golden hours, that never will return ;
Frivolity and indolence, the fruit
Of Poeſy, of Fiction, of Romance,
Uſurp the place of LITERATURE and SCIENCE.

EPIGRAM.

" IF Nature never acts a part in vain,
" Who, ſaid an Atheiſt, ſhall this fact explain ?
" Why in the glow-worm does her power produce
" Such laviſh luſtre, for ſo little uſe ?"

A plain blunt fellow, who, by chance, ſtood by,
Heard what he ſaid, and made him this reply :

" Nature, quoth he, explains her own deſign ;
" She meant to mortify all pride like thine,
" When o'er an inſect's tail ſuch *light* ſhe ſpread,
" And left ſuch *darkneſs* in a coxcomb's head."

PATENT MEDICINE.

Ramrod's Essential Tincture of Gridiron,

OTHERWISE CALLED

Nature's Grand Restorative.

DOCTOR SIMON RAMROD, by a scrutinous and chemical analyzation of vegetable substances, has recently discovered that Gridirons contain a subtle, invigorating fluid, sympathetically allied to the nervous or magnetic fluid of the human body, which, being skilfully extracted, and properly prepared, becomes a specific and infallible remedy for almost every complaint, both of mind and body, to which nature has been subject since the flood. It is found also, to have a powerful effect upon the brute creation, and on various inanimate substances; to give relief against accidents, to be a wonderful quickener of the circulations, and to give renovated strength to all muscular exertions; from which it is found useful to persons travelling by sea or by land, and to those exposed to extraordinary dangers.

To announce the instances in which Ramrod's Tincture of Gridiron has proved beneficial, would be but to give a detail of all the diseases to which men, women, and children are subject. The following are but a few, out of a thousand and *upwards*, of certificates, which have been, or may be, procured, as a testimony of its efficacy—

The subscriber has long been afflicted with the tooth-ache, to such a degree that nearly all his teeth had been drawn out; and, by an unjuſt ſentence, he alſo unfortunately had both his ears cut off. On applying a little of the Tincture of the Gridiron to his head, his teeth were reſtored, and his head was inſtantly ſupplied with as fine a pair of ears as he could boaſt of the day he was born.

JOHN EARWIG.

Not long ſince, riding on the highway, my horſe ſtumbled and fell, and ſo lamed himſelf as to be unable to proceed. I *heard* of a phial of the Tincture of Gridiron in the neighbourhood, and ſuddenly found myſelf at the end of my journey, without further trouble.

JONA. SPEEDWELL.

Having from my infancy had an uncommon reliſh for Barbecues, I not long ſince attended one; and, notwithſtanding the ſplendid variety which a ſumptuous table afforded, I was unable to eat a mouthful. I took a ſpoonful of the Tincture of Gridiron, and felt as perfectly ſatisfied as if I had eaten all on the table.

S. GORMANDIZER.

Sometime ago my houſe was very much infeſted with rats; and one day, while I ſat brooding over my misfortunes, a large number of them ſuddenly came upon me and ate me up. I inſtantly took ſome of the Tincture of Gridiron, and found myſelf at eaſe, and have never been eaten ſince.

JACK RECOVER.

I was, not long ſince, ſubject to extreme fatigue from dancing and other exerciſe. I took a ſmall quantity of the Tincture of Gridiron, and have been dancing ever ſince, without the leaſt inconvenience.

SAML. RIGADOON.

Riding out the other day, I accidently fell into a ditch, and broke my legs, my arms and neck. On taking a little of the Tincture of Gridiron, I inſtantly recovered, and have never been near a ditch ſince, nor felt a deſire to approach one.

TOM. TUMBLE.

Walking, not long ſince, near the machinery of a mill, I was caught and carried between two cogwheels, and every bone in my body broken to pieces. A phial of Ramrod's Tincture of Gridiron being thrown into the mill-pond, I found myſelf reſtored, and as whole and ſound as a roach.

DICK WHIRLIGIG.

NOTE.—Gridirons, taken in their natural ſtate, and particularly taken whole, are, by ſkilful chemiſts, deemed extremely dangerous: but the recent diſcovery of a mode of preparing the Tincture from them, places them in the firſt rank of valuable plants.

☞ BEWARE OF COUNTERFEITS!

Each bottle is ſtopped with a gimlet, and ſealed with juniper-berries, and labelled "RAMROD's TINCTURE OF GRIDIRON." To be ſold *only* in Frying-pan Alley, at the ſign of the Tea-kettle.

AN OLD BATCHELOR'S LAMENTATION.

TIME, ſwift as a poſt, yea, as ſwift as the wind,
Flies off with my life, and leaves nothing behind;
Flies aff with my joys, and leaves nothing in place,
But a painful review of a whimſical chaſe.

How light danc'd my ſpirits! how joyous the hours,
While youth lent me vigour, and love lent me pow'rs;
But I ſee with ſorrow thoſe pleaſures decay;
Yet alas! when I had them, I flung them away.

Young Cupid oft threaten'd to play with his dart,
And ſometimes he wounded—one ſide of my heart;
But now I could wiſh, when his pranks I review,
His godſhip had ſtricken my heart through and through:

Then Hymen's ſoft bands had per chance been my fate,
Nor had I lamented my folly too late;
Nor Chloe had frown'd with an air of diſdain,
Nor the world had condemn'd me for living in vain.

No innocent prattlers now cling to my knees,
No tender endearments to ſooth and to pleaſe;
No boſom-companion to heighten my bliſs,
Say, can you imagine a ſtate worſe than this?

No more the gay ſpring in her bridal attire
Excites my fond boſom ſome nymph to admire;
A ſtupid indiff'rence pervades my dull veins:
Hear this, and be wiſe, oh ye nymphs and ye ſwains.

Ye youths and ye virgins, Columbia's firſt pride,
Indulge the ſoft poiſon while youth's on your ſide;
Join hearts and join hands, and with rapture you'll find
How happy the lot of the faithful and kind.

Ye bachelor drones, who intrude on the hive,
You moſt inſignificant creatures alive,
Go, quit you like men, that no more it be ſaid
You are uſeleſs alive, and deſpis'd when you're dead.

If lawleſs intrigue be the pride of your liſe,
And a miſtreſs your glory inſtead of a wife,
Your boaſted enjoyment is all a miſtake,
And the height of your pride is the pride of a rake.

A rake is the bane of all permanent blifs;
'Tis pleafure they feek, but true pleafure they mifs:
For boaft what they will of their favourite lafs,
She's a thorn in their fide, and a fnake in the grafs.

Beware, oh ye fair, or with forrow you'll find
Their oaths are deceit, and their vows are but wind;
Let virtue and honour and truth be your care,
And then you'll be happy, as now you are fair.

Return, ye bleft moments, young days of delight;
What, muft you for ever be chas'd from my fight?
Then adieu to all pleafure this earth can beftow,
For a heart void of love is a heart full of woe.

BENEVOLENCE.

Benevolence, thou facred aid,
And attribute of heav'n;
May thy bleft influence ftill pervade,
This world to mortals giv'n!

Thy genial influence cheers the heart,
Of many a wretch forlorn;
When doom'd from home and friends to part,
By dire misfortune torn.

'Tis like the fweets which erft were dropp'd,
From Hybla's thymy hill;
The wandering ftranger gladly ftopp'd,
To tafte the bounteous rill.

Thus have I feen on Mary's cheek,
The tear of pity fall,
The "little brilliant" feem'd to fpeak,
Its generous wifh for all.

'Twas then my bofom felt the flame,
Of SYMPATHETIC LOVE,
The fweet fenfation ftill remains,
Grant Heav'n, it never rove.

FRIENDSHIP.

HOW fweet the ties of nature prove,
When bound in friendfhip's chains,

They cherish life, they ease its load,
 And lighten all its pains.

When fortune frowns, and traitors flee,
 And turn their smiles to jeers;
When o'er the waves we're forc'd to roam,
 How sweet are friendship's tears.

When disappointed love has wrought
 A pang within our breast;
How sweet the victim's soul reclines
 On friendship's downy nest.

When o'er the steeps we catch at fame,
 And lose the gilded prize;
How blest the sound! how sweet the tears,
 That flow from friendship's eyes.

When age o'erspreads the hero's brow,
 And checks his " wild career;"
When he reflects how short is life,
 He sighs for friendship's tear.

When death shall come to seal our doom,
 And bear us to the skies;
How blest the soul who views the tears
 That moisten friendship's eyes.

THE SEASONS.

HOW mild the balmy breath of SPRING!
 How fair the fostering vernal sky!
Hark! how the woodland minstrels sing!
 Hark! how the whispering zephyrs sigh.

Usurping SUMMER shifts the scene,
 And boldly flames in brighter day;
How transient is his fervid beam!
 Shot but to dazzle, and decay.

Brown AUTUMN comes in solemn grade;
 Unlocks her bounteous stores in vain:
How quick her boasted honours fade!
 How faint her strength, how short her reign.

See WINTER fierce, in mad career!
Expiring nature blooms no more;
No flowers bloom to deck the year;
For mufic—hark! the tempefts roar!

Thus LIFE's progreffive feafons pafs
Our vernal blufh, our riper bloom,
Our fober Autumn's finking glafs,
Sad prelude to a wintry tomb.

MARIA.

MARIA was among the faireft and fweeteft girls that I have ever known. If the love of the fondeft and beft of parents—if the moft enchanting grace and beauty—if the pure fpirit and difpofition of a feraph could have faved her from mifery, Maria had been faved. My heart bleeds at the recollection of her. But let me try to command myfelf, while I tell this tale of joy turned into forrow; of the faireft hopes reverfed and blafted of the brighteft luftre and beauty extinguifhed for ever.

Her parents were not rich, but they were good. Although they had lived much in the world, they retained a fimplicity of character which is now rarely encountered except in the defcription of poets. Their benevolent breafts were fraught with a tendernefs of feeling, whofe luxury is known only to the poor and humble. The rich and the profperous know it only by name. Their fimplicity, their benevolence, their fenfibility, were concentrated in the bofom of the young Maria—they gave an emphafis to her opening beauty—fuffufed her cheek with a richer hue—and rode, in triumph, on the beams of her eyes, through the heart of every beholder. I remember Maria at her first appearance in the ball room. She was then about fourteen years of age. The inquiry ran—"what rose-bud of beauty is this!" The epithet was applied with peculiar propriety: it depicted in one word, her youth, her beauty, her innocence and sweetness. She danced; when light and etherial as a sylph, she surpassed whatever we have read of the wild, the striking, the captivating graces displayed by the rural beauties of the flowery side of Ætna. It was easy to read in the countenance of this gay and artless young creature, the exulting expectations with which she was entering into life. Her childhood had passed away amid the blandishments and caresses of her fond parents; all had been ease, indulgence, and gratification; admired, applauded, and beloved by every body who saw or knew her, every day, every hour, every minute had been filled with animation, joy and rapture. As yet she frolicked only on "life's velvet lawn," covered with a canopy of amaranth: and her young fancy was teeming with visions of bliss, to bright and boundless prospects. Alas! poor Maria: How soon was the serene and joyous morning to be overcast! A lover presented himself. Like Maria, he was in the bloom of youth, and had every advantage of person and address; but his breast was not like Maria's the residence of pure and exalted virtue. He loved her indeed; or rather he was infatuated by her beauty; but he was incapable of forming a correct estimate of the treasure which was lodged in her bosom; of that heart whose purity, delicacy, fidelity, generosity, and sensibility, an angel might have owned without a blush. The dupe, however, of fervent and pathetic professions, she accepted this man; and Maria, who was formed to crown the happiness of a sensible and virtuous man, became the miserable wife of a weak and vicious one. Merciful God! Must I remember the contrast which I so often witnessed, in agony! Poor Maria! her velvet lawn was exchanged for a wilderness of briars and brambles; her amaranthine canopy for the keen cutting blasts of a winter's sky. I have seen Maria in the thronged assembly room, when every eye was fixed upon her with delight, and followed her in speechless admiration through the mazes of grateful dance; and I have seen the same Maria far removed from the world's society, and even yet in the bloom of youth, all lonely and drooping like a wounded flower. I have seen the lovely girl presiding, like a bright propitious planet, at her father's hospitable board; and I have seen her the solitary and menial drudge of her own gloomy and forsaken household. I have beheld her the animating soul of the polished circle, dispensing light and life by her smiles——and my own soul has sunk within me, to see her insulated from the world, and pierced and languishing under the neglect of her once arduous and aſſiduous huſband. She had ſeen the time when every tranſitory dejection of countenance had been watched by him, its cauſe aſſiduouſly explored, and conſolation adminiſtered with a tenderneſs that could not fail of its effect. But now, without a ſingle inquiry, without one touch of pity, he could ſee her face pale with ſorrow, and her once radient eyes dim with weeping At ſuch a moment, inſtead of bending before her as he had once done, and preſſing his hand to her ſympathetic heart, he could caſt on her a look ſo cold and chilling as to freeze the vital ſtream of life even in its fountáin, fling out of his houſe with contempt and diſguſt, and laviſh on the vicious and impure thoſe affectionate attentions which he had ſolemnly vowed to her alone. He might have been happy, and might have realized for his beauteous wife all thoſe dreams of conjugal innocence and bliſs with which her youthful fancy was wont to regale her. But inſtead of theſe pure and calm joys, whoſe recollection might have gilded the moment of death, he choſe riot, debauchery and guilt; to his own virtuous and celeſtial bed, he preferred habitual impurity and proſtitution; and inſtead of the perpetual ſpring which ſhe had fondly anticipated. poor Maria experienced only perpetual winter. She is gone; and, with her ſiſter angels, ſhe has found that peace which her unfeeling huſband refuſed to her on earth. Her death ſtunned him into his ſenſes. In vain he endeavoured to recal her fleeting breath : in vain he promiſed and vowed if ſhe could be reſtored to him, to atone for his paſt neglect by future tenderneſs. To him the reſolution of amendment came too late.

AFFECTION.

DOES the boſom ceaſe to glow,
Muſt the lyre in ſilence lie ;
Does the heart beat languid ?—No—
Friendſhip's flame can never die.
Never will it quit the breaſt ;
Where it once had been a gueſt.

Dance the ſpirits nimbly round,
Does life's current lightly flow ;
At the viol's ſprightly ſound
Beats the heart reſponſive ?--No.
When our deareſt hopes are croſt,
Muſic's magic power is loſt.

Is the boſom caſed in ſnow,
Are its beſt emotions chill'd ;
Does it ceaſe to vibrate ?--No.
'Tis alone with ſorrow fill'd :
But death's ſtern hand muſt ſet it free,
Before it can be cold to thee.

SCIENCE.

O ſay fair ſcience, darling child
Of induſtry and toil ;
When wilt thou quit the great, the gay,
To bleſs—my humble ſoil ?
The ſons of vanity and wealth,
Pay not their court to thee ;
Canſt thou not leave their ſplendid ſphere
To lend one ray to me ?

Me, who have toil'd the live long day,
Nor other joys have known ;
And waſted out the midnight lamp,
To call thy ſmiles my own.

But ah! to me, the nymph so coy,
Imparts no friendly ray;
In penury I'm doom'd to pine,
And linger out the day.

RECEIPT TO MAKE A MODERN POET.

IN a cogitative state,
The poet Mr. Plodder sat,
Lab'ring to pen a handsome lay,
Upon his Delia's natal day,
But e'er he'd written one short line,
He found himself in want of rhyme,
He rubb'd his forehead, till it bled,
And then he scratch'd his mop-like head,
He chew'd the quill, each word he writ,
And then his finger nails he bit.
At length he threw the paper by,
And with a very heavy sigh
Address'd his muse in such a tone,
As would have mov'd a heart of stone.
Swift from high Shockœ hill* the maid
Descends, and brings her poet aid,
Plodder, she cries, "no more complain,
"I will assist you, in your strain,
"Mind what I say, and then your rhyme
"Shall flow with ease at any time,
"Put down, for instance, words like these,
And fill the space with what you please:—

Delia thou my nymph, above all others—fair,
Thou angel with the carrot colour'd——hair,
By nature form'd to storm each youthful—breast,
And e'en to rob an anchorite of————rest,
With eyes to dim the twinklers of the——skies,
And raise a hurricane of lovers'————sighs,
Permit the bard upon thy natal————day,
Submissive at thy feet his verse to———lay;
Long may you live revolving years to——see,
From time's rude hand and ev'ry danger—free:

To cheer the world with thy reſplendent—charms
But only bleſs thy loving poet's———arms.

" This is the rule that's now in uſe,
" You ſee how ſoon it can produce,
" Adopt it, and no doubt you'll ſhine ;
" Many will deem your verſes fine,
" For men now think, and moſt works ſhew it,
" That *ſound* alone,† can form the poet,
" To fancy, genius and invention,
" Our modern bards make no pretenſion,
" Nor do they--I mean no offence,
" Care much for good old common ſenſe.

—

* This proves that Parnaſſus is not the only ſeat of the muſes. I dare venture to aſſert that there are three times nine muſes on three ſeveral hills about Richmond, who if properly *encouraged*, would ſing delightfully. This is the age of diſcoveries.

† What an old gander the once celebrated Dryden, at preſent ſeems to us great geniuſes, when we read his advice, viz.

" Learn to riſe in ſenſe, and ſink in ſound."

Riſe in ſenſe, and ſink in ſound ! ha ! ha ! ha !— Why is not muſic allowed by Congreve, to be capable of ſoftening rocks and bending knotted oaks—and muſt we give up ſound for dull ſenſe ? Beſides, there's another fellow, one Matt. Prior, he ſeems to have been an enemy to improvement—ſays he, as a precept,

" Let him be kept from paper, pen, and ink,
" So he may ceaſe to write, and learn to think."

That would be a pretty joke, if authors in our country, were to be reſtrained from the above materials, until they *think*. Why, writers would for twenty years to come, be as ſcarce among us as the growth of nutmegs.

An impudent fellow had the aſſurance the other day, to ſpeak extemporaneouſly to a poeteſs,

Madam, I think, you're very wrong,
Thus to be delving at ſing ſong,

It ſounds ſo like a ſcraper's tweedle,
Throw down your pen, take up the needle.

Would not a rhyming dictionary be very ſerviceable to our 1805 poets—for it is preſumed they never intend to write in blank verſe, becauſe it is ſo dry—ſhould they however condeſcend ſo far, would it not be adviſeable for them to gut old Milton, Thompſon, and others, and then introduce them in a new form. If they chuſe to have ſenſe in their compoſitions, and yet are addicted to rhyme, ſuppoſe they haſh up, as is the cooks' ſaying, poor Gray, beginning,

"Lo where the roſy boſom'd hours
"Fair Venus' train appear," &c.

Or any other old animal, that can be ſo dreſſed as to ſuit the palate of the public.

I do not at preſent recollect any more notes that I ought to ſubjoin, although, true it is, I wiſh to imitate ſeveral modern bards, who ſeem to have compoſed poems, merely for the purpoſe of writing addenda, three times as long as thoſe poems themſelves.

A SERMON IN PRAISE OF SWEARING IN CONVERSATION.

Deut. vi. 13.
And SHALT ſwear by his name.

THERE is a ſet of men in the world, who need to be known only in order to be deſpiſed; men who are a conſtant ſubject for ridicule, and juſtly the deriſion of the gay and more refined part of the human ſpecies: men who are ſo ſtupid, as to be more enamoured with the pleaſure of a benevolent action, more charmed with giving joy to the helpleſs and miſerable, with drying up the tears of the diſtreſſed, or ſoothing the agonies of the burſting heart, than with the lordly pride of wanton power, than in rendering the wretched more wretched, than with ſpurning at patient merit, or even the ſatisfaction of racking tenants, hoarding wealth, or all the high gratification of a debauch; more delighted with the viſionary pleaſure of indulging their own reflections, and the applauſe of a good conſcience, than with the charms of a bottle, the tranſports afforded by the laſcivious wanton, or all the high-wrought indulgences of a luxurious appetite. And, in one word, to ſum up their character, more afraid of a falſe, or even an unneceſſary oath, than of the point of a ſword.

It is with theſe poor mean-ſpirited wretches that I am now to combat, in order to ſhew the great advantages that attend a ſtrict compliance with the injunction in my text, *And thou ſhalt ſwear by his name.* I ſhall not here take up your time in examining the context, or even in conſidering what is meant by the command in my text, which ſome would confine to the neceſſary oaths, taken in a court of judicature; but, like all ſound divines, and in compliance with the cuſtom of all good commentators and diſputants, conſider the paſſage before us in that latitude, which is moſt adapted to anſwer my particular deſign.

One man takes his text, and endeavours, with the moſt elaborate eloquence, to prove, that the bible he preaches from is a work not fit to be read; that it never was deſigned for the inſtruction of ſuch blockheads as his audience, who, by looking into it, incur damnation. What concerns all to know, muſt be read by none but the prieſt, or whom he ſhall appoint. How glorious that revelation, which, in the hands of the multitude, points the way to miſery, but, in thoſe of the church, to eternal life! It is ſhe alone, who can infallibly inform us, that love, and charity, and compaſſion, and tenderneſs, ſo often mentioned in that old book, the bible, mean ſpite, and hatred, and the inquiſition, and burning fagots.

Another proves, that the God of truth is the God of falſhood; and, finding his ſcheme contradicted, by the language of ſcripture, from ſcripture nicely diſtinguiſhes between a revealed and a ſecret will, both oppoſite, both contradictory to each other. Scripture he proves to be a lye; his opinion he proves to true from ſcripture. Ye deiſts rejoice in theſe your friends! Admit them into your ſocieties! They, like you, can darken truth, they have aſſiſted you in ſetting fragment againſt fragment; and, when the dazzling ſun-beams ſhine too bright, can wiſely cloſe their eyes. Let me too be permitted to rank myſelf on this ſide, and, countenanced by ſuch great authorities, to take a text that ſuits my preſent purpoſe, regardleſs of every other paſſage that may be ſuppoſed to contradict it: nay, regardleſs of the text itſelf, any further than as it may ſerve for a plauſible introduction to what I have to offer.

It is ſufficient, therefore, that we have here a command to ſwear by the name of God; which I ſhall take, in the common and vulgar ſenſe of the word ſwearing, to mean, not only all manner of oaths, but whatever goes under the denomination of ſwearing in converſation, or oaths, curſes, and imprecations.

In treating this ſubject I ſhall conſider,

I. The many advantages attending the frequent uſe of oaths, curſes, and imprecations; in which will be ſufficiently proved, the falſeneſs of the aſſertion, that ſwearing is attended with neither pleaſure nor profit.

II. Anſwer ſome objections. And,

III. Make a ſuitable application.

I. I am to conſider the many advantages ariſing from a frequent uſe of oaths, curſes, and imprecations.

In the *firſt* place, this genteel accompliſhment is a wonderful help to diſcourſe; as it ſupplies the want of good ſenſe, learning and eloquence. The illiterate and ſtupid, by the help of oaths, become orators; and he, whoſe wretched intellects would not permit him to utter a coherent ſentence, by this eaſy practice, excites the laughter, and fixes the attention of a brilliant and joyous circle. He begins a ſtory, he is loſt in a vacuity of thought, and would inſtantly, to his eternal diſhonour, become ſilent, did not a ſeries of oaths and imprecations give him time to gather up, or rather ſeek the thread of his diſcourſe: he begins again, again he is loſt, but having complimented his friends, by calling for eternal damnation on them all, he has thought what to ſay next, and finds himſelf able to proceed with a ſentence or two more. Thus he ſtill talks on, while thought follows ſlowly after. Bleſt expedient! by the uſe of which polite converſation glides on uninterrupted, while ſound is happily ſubſtituted in the place of ſenſe: by this, mankind communicate familiar noiſe to each other, with as little intellectual ability and labour, as a pack of well-matched hounds; ſo often the object of their delight and admiration! O how prepoſterouſly abſurd then! how falſe, and contrary to experience, is that ridiculous aſſertion, that ſwearing is attended with neither pleaſure nor profit! For what higher pleaſure, what greater profit and advantage can a man enjoy, than to find, that, *in ſpite of nature, who has directed him to be ſilent*, he can hear himſelf talk—talk without ſtammering, or drawling out each heavy ſentence, that lags behind to wait on thought. Ye idiots rejoice! ye coxcombs, whoſe coſtive brain never dictated the flowing ſentiment, be glad! Ye whom learning never fired, in ſtupid ignorance loſt, exult! Bleſt with eaſe and indolence, you talk, and thoſe, like you, admire; while liſtening dæmons clap their wings, and grin applauſe.

Forgive me, if fired with my ſubject, I loſe my uſual moderation, for who can help being warmed at the mention of ſuch glorious advantages as theſe? Advantages, which level the converſation of the mighty, and raiſe the oratory of the carman and the porter. Here the loweſt frequently excel; the ploughman, with clouted ſhoon, outvies his competitors, and practiſes the vices of the gentleman, with more ſucceſs than the lord of the manor, or the ſplendid courtier, though adorned with ſtar and garter. Here no abilities, no learning are neceſſary, no ſtudious hours are required to attain perfection. Tropes and figures, all the flowers of oratory, all the pedantry of the ſchools, are vain and uſeleſs trumpery, compared with theſe ornaments: they require pains and ſtudy, nor can be applied without judgment, and the toil of reading what are fooliſhly called, the ingenious and polite authors: but ſwearing is, as I have ſaid, learning to the ignorant, eloquence to the blockhead, vivacity to the ſtupid, and wit to the coxcomb.

Secondly, Oaths and curſes are a proof of a moſt heroic courage, at leaſt in appearance, which anſwers the ſame end. For who can doubt the valour, the intrepidity of him who braves the thunder of heaven, who affronts the moſt formidable being in the univerſe, and treats with contempt, that all-enlivening principle which ſuſtains and animates the whole creation? Of what a noble elevation is the heart of a coward conſcious, when he thus defies the Almighty, and imprecates the fires of Hell! Let the bluſtering bully domineer, let him roar out his curſes, and threaten all who dare provoke the vengeance of his potent arm; let him terrify by a ſurly frown, and intimidate when, with portly gait, he vents ten thousand curses on the wretch, who impudently, presumes to oppose his mighty will —who dares doubt his courage? Who can believe, that the cane, or the toe, when duly applied, can have such magic power, as to make him twist, and writhe himself like a serpent, till, with this exercise, his joints and his mind, become so supple that he can bend and cringe and ask for pardon? Let the meek soldier boast his deeds in war, and with oaths and execrations lace the self-flattering tale; who can believe that so great a hero should have an antipathy to the sight of steel? Or that he, who challenges the blasting lightning to fall on his head, would tremble and turn pale at the flash of a pistol? No, this must never be imagined; for can it be supposed that he has less bravery in the field than in the tavern? With these blustering expletives then, the coward may strut and look big, and every minute give fresh proofs of an invincible courage: he may bravely sport with that being whose frown would make the heavens and earth to tremble: he may seem to snatch the vengeance from his uplifted hand, and throw it on his foe: he may invoke the wrath of heaven; and who can imagine that he is afraid of death, when he is continually calling for all the horrors of hell?

Thirdly, He hereby not only gives a proof of his courage, but informs the world, that he is entirely divested of all the foolish prejudices of education and has unlearnt ——

"All that the nurse, and all the prieſt have taught;"

that he has not only ſhook off the ſhackles of enthuſiaſm, but has baniſhed from his mind, that reverence of the deity, which is the foundation of every ſyſtem of religion. He is not ſuſpected of being ſuch a fool as to want inſtruction, ſince it cannot be imagined, that he has ſo dull a taſte as to go to church, unleſs, if he be a gentleman, to ogle the ladies; if a clown, to ſleep; or, if a tradeſman, in complaiſance to the ſober old women of both ſexes, who happen to be his cuſtomers: and he has this advantage, that he will never be taken for a pious churchman, a preſbyterian, a quaker, or a methodiſt. And in reality, he is ſo far from being a bigot to any religious principles, that he belongs to no religious ſociety upon earth. That he is not, nor cannot be a Chriſtian, is evident; for what is chriſtianty? It is extenſive benevolence, humanity and virtue, to which he bids defiance with every curſe. He cannot be a deiſt, becauſe they openly profeſs the utmoſt reverence for the deity; and for the ſame reaſon, he can neither be a Jew, nor a Mohamedan, or a follower of Confucius. No, nor even an atheiſt; ſince we cannot conceive that he would ſo often call upon God, if he were thoroughly convinced there was no ſuch being in the univerſe; however, he every minute lets us ſee, that he does not fear him. How unlicenſed is his freedom, how glorious and unconſtrained! Let the wretches, who meanly bend their wills, and regulate their actions, by the ſage dictates of reaſon and conſcience; who ſtoop to follow the rules of religion, and call them ſacred; let theſe bridle their tongues, let theſe confine themſelves within the narrow limits preſcribed by reaſon and good ſenſe: the ſwearer knows better; ſenſe, and reaſon, and religion, are all ſubſervient to his will, he diſdains their fetters, and rules thoſe which rule all the world beſide.

Fourthly, and laſtly, another advantage which attends this vice of the gentleman, this noble accompliſhment, is, that it ſometimes raiſes him to dignity and honour.

Under this head indeed, I take a greater latitude, and advert to a remote conſequence of the practice of ſwearing: but, as there is ſuch a cloſe concatenation in all our habits, and virtue and vice are progreſſive in their very nature, I ſhould not do complete juſtice to my ſubject, if I omitted the conſideration of it in this particular view. When a man, therefore, by a happy aſſociation of ideas, joins to the other advantages of this vice, ideas of wealth and grandeur: when he ſees no argument, that appears of any weight, to bind him down to the unthrifty rules of honeſty, and his regard for his own private advantage is too ſtrong, to let him have any for the private property of his neighbour; what ſhould hinder him, when a fair opportunity offers, from raiſing himſelf, by the ruin of his neighbour, his companion, or his deareſt friend? He has ſworn to a thouſand lies in company, without any view of private advantage; what ſhould prevent him then from taking one falſe oath, when the advantage is ſo conſiderable? Surely, neither conſcience, nor reaſon, nor religion, can do this: no, that is impoſſible; for I, who am as infallible as any dignified prieſt, that ever mounted a pulpit, have aſſerted, that theſe are all ſubſervient to his will.

Here the ſwearer, with an unbounded ambition, aſpires to ſeize on wealth, and boldly to graſp at thoſe riches, which fortune has fooliſhly given to a more deſerving perſon; and this in ſpite of JUSTICE and EQUITY; who are his profeſſed enemies. Thus he riſes above the multitude, and gains a laſting fame; not by blood and ſlaughter, but by cunning, deceit, and artifice; by burſting through the moſt ſolemn engagements, breaking in ſunder the bonds of ſociety, and only violating what all honeſt men hold ſacred. Suppoſe, that he fail in his attempt, and the property of the perſon he has attacked remain inviolate: he is conveyed to a caſtle, ſtrong as that of a crowned head; where no impertinent intruders dare appear to diſturb his repoſe: for in the day time he has a porter to ſtand at his gate; in the night his faithful attendants lock and bar his doors.

Surrounded with guards, he pays a ſolemn viſit at the ſeat of JUSTICE; he has the honour of being admitted to the royal bench; he converſes with that ſovereign perſonage herſelf, and, for a conſiderable time, takes up the whole attention of her prime miniſters, the lords of her court, who, aſſiduous to pay him all due reſpect, wait his coming, in their proper habiliments; and, though it be ever ſo early in the day, he is never received with the diſreſpectful negligence of an undreſs. The ceremony being over, he is reconducted by the ſame guards who brought him thither, and who dare not preſume to leave him, till he is ſafe within his palace. He now ſoon receives the reward of his baffled dexterity, the glorious fruit of his ambition. The day arrives, devoted to mirth and jollity; buſineſs and care are laid aſide, and every labouring hand has now a holiday. He walks, or rides in his triumphal car, attended by a numerous throng of gazing ſpectators; he is mounted above their heads, and his neck, not his temples, adorned with a civic wreath, and his wriſts with an embraſure, compoſed of a matter, ſomething coarſer, indeed, than that of pearls and diamonds. This is no ſooner done, than gaping thouſands ſend forth ſhouts of joy, and bending low, even to the ground, pay him homage; then riſing up, with loud acclamations, preſent their tribute, ſtriving who moſt ſhall pay, who ofteneſt bend. He is covered, he is loaded, with their gifts, and ſenſibly touched with their bounty. The more he gains, the more unenvied here he ſtands, while all rejoice, and give the applaufe that is his due. But, let his modefty be ever fo great, let his blufhes be like the trickling drops of crimfon, painting his bafhful cheek, and prompting a willingnefs to retire from thefe honours; yet one hour, at leaft, he is conftrained to ftay, to receive the willing offers of the multitude. Thrice happy man! had confcience, or had reafon fwayed, thou never hadft thus been bleft; unknown thou mighteft have lived, unknown have died.

II. I come now in the next place, to anfwer fome objections: but as thefe, after what has been faid, muft appear extremely trifling, I fhall be as concife as poffible, and haften to a conclufion. It is faid,

In the *firft* place, that the fwearer acts in direct oppofition to all the rules of right reafon.

But how can this be called an objection againft fwearing? What have we to do with right reafon?—We leave it to the dull wretches, the men of reflection: and yet there are fome of thefe, who attempt to mimick us: but if they act inconfiftently with their own abilities, let them look to that. An upright man is a downright fool, if he fwears at all. Let thofe who can talk without, extol their wonderous talents; they have no need of this polite vice to recommend them to the world. The fqueamifh wretch, who is afraid of a lie, has no need to fwear to what he fays, for he is certain that his word will be readily taken. But away with these *yea and nay* wretches, men born to be pointed at; the sheepish, the sober fools, who, regardless of the boundless liberty which we enjoy, talk of rectitude of manners, religion, and conscience.

Secondly, and lastly, it is objected, that it is one of the most senseless, unnatural, rude, and unmannerly vices, that ever was invented.

This, it must be confessed, is paying a fine compliment to at least half the polite world. How can that be *rude* and *unmannerly*, which gives such a grace to conversation? It is true, we express ourselves strongly, and use none of those languid, sneaking epithets in our discourse, which your modest men, your men of humanity make use of: but as we talk without meaning, nobody can say that we mean ill. And indeed, it is a very injurious expression, to say that this is *unnatural*, when so many of us have the honour of being universally deemed to be little better than *naturals*.

Now I have proved so effectually the great advantages attending the practice of this genteel and fashionable vice, that there needs but one word by way of application.

Consider, O consider, how inestimable are the advantages whicIsih have mentioned! If there be any one here desirous of obtaining these, and yet is troubled and intimidated with the impertinence of a restless conscience flying in his face, and threatening to haunt him, like a ghost, let him follow my advice, and conſcience will fall aſleep. Would he ſteel his heart againſt compunction, let him advance by degrees; if he be afraid of an oath, let him come as near it as he can, let him cry, *Egad*, *ramnation*, and *o dram ye*; let him thus chip and carve a few common-place expreſſions, to fit them to his conſcience, and the buſineſs will be done. This, practice will render familiar, and the coward, who firſt trembled at the thought of hell, will ſoon have the courage to call for damnation.

And now, ye, who have long indulged this vice; who have arrived at perfection in this great accompliſhment, and, by this mean, have gained that applauſe, which nature would have denied you, which reaſon refuſed, and conſcience condemned: you, I ſay, who, by the aſſiſtance of this vice, have diſtinguiſhed yourſelves, either as the orator, the pimp, or the bully: you who, with more diſtinguiſhed glory have graced the lofty pillory; and you who, under ſpecious oaths of ſpeedy marriage, have violated virgin innocence, and rewarded the maid, that loved you, with eternal infamy; conſider theſe noble advantages, applaud, congratulate yourſelves, and rejoice: you have not ſtopped at the moſt flagrant impieties; you have challenged, and defied the blaſting power of heaven to do its worſt, and with a diſintereſtedneſs peculiar to yourſelves have generouſly ſold the reverſion of eternal, inexhauſtible happineſs, merely for the pleaſure of affronting that great beneficent being, who has prepared it for you; your indulgent creator, and almighty friend. How nobly ungrateful! how unſelfiſh your conduct! Boaſt your bravery, and conſider the wiſdom of the exchange: for how blind muſt you be to every ſelf-intereſted view, how deaf to the calls of ſelf-love, while infinite unbounded felicity has no charms, when ſtanding in competition with the delight of affronting a benefactor, with the pleaſure of a curſe, and the ſatisfaction of hearing your own impertinence! STUPIDITY, IGNORANCE, and FOLLY, are on your ſide: act, therefore, like men, who profeſs to be their friends, and like the true enemies of REASON, RELIGION, and COMMON SENSE. You have ſeen your practice juſtified with advantages, which you never thought of: if theſe have any weight, if theſe have any claims, let them have all their influence. To ſum up all, let every man act conſiſtently with his real character, and, by his indulgence of this practice, or his forbearance, let his abilities, or his follies, ſtand confeſſed.

EDUCATION.

YE happy youths who tread, with willing feet,
The path of learning's venerable ſeat;
Where Truth's fair form in claſſick ſhades is found,
And Science breathes her inſpiration round—
Oh ſay, while youth yet folds you in her arms,
And hope yet flatters with deluſive charms,
While joy attends, Companion of your way,

And no dark cloud obſcures your infant day,
How ſweet to range the Academick bow'r
And cull with eager hand each claſſick flow'r:
To dwell with rapture on each mighty name
That ſhines reſplendent on the Roll of Fame,
And catch a ſpark of that celeſtial fire
That rous'd the Hero, or that wak'd the Lyre!
How ſweet to dwell on Homer's glowing line,
Homer the Great High Prieſt of all the Nine:
And heard the letter'd Prince of Roman ſong
Pour the rich tide of melody along:
With feſtive Horace—ſprightlieſt ſon of mirth,
Whom Attic doves inſtructed at his birth,
Preſs the rich cluſters of the teeming vine
And pledge, in Lyric draughts, the tuneful Nine.
Or liſt the Teian Bard, whoſe ſportive ſoul
Glows in his verſe and ſparkles in his bowl,
Thrill all the madd'ning raptures of his lyre,
While melting ſpirits wanton on the wire.
Or if the mind in ſorrow love to ſhare,
And ſeeks another's load of grief to bear;
Then penſive pour o'er Curtius' flow'ry page,
And mourn th'effects of Macedonian rage,
Sigh for Darius from his empire hurl'd,
A ſplendid ruin to inſtruct the world.
Not to the ancients only are confin'd
The various pleaſures of the ſtudent's mind.
'Tis his with fancy's eye to range each clime,
And even arreſt the "feather'd feet of time,
To pierce wherever truth or ſcience ſhone
And make the labours of the world his own.
Hence, tho' to one ſmall ſpot of earth confin'd,
We view the daring ardour of his mind
Look through all nature with a ſingle glance,
Shew what depends on fate, and what on chance,
With Newton trace the comet on its way,
Or count each beam of light that gilds the day,
Delighted mark the varied planets roll,
And own the wiſe concordance of the whole,
With Locke and Reid unfold the inward man
And each fine ſpring of human action ſcan,
The ſecret chambers of the mind explore,

And feaſt the ſoul with metaphyſick lore--
Theſe are the ſweets that crown your riſing hours,
That ſtrew your infant path of life with flow'rs,
That in yon hallow'd walls delight to dwell
And lure her votaries to learning's cell;
For you the world yet ſpreads no wily ſnare,
For peace and angel innocence are there.
Oh may ye learn, beneath his foſtering hand,
To whom is lent the promiſe of our land,
Whoſe liberal ſoul enlighten'd and refin'd
Delights in all the good of all mankind,
Delights to form to truth the infant breaſt
And bleſſing others is himſelf moſt bleſt,
Oh may ye learn t' improve the precious hour
Which Heav'n indulgent places in your pow'r;
To wake each noble impulſe of the ſoul,
Reſtrain each paſſion under juſt controul,
To own the finer feelings of the heart
And bid the ſigh at others' ſorrows ſtart,
To view misfortune with a pang ſincere
And give to mis'ry pity's tendereſt tear—
Oh cheriſh in your commerce with mankind
The dear inſtinctive ſympathies of mind,
And ever be with this great truth impreſt,
'Tis virtue beams the ſunſhine of the breaſt.
But moſt of all religion's ſacred pow'r
Cheers pilgrim man thro' life's ſad varying hour;
To her in awful reverence we bend;
The atheiſt's terror--but the chriſtian's friend.
Hail! meek religion, 'tis to thee we owe
Each ſource of bliſs—each antidote of woe;
'Tis thine when clouds life's tranſient day deform
To lift the ſinking ſoul above the ſtorm,
To beam the ſmile ſerene, the tranſport ev'n,
And grant a foretaſte of the bliſs of Heav'n.
And thou to whom in gratitude belong
The heart's warm tribute, and the muſes ſong,
Who led'ſt my infant ſteps to learning's ſhrine,
And taught'st me to revere her form divine,
Taught'ſt me when journeying thro' life's turbid ways,
Where ſorrows thicken and where hope decays,
Where thoſe deſert us whom we held moſt dear

And nought is left for misery but a tear,
To raise, like Anaxagoras, my eyes
And place my hopes of bliss beyond the skies,
To seek resign'd religion's fair abode
And rest my hopes and sorrows with my God.
Oh may'st thou long, to us and science dear,
Defer thy flight to heaven and linger here;
Still linger here a blessing to mankind
And perfect what thy mighty soul design'd.
And when at length, thy course of virtue run,
We mark the lustre of thy setting sun;
When the last hour shall come when we must part,
(Oh fatal truth that rends the poet's heart)
May no rude pangs thy parting soul annoy,
But dreams of bliss thy latest hour employ;
May soothing recollection of the past
Beam comfort round, and cheer thee to the last,
While joyful angels point thy trackless way
To blisful regions of eternal day.

SPRING.

HARK! it was sure the Turtle's note,
The breezes bore along,
At Spring's return she tunes her throat,
Moaning these woods among.

Sad songstress! let thy music flow,
In murmurs on my ear,
And I will hail thy plaint of woe,
While Spring's sweet buds appear.

Soft breezes catch the soothing sound,
And fancy loves thy lay,
While echo swells it all around,
At morn and close of day.

Now nature mourns no more decay,
But wakes again in smiles,
And blooming sweet in rich array,
Her vot'ry's time beguiles.

And oh, may swift the genial year,
A brother's health restore,

Spread o'er that languid form fo dear,
Hygeia's tints once more!

Spring breathes! the balmy power breathes,
And infant buds expand,
Op'ning they twine in rofy wreaths,
Bath'd by Aurora's hand.

And now appear the finifh'd bow'rs,
Adorn'd with vivid hues,
Foliage creeping with the flow'rs,
That blufh through morning dews.

Zephyr exhales, and from his wing,
Does grateful odours fhake,
While birds their matin chorus fing,
And fweeteft concert make.

The waves no longer hoarfely roar,
Their dafhings rude they ceafe;
And flowly paffing gently pour,
Soft founds infpiring peace.

Oh nature! pleafure giving pow'r
And great in ev'ry fcene,
Belov'd is e'en thy ftormy hour,
But more thy fmile ferene.

CLOSE OF AUTUMN.

OFT through thefe fcenes I filent rove,
And mark the changeful year;
See the firft tints adorn the grove,
Or view the profpect drear.

And now the haunts late green and gay,
Awake the fombre thought;
I mourn to fee this fwift decay,
And nature's ruin wrought.

For autumn now a mantle fpreads,
Of brownifh yellow hue;
No flowers fhew their blufhing heads,
Impearl'd with morning dew.

But blaſts now tear the faded bow'r,
 And howling fright the ear,
While fancy at the duſky hour,
 Bids airy forms appear.

The foaming waves, they daſh the ſhore,
 And melancholy found ;
And while the winds that widely roar,
 Make ſolemn muſic round ;

I mark the ſcenes with penſive care,
 And ſympathetic ſighs,
For ſummer flown I drop a tear,
 Then on it moralize.

THE RECLUSE.

" And he made Man a little lower than the
Angels."

" In joyous youth, what ſoul hath ever known
Thought, feeling, taſte, harmonious to his ear ?
Who hath not pauſed, while beauty's penſive eye
Aſk'd of his heart the tribute of a ſigh ?
Who hath not own'd, with rapture ſmitten frame,
The power of grace—the magic of a name ?"

THE moraliſt may lament the depravity
of human nature—he may paint in the live-
lieſt and moſt faſcinating colours the beauty and reality of VIRTUE—diſplay the hag-
gard face of VICE—exhibit her to our view
ſtripped of her falſe and deceptive glare, in
all her original deformity ; but unleſs ſome
more powerful auxiliaries are enliſted on his
ſide, ſhe will ſtill triumph in ſecurity, and
continue to defy the powers of reaſon and
of truth. For theſe auxiliaries we need not
wander into the regions of fancy, or call on
" ſpirits of the vaſty deep"—They are at

our doors, have nurtured us before we ſaw the light, are the nurſes of our infant years, and the loved companions of our lives. In ſhort, I would call on the female part of our race for their aſſiſtance in this momentous work. *Their* influence on ſociety has ever been univerſally acknowledged, and ſhould they with one accord join heartily in ſo great, ſo good a cauſe, nothing could withſtand that influence. If they would not only purſue virtue themſelves, but, enamoured with the beauty of holineſs, and truly ſenſible of the dignity of the female character, give an open and decided preference to thoſe who exult in virtue—what a wondrous change in our national manners would be ſpeedily effected. Men, ſenſible that their only paſſport to the favour of the fair, was an honourable and virtuous name, would fly, as from a peſtilence, the haunts of vice and depravity, where their morals are now corrupted, and their health becomes a prey to loathſome diſeaſe: they would be ſeen the delighted companions of rational ſociety, and the faithful guardians of innocent credulity. The moſt lovely part of the creation would alſo be charmed with the change. They would inſtantly be exalted to that ſtation in ſociety to which their influence on idolizing man juſtly gives them a claim. They would be courted with all the ardent veneration that a pure and virtuous heart is capable of feeling; and they would riſe in the idea of their faſcinated lovers, until they in truth beheld them but a little lower than those Celestial Hosts that chaunt Hosannahs in the Highest Heaven; and the epithet of angelic, now given in derision, we should scarcely doubt them entitled unto.

> " Come bright improvement, on the car of time,
> And rule the spacious earth from clime to clime!
> Come, Heavenly Powers, primeval peace restore;
> Love, mercy, wisdom, rule for evermore."

Let the hardened sensualists laugh virtue to scorn, and seek for joy in the haunts of illicit love—Let the man of the world, whose mind hourly pursues every calculation of interest, and whose dreams each night are the golden treasures of Golconda, despise what he, without doubt, will call the foolish imagination of an enthusiast.—I write not for them, but to souls of softer mould; and *they* will believe when I avow that I have beheld VIRTUE in a female form, have been the delighted witness of its fascinating influence on society, and have paid a willing homage to its power. And if such have been the power of an individual, what can possibly withstand the whole sex armed in all the loveliness of virtue, and marching on conquering and to conquer?

Yes I repeat, I have known the influence of the propriety of principles and conduct; and who, that has been blessed with an acquaintance with the gentle ASPASIA, but will gladly assent to its truth. Born in one of the great cities of America, of parents who delighted in teaching the young idea how to ſhoot, her mind at an early age acquired the power of diſcrimination: as ſhe grew in years, ſhe alſo grew in knowledge; and ſhe at an early age became the delight of her friends, and the admiration of her acquaintance. Whilſt with true politeneſs ſhe ever, in the trivial and common intercourſe of life, preferred the wiſhes of others to her own, and was perfectly willing to ſing, to ride, to walk, to ſit, and converſe, as the ſtate of her companions would dictate—in matters of eſſential right and wrong, ſhe was immovable. No intreaties, no artifice, could engage her to countenance, or commit an action which that Divine Monitor, conſcience, told her was evil; and nothing could deter her from purſuing what ſhe was convinced was her duty. The dignity of her deportment put inſolence to the bluſh, and vanity became abaſhed in her preſence. The boldeſt libertine was awed into ſilence, and the half-formed jeſt died unpronounced from his tongue. Yet this was not in conſequence of any haughtineſs of manners, natural or aſſumed; ſhe was ever cheerful, eaſy and condeſcending. But ſhe diſguiſed not that ſhe preferred virtue to vice, was a believer in the ſacred ſcriptures, and an humble follower of Him who died for her.—— Poſſeſſing a perſon gracefully elegant, manners eaſy and polite, a countenance beaming with ſenſibility and good will, it cannot be ſuppoſed that ſhe was without profeſſed admirers. A number of gentlemen, ſuppoſed by the world to be unexceptionable, offered her their hands; but ſhe had drawn a picture of her intended, of which theſe were not the likeneſs. Aſpaſia therefore, with great gratitude and gentleneſs, ſuppreſſed their hopes, but in ſuch a manner as, while it increaſed their admiration and filled them with regret, left them without the leaſt reaſon to complain, and they became the *friends* of her whom they had aſpired to call by a more endearing name.

I knew her well, was the delighted witneſs of her virtues; was honoured with her approbation; made happy by her friendſhip, and was admitted into her moſt unreſerved confidence; and although accident has drawn me from her ſociety, and cut me off from all direct communication with her—although I do no more imbibe inſtruction from her lips, nor am bleſſed with her ſentiments warm and undiſguiſed from the heart, drawn in language correct and impreſſive—I once owed much of my happineſs to her friendſhip, and even now thus retired, I am not without the conſolation of believing that her heart bears teſtimony of my truth and faithfulneſs, and that ſhe would ſtill greet with joy him ſhe has long called her friend.

I have ſometimes, in my accidental intercourſe with the world, heard her name coupled with praiſe; and truly rejoiced on finding that ſhe ſtill continues her virtuous and brilliant courſe, that ſhe is the ſupport and consolation of the widow and fatherless, the instructor of the ignorant and defender of the oppressed.—Go on, ASPASIA, thou art blessed with the approbation of Men and Angels, and hast prepared for thee in another and a better world, a Crown of Eternal Glory.

PETITION OF A GOOSE.

PITY the sorrows of a poor old Goose,
Whose feeble steps have borne her to your door,
Broke down with sorrow, lame, and past all use,
O! give me corn, and Heav'n will bless your store.

My feather'd coat, once lily white, and sleek,
By cruel pluckings grown so bare and thin;
These rags, alas! do misery bespeak,
And show my bones, just starting through the skin.

"Come, Biddy, come," that well known, pleasing sound,
Stole in soft murmurs from Dame Parlet's farm;
For plenty there, in youthful days, I found,
So waddled on, unconscious then of harm.

Soon as I reach'd this once blest, happy cot,
Feeding the pigs, came Parlet from the sty;
More kicks than half-pence I too surely got,
She seized a broomstick, and knock'd out my eye.

A bandy cur, sworn foe to all our race,
Some few years past, when I was strong and plump,
Who, if I hiss'd, would run and hide his face,
Now boldly tears my breeches from my rump.

The wall-eyed brute next bit me through the leg;
A snotty boy, too, out of wanton joke,
For whom I've laid, aye, many and many an egg,
Snatch'd up a stone, and this left pinion broke.

To go from hence you ſee I am not able;
Oh! take me in, the wind blows piercing cold;
Short is the paſſage to the barn or ſtable,
Alas! I'm weak, and miſerably old.

St. Michael's fatal day approaches near,
A day we all have reaſon ſure to curſe;
Ev'n at the name my blood runs cold with fear,
So inimical is that ſaint to us.

You have misfortunes; why ſhould I repine?
We're born for food to man full well I know:
But may your fate, ah! never be like mine,
A poor old Gooſe, of miſery and woe.

A numerous flock elected me their Queen;
I then was held of all their race the pride;
When a bold Gander waddling from Brook-Green,
Declar'd his love, and I became his bride.

Goſlings we had, dear comforts of my life;
But a vile cook, by ſome mad fancy bit,
My pretty cacklings kill'd, then ſtuff'd with ſage,
And their ſweet forms expos'd upon the ſpit.

The murd'reſs next ſeiz'd on my tender mate;
Alas! he was too fat to run or fly;
Like his poor infants yielded unto fate,
And with his giblets, Cook, ſhe made a pie.

Pity the ſorrows of a poor old Gooſe,
Whoſe feeble ſteps have borne her to your door,
Broke down with ſorrow, lame, and paſt all uſe,
O! give me corn, and Heav'n will bleſs your ſtore.

THE TEST OF FRIENDSHIP.

WHEN cloth'd in power, and eager hoſts,
With ſmiles and greeting lowly bend,
Ah! can the erring mortal boaſt,
Of all his flatterers, *a Friend?*

When bleſt with wealth, amid the crew
That crowd our feſtive boards around,

Is he—the man fincerely true
  In pure affection, always found ?

No ! when degraded, fcoff'd, opprefs'd,
  The victim of unfeeling fway ;
When want and ficknefs from our breaft,
  Have driven the cherub HOPE away—

The very knave, who fwore he'd bleed
  Rather than view our bleffings fhorn ;
The very wretch, we wont to feed,
  Will treat ourfelves and woes with fcorn.

'Tis he alone, who ftill the fame
  In power, in ficknefs, and in need,
Aye, owns with joy the facred flame,
  He only is *a friend indeed.*

ODE

CANTABILE.

THE night was calm—the fky ferene,
  And darknefs veil'd the face of day,
Tir'd nature clos'd her active fcene,
  And bound in fleep, her offspring lay.
The midnight watch had juft been fpoke.
  Who guards the peaceful hours of night ?
When from the roof burfts forth the fmoke,
  And horror ftrikes th' aftonifh'd fight.

ALLEGRO.

Now fee th' affrighted mother run,
  Her tender offspring yet to fave,
While round the father clings the fon,
  Whofe piercing cries protection crave.
The crackling flames, like lightning darts,
  From fide to fide deftructive fly
The frame gives way, the roof now parts,
  And all will foon in ruin lie.
When from the crowd a youth afcends,
  Who dar'd the fcorching flame to brave,
Fearlefs of death, he thus defends,
  And tries his fellow man to fave.

ADAGIO.

Bleſt Providence, whoſe power we own
To ſave or periſh, though unknown,
Thy myſtick will, we muſt obey.
And thou ſweet Charity beſtow,
Thy bounteous gifts to heal the woe,
And cheer the ſuff'rers gloomy way.

LOVE.

LOVE! thou ſacred, tender paſſion,
Kind refiner of our youth,
Fly the ſeats of pride and faſhion,
Haſte to virtue, peace, and truth.

Here thy watchful vigils keep,
Never—never from us flee,
Softly let my Ellen ſleep,
Let her dream of love and me.

Let my breaſt her pillow be,
Let me taſte the fond delight;
Still, beneath the hawthorn tree,
Let me watch her ſlumbers light.

Let no thoughts approach alarming,
Gentle love, the hours beguile;
Let me ſee her eyes, ſo charming,
Open on me with a ſmile.

Let me ſee her, with confuſion,
Hide her bluſhes in my breaſt;
When I preſs her to my boſom,
Let me hear her ſigh ſhe's bleſt.

Soft ſenſations crowd upon me;
Never may my heart repine;
Why ſhould care or ſorrow preſs me
Since Ellen, lovely Ellen's mine.

FRIENDLY HINTS.

AS you are beginning buſineſs in trade, I am induced by perſonal affection and moſt ardent wiſhes for your welfare and proſperity, to offer you my advice. I well know that advice is ſeldom welcome: but to you I tender mine in confidence that it will be well received, inaſmuch as ſince the mournful period when it pleaſed heaven to bereave you of your excellent father, I have in a manner ſtood in that endearing relation toward you, and have hitherto received from you the conſtant tokens of filial gratitude and love.

In the firſt place, deal fairly and hold faſt to integrity. Let no temptation of gain on the one hand, nor any embarraſſment on the other, ever lead you to ſtep aſide from the path of ſtrict honeſty. For aſide from the conſideration of a ſolemn reckoning hereafter, "honeſty is the beſt policy:" it is the ſureſt way to worldly thrift and proſperity. But to honeſty there muſt be added a great degree of caution, leſt you become a dupe to the arts of the knaviſh. Many a hopeful young man has been led by the conſcious integrity of his own heart to ſuch an overweening confidence in mankind as rendered him a prey to cunning ſharpers and ſwindlers.

Unite care with diligence. Care preſerves what induſtry gains: but the man who attends to his buſineſs diligently, but not carefully, throws away with one hand what he gathers with the other. A man in buſineſs ſhould, as much as poſſible, make uſe of his own eyes; at leaſt, he ſhould have a conſtant overſight of all his concerns; for if he leave this chiefly to others, it is ten to one, that he will ſoon find his circumſtances embarraſſed.

Endeavour to poſſeſs at all times a critical knowledge of your real circumſtances. For this purpoſe, and indeed in every reſpect, exact order or method in buſineſs is highly neceſſary Men who do buſineſs without method, act in the dark; they plunge along at random, not knowing where they place their ſteps. They quickly find themſelves bewildered and embarraſſed; and there are many chances againſt them for one in their favour.

Prudently beware that your expenditure do not out-run your income. The ſtyle of living ſhould conform to one's perſonal circumſtances; and ſuch expenditures as can be well afforded by a man of fortune, might be inevitably deſtructive to him who has his fortune yet to make. "Money," ſays the old proverb, "makes money. When you have got a little and carefully ſaved it, it is often eaſy to get more. The great difficulty with the beginner, is to get that little." But if frugality does not ſtore up what induſtry acquires, there can be no increaſe of capital.

Take heed of over-trading.—If you adventure beyond your depth, if depending upon a fictitious capital, you extend your buſineſs very far beyond your capital, the hazard of bankruptcy will be great. Indeed in this case you would hazard not only your own property, but that of your creditors; which is hardly reconcilable with honest principles. "When the profits of trade happen to be greater than ordinary, over-trading becomes a general error, both among great and small dealers;" and a sudden shift in the state of commerce, (such as frequently happens) produces general distress.

Reckon nothing your own that you owe for: it is a deposit placed in your hands by your creditors; which it would be fraudulent for you to use in such a manner as to endanger their interest. Debts are sacred; and every honest man will use his endeavour to discharge his *bona fide* debt with punctuality and honour.

Be ever cautious of running deeply into debt. Flattering prospects of great gain in this way some times occur, but they often prove delusive, and leave the too rash adventurer under an insupportable load.

Beware of entangling yourself by imprudent suretyships. There are divers caveats in the sacred volume against this kind of adventure; and its fatal consequences have been often witnessed in our own times, and in almost all parts of this country.—Especially beware of dealing too largely in *accommodation paper*; for as in such a case, you must borrow the names of others as endorsers, you will frequently find yourself under the necessity of lending your own name in return, further than prudence would dictate.

And as a large number become linked together in this way, the failure of a few of them ſhocks the whole.

Perſuaded that you will take theſe friendly hints in good part, and give them their due weight in your mind and practice, I only add the ſincere expreſſion of my ardent wiſhes that your honeſt and laudable efforts may be crowned with the divine bleſſing.

Hints to authors in general, but eſpecially to thoſe whoſe ſtock of ideas will enable them to fill a pamphlet only—ſhewing the proper method of *book-making*, let the ſubject be ever ſo barren in itſelf.

Propoſal for a Hiſtory of Snuff, from the earlieſt period down to the preſent time—in 12 *vols. fol. with a copious index.*

Vol. 1. Word Snuff—whence derived.—General hiſtory of Snuff—by whom firſt manufactured. Sir Walter Raleigh firſt brought tobacco into England. Hiſtory of Sir Walter's family from the time of William the Conqueror, proving indiſputably, that the name ought to be written and pronounced *Rawleighe*.

Vol. 2. The life of Walter, with a copy of his commiſſion from Queen Elizabeth for making diſcoveries in North America—with a defence of the Queen from the many *unfounded* aſperſions caſt on her character, concerning her intimacy with Sir Walter—the earls of Leicester and Essex, &c *Tobacco* a native plant of Virginia—History of Virginia and Maryland down to the present time.

Vol. 3. General Arnold burnt large quantities of tobacco last war—Cause of the American war—History of the stamp-act, with an estimate of the number of pinches of snuff taken previously to its passing both houses of parliament.

Vol. 4. History of the American war—Large quantities of snuff taken by the *quidnuncs* of London during that time, and proving clearly that the government of England was brought to *a pinch*.

Vol. 5. Account of the principal snuff-shops in and about London since the great fire Anno Domini 1666—Consequences of that fire—Table the 1st, shewing the quantity and value of snuff and tobacco destroyed. Table the 2d, the number of pipes and snuff-boxes broken, and otherwise destroyed, with a very particular account of two steel boxes in perfect preservation, and three pipes *burnt out* remarkably well during the conflagration, and taken from the ruins after the fire.

Vol. 6. Biographical accounts of the principal snuff-takers and smokers from the first introduction of tobacco into England—Name of the first person in England who carried a snuff-box—Hints for raising a sufficient sum to erect a monument to him in Westminster Abbey, in the shape of a tobacco-hogshead.

Vol. 7. A dissertation on *sneezing*, proving fully to any reasonable man that the faculty are entirely unacquainted with its causes; together with a criticism on the *term* "snuffing," in consequence of its being sometimes applied to the action of candles.—When tallow-candles first came into use.—The ancients generally used oil.—Large quantities of tallow imported from South America—History of Mexico and Peru, with an account of its subjugation by Cortez—with a critical dissertation on the materials of which the fire was made which was constantly kept burning in the temple of the sun.

Vol. 8. The names of the different kinds of snuff now in use, wherein their comparative merits are ably and fully discussed—*Macaboy* snuff made from tobacco growing only in a very small district in the island of Martinique.

Vol. 9. History of Martinique from its first discovery down to the present time—Quantity of snuff consumed in that island—the ladies remarkably fond of snuff.

Vol. 10. Tobacco generally made by slaves—a dissertation on slavery with a history of the slave trade.

Vol. 11. Mr Wilberforce's speeches in the British parliament respecting the abolition of the slave-trade.

Biographical account of Mr. Wilberforce.

Vol. 12. Snuff-taking rather on the decline, causes of it deduced—the late excise-law supposed to be one, &c.

A copious appendix in four large folio lolumes, containing *a brief* account of ſnuff-takers and ſnuff in the United States of America—an attempt to prove that it would be more to the advantage of the United States to import than manufacture their own ſnuff, inaſmuch as the inconvenience reſulting from having the tobacco on the ſpot, deters numbers from purchaſing, and determines many others to import for their own uſe—together with the different authorities made uſe of in the book, with an index, &c. &c. &c.

One ſmall volume of plates conſiſting of about 1500, containing views of the principal tobacco and ſnuff manufactories, ſnuff-ſhops, &c. &c. with ample references. As a ſpecimen of the authorities alluded to in the Appendix, take the following:

Syrre Wallterre Rawleighe, whoe waſſe a greate favouritte offe the Queene's highneſſe, ande a manne offe faſhionne aſſe welle aſſe a phylloſſophere, introducedde the ſmoakynge offe Tobaccoe intoe Englande. Inne a ſhorte tyme the practyſe became quite the *tonne*; nay, the Queenes Majeſtye herſelffe, grewe fonde offe itte, ande woulde oftenne indulge herſelfe, wythe a ſocyalle Pype withe herre maides offe honoure, ande ſomme offe the more favourede gentlemene offe the courte.

Inne one offe thoſe ſmoakynge partyes, her Highneſſe havynge much agytatedde the nature offe theire preſente enjoymente, atte lengthe broke uppe the commpanie, verie facettyouſlye and wittyllie remarkynge, That "alle the pleaſſure offe the evennynge aſſe did the pleaſſures offe thiſſe tranſitorie ande uncertaine worlde, hadde endedde in ſmoake!" Aſſe thiſſe notable ande pleaſaunte obſervacyonne waſſe utteredde bye herre Highneſſe with herre accuſtomydde gravittye offe countenaunce, the courtlie Barronnes ande noble ladyes preſente didde notte welle knowe whetherre they were toe looke grave orre ſeryouſe, toe laughe orre toe crye; ande ſoe, eche offe themme puttynge a fore fingerre upponne theire lyppes, theye didde inne concerte ſneeze, ande inne a lowe voice cryed—"*te he!*"

THE GRAVE.

There is a calm for thoſe who weep,
A reſt for weary pilgrims found;
They ſoftly lie, and ſweetly ſleep,
Low in the ground.

The ſtorm that wrecks the winter ſky,
No more diſturbs their deep repoſe
Than ſummer evening's lateſt ſigh
That ſhuts the roſe.

I long to lay this painful head,
And aching heart beneath the ſoil,
To ſlumber in that dreamleſs bed
From all my toil.

For Miſery ſtole me at my birth,
And caſt me helpleſs on the wild;
I periſh—O my mother Earth!
Take home thy child.

On thy dear lap theſe limbs reclin'd,
Shall gently moulder into thee:

Nor leave one wretched trace behind,
Refembling me.

Hark !—a ftrange voice affrights mine ear ;
My pulfe—my brain runs wild—I rave ;
—Ah ! who art thou whofe voice I hear ?
" I am the GRAVE !

" The GRAVE, that never fpake before,
Hath found at laft a tongue to chide ;
O liften !—I will fpeak no more ;
Be filent, Pride !

" Art thou a *wretch* of hope forlorn,
The victim of confuming care ?
Is thy diftracted confcience torn
By fell defpair ?

" Do foul mifdeeds of former times
Wring with remorfe thy guilty breaft ?
And Ghofts of unforgiven crimes
Murder thy reft ?

" Lafh'd by the furies of the mind,
From wrath and vengeance would'ft thou flee,
Ah ! think not, hope not, Fool ! to find
A friend in me.

" By all the terrors of the tomb,
Beyond the powers of tongue to tell !
By the dread fecrets of my womb !
By Death and Hell !

" I charge thee *live !*—Repent and pray ;
In duft thy infamy deplore ;
There yet is mercy !—Go thy way,
And fin no more.

" Art thou a *Mourner ?*—Haft thou known
The joy of innocent delights ?
Endearing days forever flown
And tranquil nights ?

" O *live!*—and deeply cherifh ftill
The fweet remembrance of the paft:
Rely on Heaven's unchanging will
For peace at laft.

" Art thou a *Wanderer?*--Haft thou feen
O'erwhelming tempefts drown thy bark?
A fhipwreck'd fufferer haft thou been,
Misfortune's mark?

" Though long of winds and waves the fport,
Condemn'd in wretchednefs to roam,
" LIVE!--thou fhalt reach a fheltering port,
A quiet home.

" To Friendfhip didft thou truft thy fame,
And was thy friend a deadly foe,
Who ftole into thy breaft to aim
A furer blow.

" LIVE!--and repine not o'er his lofs,
A lofs unworthy to be told;
Thou haft miftaken fordid drofs
For friendfhip's gold.

" Go, feek that treafure, feldom found,
Of power the fierceft griefs to calm,
And footh the bofom's deepeft wound
With heavenly balm.

"—In *Woman* haft thou plac'd thy blifs,
And did the Fair One faithlefs prove?
Hath fhe betrayed thee with a kifs,
And fold thy love?

" LIVE!--'twas a falfe bewildering fire;
Too often love's infidious dart
Thrills the fond foul with fweet defire,
But *kills the heart.*

" A nobler flame fhall warm thy breaft,
A brighter maiden's virtuous charms!
Bleft fhalt thou be, fupremely bleft,
In beauty's arms.

"——Whate'er thy lot—whoe'er thou be ;
Confefs thy folly, kifs the rod,
And in thy chaftening forrows fee
The hand of God.

" A bruifed reed he will not break ;
Afflictions all his children feel ;
He wounds them for his mercy's fake,
He wounds to heal.

" Humbled beneath his mighty hand,
Proftrate, his Providence adore :
'Tis done !—Arife ! he bids thee ftand,
To fall no more.

" Now, Traveller in the vale of tears,
To realms of everlafting light,
Through time's dark wildernefs of years,
Purfue thy flight.

" There is a calm for thofe who weep,
A reft for weary Pilgrims found :
And while the mouldering afhes fleep,
Low in the ground,

" The Soul, of origin divine,
GOD's glorious image freed from clay,
In heaven's eternal fphere fhall fhine,
A ftar of day !

" The SUN is but a fpark of fire,
A tranfient meteor in the fky,
The SOUL, immortal as its fire,
" Shall never die !"

BOTANICAL GARDEN.

IT ver, et Venus, et Veneris prænuncius ante,
Pennatus graditur Zephyrus veftigia propter,
Flora quibus mater præfpergens ante viæ
Cuncta, coloribus egregis et odoribus opplet.
LUCRET.

A ſpacious plain extends i s upland ſcene,
Rocks riſe on rocks, and fountains guſh between;
Soft Zephyrs blow, eternal ſummers reign:
And ſhowers prolific, bleſs the ſoil—*in vain.*

DARWIN.

From different climes, from various regions brought,
All that can charm the eye, or fix the thought;
From cleanſing Hyſſop, ſtill the theme we greet,
Till all Libanus lie beneath our feet.

MY OWN!!!!

I was moſt aſtoniſhingly gratified, and wonderfully pleaſed, to ſee ſome hints on the ſubject of a Botanical Garden—from the immenſe advantages which would attend ſuch an inſtitution, I am really at a loſs to divine, why the *thing* has only been ſpoken of —and why it has not been written upon, read, and put in practice long ſince.

There are but two objections, which preſent themſelves at this time to my view—the firſt is, that from the increaſed, and increaſing population of this flouriſhing city; the land in the vicinity cannot be purchaſed, but for a price far exceeding what *ſome people* might think its real worth: and the ſecond is, that if we ſhould *be ſo fortunate* as to ſucceed in making the purchaſe, the ſoil I mean of a ſufficient quantity very near the city, is of ſuch a quality, as not to afford even variety enough, to anſwer every purpoſe of the inſtitution.

To the firſt I would anſwer, that although ſome one of the community might make a profitable *job* of it, yet every one knows that public advantage is ſo connected with private intereſt, that we ſee them walking hand in hand through the ſtreets, lanes, alleys, and over the bridges of this city every day; and no one will doubt, that public advantage will always increaſe private emolument: and it muſt alſo be conſidered by every perſon, that even under the ſuppoſition that ſome *patriotic* individual ſhould be entitled by means of this ſcheme being carried into effect, to receive from the *generoſity* of the director s*that are to be*, 150, or 200 per cent. more than his lands are worth—it will very probably convince that very man of the ſalutary effects reſulting from ſuch an inſtitution, and of courſe he might be induced to ſubſcribe for 40 or 50 ſhares—when, if the tranſaction had not taken place—he would not perhaps have advanced a ſingle dollar to tranſplant all the exotics in the four quarters of the globe to our ſoil, even if he knew that they might with time and care become naturalized to it.

To the ſecond objection I muſt anſwer, that it is by no means apochryphal, but a well atteſted fact, that the Malteſe and for ought we know many other nations, are ſo extremely choice in the culture of ſome of the fruits of that iſland, as to import earth from Sicily; their own ſoil not being ſufficiently ſtrong for every purpoſe of horticulture:—Now I am very well convinced, that we might not import earth from Sicily only, but from every part of the known world, except Paleſtine, where I am told it is rather ſcarce—but even there, when we come to our rock-plants, we might receive very confiderable benefit by importing huge maffes of folid rock, much larger than can poffibly be met with in this country—to give an inftance or two—for that particular place in the garden fet apart for the culture of tea, a fhip might be fitted out at a *trifling* expence to take in a load of earth for the exprefs purpofe—to Botany-Bay it would anfwer a double purpofe; for according to *Sir Jofeph Banks*, the garden might be half filled not with earth only, but with plants of every kind which are not *come-atable* in this country, and which are of courfe highly valued by the virtuofi. The charge confequently attendant on thefe imports, might be confidered as enormous by fome plodding, calculating, miferly perfons, but when we view the aftonifhing utility of the *thing*, fuch a *paltry* objection will immediately vanifh.

There is another objection, which however did not ftrike me when I firft began to write this plan, viz. that although we may fpend our money in importing earth and rocks, yet it will be impoffible to import climate from the frozen or torrid zone, d y weather from Peru, a whole rainy feafon from the Weft-Indies, or an inundation from the Nile or Miffiffippi. Luckily, however, this objection, which appears to be irremediable, may in a great meafure be fo difpofed of as to be reduced to a mere nothing, in comparifon, to what it was at firft fight.—Now be it known to all thofe who have been ſo unfortunate as not to have read the life and magnificent works of the great CATHARINE of Ruſſia *of bleſſed memory*, that ſhe had, and perhaps the preſent Emperor now has, a garden wherein all the productions of the globe have been tranſplanted with the moſt aſtoniſhing ſucceſs—This garden is planted over a vaſt number of arches, in the interior of which are furnaces, properly arranged, the heat of them being continually regulated by thermometers in ſuch a juſt proportion, that the ſame degree of heat is conveyed to each plant that it would have received had it remained in its native ſoil:—her not being acquainted with Swift's works, immediately accounts for the inconvenience attending the want of ſunſhine, a ſufficient quantity of which, one of his projectors confidently affirms, may very eaſily be extracted from cucumbers!!!

But I am ſtill more aſtoniſhed, that although many have given their ideas as far as reſpects the utility of ſuch an inſtitution, yet not one of them all has given a plan, or even a proſpectus of one; and as this leaves an immenſe vacuum in the minds of many, who would perhaps, after reading this ſcheme, cheerfully ſubſcribe, I beg leave humbly to propoſe the following outlines of a plan, which, if carried into effect, although it will be attended with ſome *little* trouble and expenſe, yet the pleaſure it will give every true Darwinian ſoul, will be at leaſt commenſurate, and not only comport with the dignity of our city, but alſo add conſiderably to the beauty of its ſuburbs.

It will be nec ſſary in the firſt place, every body knows, to raiſe the funds; therefore, to give all perſons the opportunity of coming forward on ſo noble an occaſion, let the capital ſtock, which muſt at leaſt be *ten millions of dollars*, be divided into one million of ſhares at ten dollars each, theſe, I am certain, will be very ſoon ſubſcribed for, and then begin the garden on the FOLLYING plan, which is as near to one I have read in ſome European publication as circumſtances will admit:

Plan of a Botanical Garden.

Let the ground plot be ſufficiently large, ſay at firſt 5000 acres, to embrace every object which may be either uſeful or elegant, always taking care to blend the Utile with the Dulci, in ſuch an agreeable manner as not to pall the imagination of the *big* and *little Maſters and Miſſes* who may come to walk therein, either for profit or delight. The firſt grand diviſion will be called the Hortus Linnœencis, which muſt be ſubdivided into three parts—

1. Herbarum—herbs.
2. Fruticetum—ſhrubs.
3. Arboretum—trees.

This will take in all herbs, ſhrubs and trees, beginning with the firſt claſs, and proceeding regularly down to the laſt claſs of Cryptogamia.

The ſecond grand diviſion will be the Peccadarium, to be ſubdivided, with the greateſt care, as follows:

1. Hortus Ovinus, or Sheep Garden.
2. Hortus Bovinus—Horned-cattle Garden.
3. Hortus Equinus—Horſe Garden.
4. Hortus Hircinus—Goat Garden.
5. Hortus Suinus—Swine Garden.

In this diviſion the *ſwiniſh multitude* will be *allowed* to walk as much as they pleaſe, but by no means to attempt the taking any of the pigs away.

By way of variety, the third grand diviſion may be laid off for the culture of the plants denominated ſaxatile, or plants growing on rocks, huge maſſes of which may be piled *ſtratum ſuper ſtrata* in one vaſt regular confuſion!!! Here will be delightful recreation for the romantic love-ſick maiden, as well as for the amorous, but neglected ſwain; here they may ſtand on the frowning brow of ſome awful precipice, think of their abſent loves or lovers, and in an agony of deſpair, precipitate themſelves to the bottom! and for their further accommodation, a ſtream of pure water, guſhing from the ſide of a magnificent rock, ſhall wind its ſinuotic courſe, until it meets with ſome reſervoir, ſufficiently capacious for all the purpoſes of *ſubmerſion*.

The fourth grand diviſion, to include the Hortus siccus—or ſpecimens of plants which are to be kept in an apartment of the green-houſe, under the particular care of the chief manager, who ought not only to have a thorough knowledge of *botany*, but alſo, ſomething of *phyſic* and *chemiſtry*: in this diviſion will alſo be, the

FLORA AMERICANA:

Where flowers from every part of America, will rear their gaudy heads; or more humbly creep along the *raviſhed* earth, perfuming the *aſtoniſhed* atmoſphere, ſo as entirely to overpower the noiſome exhalations, proceeding from the putrid ſubſtances, unavoidably collected in a large city.

The fifth grand diviſion to be called the

Eſcarium—plants which furniſh food to man.

1 Roots,—as potatoes, beets, carrots, parſnips, &c.

2 Stocks or leaves—as cabbage, ſpinache, &c.

3 Flowers.

4 Seeds as—peas, beans, &c.

With directions for thoſe who may *honour* this part of the garden with a viſit, ſhewing the relative quantity of nutriment contained in each kind; and the probable conſequences which may reſult to the human body, from the uſe of them in their different ſtages, from their firſt putting forth until ripe.

To conclude with that grand deſideratum, the

HORTUS MEDICINALIS;

the plants of which, as it may lay me open to the criticiſm of the gentlemen of the faculty, I forbear to mention.

Now, in laying this *grand* plan before the public, I do moſt ſolemnly aver, that I do not own one inch of ground within fifty miles of this city, nor indeed but let this be a ſecret between ourſelves, any where elſe. So every perſon muſt ſee, that my motives are entirely diſintereſted; and moreover, I am ſo exceeding modeſt, as to declare, that if a better plan were to offer, I would immediately withdraw mine.

P. S. As I have entirely forgotten a *Vineyard*, you may take the liberty to *ſtick one* between any of the grand diviſions, as by the projected plan, we ſhall have land enough.

P. S. Again. As a ſupplement to this garden, a piece of land in Louiſiana, of about 100 miles ſquare, and removed at a ſufficient diſtance from any inhabited part, might be purchaſed from government, for the purpoſe of tranſplanting the *bohun upas*, or *poiſon tree from Java;* this would be a *monſtrous* addition, and perhaps of what no garden in the world would have to boaſt.

FEW HONEST COBLERS.

Why ſhould our ſhoes ſo ſoon grow old?
And why the hide with which they're ſol'd
Be worn and out of date?
Criſpin! 'tis ſtrange the thread that ſews
Millions of coats, ſhould leave our ſhoes
In ſuch a ragged ſtate!

In vain I ſought the ſecret cauſe,
Look'd in the leather for the flaws,
The tanner curs'd in vain;

Stept into ſhops where ſhoes were made,
Saw artiſts hourly ply the trade,
  But none would this explain.

Then t'ward the weſt and croſs the ſtreet,
Where folks at tall St. Michael's meet,
  I hurried, vex'd in mind ;
'Till on the bank of Aſhley's flood,
On ſoil of marſh I ſighing ſtood,
  For tanning uſe deſign'd.

Not far from thence a Cobler's ſon
Stood by his hides, and thus begun,
  With aſpect dull and ſad ;
Thrice he came o'er the lazy ſtream,
The faults of ſhoes was all his theme.
  For many a fault they had.

He ſaid, the ſpacious ample hide
That doth for all our boots provide
  No thinking man could blame ;
Since ſhap'd into ſo many ſoles,
Some would have flaws, and ſome have holes,
  To blaſt the Cobler's fame.

The artiſt wiſe who ſhap'd the ſhoe,
One hide from every creature drew,
  And ſcrap'd that hide with care :
This is an honeſt ſkin, he ſaid,
Then he reſolv'd to try his trade,
  And make a handſome pair.

Soon as the hide had left the vat,
And hung aloft, a hungry rat
  Attack'd it teeth and claws :
Ah ! cruel chance and rugged fate ;
He gnaw'd it early, gnaw'd it late—
  Starvation has no laws.

Happy the man who finds a ſhoe
That's to his expectation true—
  One real good below :

But oh! the crown of wretched wights,
That travel barefoot theſe dark nights,
And wound the bleeding toe.

Thus ſnug the Cobler's hopeful ſon:
I found, at length, his ſong was done,
And thought his reaſoning true—
Sure, then, cried I, ere I agree
For thoſe curs'd ſhoes you mean for me,
I will go barefoot too.

Some happier Criſpin tell me where,
What other ſhop affords a pair,
Where better work is found;
Swift as on Quixote's ſteed of old,
I'll fly to get my boots new ſol'd,
And wear them tight and ſound.

THE TEARS OF SCIENCE.

AT the ſeat of inſtruction, where once ſhe was bleſs'd,
Fair ſcience ſat mourning with ſadneſs oppreſs'd;
Her maps and her volumes lay ſcatter'd around,
Her globes, all in fragments, were ſtrew'd on the ground;
There lay in rude tatters, the relics of ſenſe,
The waſte and deſtruction of genius immenſe!

She ſigh'd, ſhook her head, and with anguiſh began—
"Alas! for the boy that believes he's a man,
When his ſtature grows tall, and his fingers begin,
To ſtroke the ſoft down that comes over his chin,
When he talks of aſſemblies, aſſumes the fine air,
Falls in love, *as he calls it*, and dreams of the fair.

This ſchool, and thoſe ſtudents, I claim'd for my own;
Here my precepts were utter'd my maxims made known;
I diſplay'd the fair honours for wiſdom deſign'd,
And the laſting content ſhe beſtows on the mind;
I open'd my treaſures—around me they came,

And roused their ambition for glory and fame.
They heard me with rapture—I saw in their eyes
Fair hope, emulation, and genius arise.

I hail'd the glad omen—My children, I cried,
Let no pleasing objects your bosoms divide,
'Till crown'd with fair virtue, with learning refin'd,
I restore you a blessing and joy to mankind.
Oh fond expectation! I saw with despair,
How oft they forsook me to wait on the fair;
While I talk'd of the planets that roll through the skies,
Their minds were on dimples and beautiful eyes!
I laid down positions, and strove to explain,
They thought of E****, L*****, and J***.
I saw a fine youth, as apart he retir'd,
He seem'd with the ardour of science inspir'd;
His looks and his pen were dispos'd in due place,
And deep lines of thinking were mark'd in his face.
Sweet hope in my breast was beginning to swell,
And I lov'd the dear lad that could study so well;
Nor shall my assistance be wanting, I cried:
I'll crown thy exertions—and sprang to his side.
Alas! an acrostic!!—the verses were plann'd,
The name was written, the letters were scann'd;
The initials arrang'd, to promote the design,
And his genius was working to get the first line.

I shut up my Euclid—I blush'd for myself,
I laid Blair and Murray again on the shelf;
Disappointed, ashamed, o'ercome with regret,
I utter'd a wish I shall never forget:
"That the fair maidens, my counsels would prize,
And shun every lad 'till he's learned and wise."

JACK FROST, THE DOCTOR.

When an Almighty sov'reign God,
Sent forth of late his chast'ning rod;
When Philadelphia and York City,
In deep distress, excited pity;
When black despair and sorrows keen,
Almost in every face were seen,
When every aid from man prov'd vain,

And hundreds by disease were slain ;
When thousands forced were to roam,
In sorrow from their native home,
And many looked on all as lost ;
Then came the much lov'd DOCTOR *FROST*
As messenger from heaven sent,
To ease the heart with sorrow rent.
This famous Doctor from the Pole,
He heals the body, cheers the soul.
His magick power indeed is such,
He cures his patients with a touch.
Some Doctors, as most people tell,
Make patients sick, to get them well ;
He ne'er was known to give emetick,
Or to administer cathartick.
This wond'rous Doctor of great skill;
Makes use of neither bark nor pill ;
And yet you'll think it strange to say,
He cures his thousands in a day.
At his approach, by all 'tis said,
Pale sickness quickly hides its head ;
And blooming health once more is seen,
With rosy cheek and brow serene.
'Tis true, for I will not dissemble,
He sometimes makes his patients tremble ;
But whilst they tremble they rejoice,
And hail him welcome with one voice.
Unlike the Doctors of our day,
When cure's perform'd they'll have their pay ;
But he'll not take a single shilling ;
For all he asks, is to be willing,
To render thanks to God above,
For all his mercies, all his love.

A CHARGE

Delivered to the young gentlemen of the Philadelphia Academy.

Doctrina sed vim promovet insitam,
Rectique cultus pectora roborant......

THE importance of the connexion which

hath fo long fubfifted between us, and a confcioufnefs of the high refponfibility of the character in which I have acted, coinciding with my own inclination, forbid me to difmifs you from this feminary without bidding you an affectionate farewell. For your diligence and application, your conformity to my advice, your ready fubmiffion to the difcipline of the inftitution, and the uniform urbanity of your manners, I thus publicly offer you my fincere thanks.

This day, my young friends, forms an important æra in your lives; you this day ftep forward upon the theatre of human life, with a ftamp of character, and an atteftation of merit, which cannot fail to make the moft favourable impreffion upon the public mind, and to afford a very high degree of gratification to yourfelves, your parents, and your friends.

Though you have as yet acquired the rudiments of a complete Englifh education only, and the expanfion of thofe principles into maturity, will depend upon your future application and exertion, many of you will here finifh your fcholaftic ftudies, and chiefly direct your attention to the bufinefs of the counting-houfe, and a preparation to engage in that profeffion, which, as a commercial nation opens the moft extenfive field for ufefulnefs and emolument; and of courfe attracts the notice of, and employs in its purfuits a majority of our youth. Thofe of you who are intended for what are called the learned profeffions, and are now about to enter upon a courſe of collegiate ſtudies, will find in that uſeful knowledge which you have already obtained, a ſolid foundation laid, whereon to erect the moſt ſplendid ſuperſtructure of claſſical and polite literature.

The proficiency which you have made and of which you have juſt given ſuch ample and ſatisfactory proofs, in thoſe eſſential branches of a uſeful education, Reading, Writing, Arithmetic, Grammar, Compoſition, Natural Hiſtory, Geography, and Logic, to which ſome of you have added Book-keeping and the elements of the Mathematics, qualify you to enter with confidence upon the ſtudy of any profeſſion, or to purſue with ſucceſs any path of ſcience, which does not neceſſarily involve a knowledge of the dead languages; thoſe, however, from the habits of ſtudy to which you have been accuſtomed, will be more rapidly and eaſily acquired than they could poſſibly be without ſuch previous habits. So that at all events I am confident the time which you have ſpent in this ſeminary, has been diligently and profitably employed: and I truſt that whatever may be your future occupations, you will always reflect, with ſatisfaction and with pleaſure, upon that portion of your lives which you have paſſed under my tuition and guidance.

Go then, and by your conduct, animate the hopes, increaſe the eſteem, and confirm the flattering expectations which you have inſpired. Remember that your future uſefulneſs and respectability in society, will depend upon the characters which you now form, and the acquisitions of knowledge which you now obtain. Having secured the first principles of a correct education, your faculties will now be called upon to take a wider range in the fields of science; and you will henceforth gradually begin to mix with society and to be initiated into the manners and customs of the world. Believe me the present period of your terrestrial existence is an highly important one indeed; perhaps the most so of any you will be called upon to experience, as the formation of your characters, your future safety, comfort and happiness, on this probationary theatre of human life, in this "frail feverish state of being," and also your condition of happiness or misery, of reward or punishment in that state of retribution, the world of spirits, to which we are all rapidly hastening, will in a great measure depend upon the first impressions which are made upon your yet unformed, unvitiated minds, the reception which you give to the various solicitations with which you will on all sides be powerfully assailed, and the compliance or inflexibility of those principles of action which you have been taught to adopt as your safest and surest guides, through the dangerous pilgrimage of mortality. "Lifes Theatre" to you has hitherto "been shut." Like the first parents of the human race in Eden, you have hitherto enjoyed a state of innocence and undisturbed repose—but like theirs, your scene of action muſt now be changed. "The world is all before you where to chuſe your place of reſt." As inexperienced and unſkilful navigators launched into an immenſe and dangerous ocean, you will henceforth be expoſed to rocks and ſhoals, to treacherous calms, and terrifying tempeſts. The ſoſt and aromatic gales of proſperity and of pleaſure, will ſometimes ſtrive to waft you into the alluring, yet deceitful harbours of ſenſuality and of vice, while the gay and airy phantoms of felicity which glide along the ſhore, will endeavour to enchant you with Syren ſongs of promiſed joy, and point to roſeate bowers and calm retreats, of which they will ſolicit your acceptance and court your enjoyment. Sweetly they will ſing of happineſs and pleaſure, and ſtrive to induce you to "bid the lovely ſcenes at diſtance hail;" but beware of their faſcinating deluſive charms; the phantoms, falſe diſſemblers! are fiends of deſtruction in the guiſe of angels, and the bowers and inviting retreats, to which they point, are the pits of perdition, and the caves of death.

If you happily purſue an undeviating courſe, and reſolutely avoid this *Scylla* of proſperity and of pleaſure, you will ere long probably be expoſed to danger equally imminent from the boiſterous *Charybdis* of adverſity, where the whirlpools of diſappointment, the ſtorms of calamity, and the guſts of paſſion will threaten to "make ſhipwreck of your faith," to daſh you upon the rocks of diſtraction and infidelity, or ingulph you in the vortex of despair.

To conduct you with safety through this hazardous voyage across the ocean of human life, the wise and benevolent author of its appointment, hath mercifully granted three infallible guides; whose salutary and unerring counsels, if diligently attended to, and carefully complied with, will assuredly lead you into "the haven where you would be, the promised land of rest, the heavenly Canaan," "where there is the fulness of joy, and perfection of felicity for ever more." These three friendly monitors are *conscience*, *reason* and *religion*.

By the *first* we are warned of approaching danger, or convicted of error in our course; by the *second* we are directed into a safe and unruffled channel; and by the *third* we are encouraged to steady perseverance, by the most animating promises of reward, and deterred from a relaxation of our vigilance, by the most alarming denunciations of misery and woe.

But, to pursue the metaphor no further, and to address you in that plain unimpassioned style which is perhaps better adapted to your present situation, and my own earnest solicitude for your future welfare: I shall comprize what I have yet to offer as briefly as possible, in a few plain salutary *cautions against error*, and *admonitory precepts* for the government of your futur life.

1st. *Avoid Indolence.*—Remember that idleneſs is the parent of ignorance and vice. Time is a talent committed to us for improvement; our proſperity, our reſpectability, and uſefulneſs, depending upon the proper employment, the neglect or abuſe of it. If the energies of the human mind be not called forth into action, and that at an early period of life, and thoſe energies ſtimulated and ſtrengthened by the powerful influence of habit, they will ſoon droop and become enfeebled by neglect; or, hurried into the ſervice of the paſſions, inſtead of being guided by the dictates of reaſon, they will inevitably lead their poſſ ſſor into the abſurd eccentricities of folly, or the diſgraceful and deſtructive deluſions of depravity and of vice.

Beware therefore of ſuffering a day, or even an hour, to roll over your heads, uncultivated, unregarded—By unvaried attention and diligent exertion, we become acquainted with the noble powers of our nature, and by the vigorous exerciſe of thoſe powers, we arrive at the higheſt poſſible degree of dignity and happineſs which our nature is capable of experiencing.

2dly *Avoid Bad Company.*—" Evil communications corrupt good manners." Man is an imitative animal, and when the powerful inflence of example coincides with the impulſe of paſſion, it requires great firmneſs of mind, indeed, to withſtand their united ſolicitations. Cautiouſly, therefore, avoid that vortex of temptation which is formed by aſſociating with vicious or irregular characters.

And as you would preferve the purity of your *morals* by avoiding *vicious* company, be equally fedulous to guard your *manners* by avoiding *low* company; corruption of mind, vulgarity of converfation, and a difgufting awkardnefs of deportment, are the infeparable confequences of fuch an intercourfe.

3dly. *Avoid Diffipation, or an exceffive attachment to Pleafure and Amufement.*—Relaxation of mind is as neceffary to preferve its ftrength and reftore its activity, as repofe is for the body after corporal exertions; but amufement fhould only be indulged as a medicinal relief to the mind; not confidered as the principal, or indeed a leading object of purfuit. By a temperate enjoyment of pleafure the energies of the human mind are quickened, and its original tone reftored; but by unreftrained indulgence, they are foon enfeebled and deftroyed. Idlenefs and pleafure are two moft infidious and fatal enemies to mental improvement and true dignity of character: they invariably induce fuch a degree of frivolity and infipidity, as will ever render their votaries the fcorn and contempt of the wife, the virtuous, and the good.

To thefe cautionary dictates againft error, I muft add a few precepts of advice, by a compliance with which, you will not command refpect and efteem only, but enjoy the conftant delight of an approving confcience, the foothing reflections of a cultivated mind, and the fatisfactory confcioufnefs of rendering yourfelves ufeful and ornamental to fociety.

1st. *Be ambitious of excelling.*—The passions, if under the guidance of reason and religion, they be directed into proper channels, are calculated to promote happiness and prosperity.

Were, for instance, the passions of pride and ambition, which, when intemperately and injudiciously indulged, have caused such misery and havock in the world, always directed to the pursuit of laudable and virtuous objects, how different would be their effects! Instead of agitating the bosom with plans for the destruction and degradation of our fellow creatures, that we may rise conspicuously on the ruin of their fortune or their fame, those passions would teach us to promote as much as possible their interest and honour, and to command the powerful influence of example, by endeavouring to outvie them in noble sentiments and in geneous and useful actions.—Be it your part then, to employ the infant energies of those principles in striving to obtain superiority in those pursuits which are accommodated to your time of life, and the views which may be taken of your future employment and establishment in society, viz. in the acquisition of useful knowledge, in the cultivation of benevolent affections, in the exercise of a respectful, submissive deportment to your superiors and elders, in kindness and gentleness to your inferiors, and in a general expression of urbanity and good nature towards all.

2dly. As the operation of the paſſions, if judiciouſly directed, tends to promote our happineſs and honour, ſo, if ſuffered to have an unreſtrained ſway, they will inevitably hurry the victim of their authority into the moſt extravagant and fatal exceſſes. Juſtly are they ſtyled by a celebrated poet "The tyrants of the human breaſt," and certainly no period of life is more favourable to the obtaining of victory over them than yours; becauſe at no period of your lives will their exertions be leſs powerful. Vigilantly therefore guard againſt the indulgence of anger, revenge, malice, and all thoſe paſſions and propenſities which endeavour to dethrone reaſon, and are in direct oppoſition to the precepts of religion.

"Reaſon in man obſcur'd, or not obey'd;
"Immediately inordinate deſires
"And upſtart paſſions catch the government
"From Reaſon, and to ſervitude reduce
"Man till then free."

3dly. *Aſſociate as much as poſſible with your ſuperiors*, and with thoſe who are further advanced in age than yourſelves, and are diſtinguiſhed for their talents and virtuous accompliſhments; from whoſe experience and knowledge you may derive uſeful inſtructions, and from whoſe language and deportment you will inſenſibly acquire a poliſh and refinement of character, which will render you pleaſing and acceptable to all with whom you may aſſociate.

It was ſaid by the juſtly celebrated Edward Hyde, Earl of Clarendon, who raiſed himself by his personal merit to the office of Lord High Chancellor of England, "that he never was so proud, or thought himself so good a man, as when he considered himself inferior to the rest of the company:" a saying strongly expressive of his sense of the benefits which he had derived from having been early introduced to, and continuing an acquaintance with, the most eminent persons of his time for learning, virtue, and talents.

4thly. *Cultivate a taste for reading and for study.* The human mind is naturally desirous of acquiring knowledge, conscious that true dignity and respectability of character depend upon it; but, there is a variety of principles which powerfully oppose that acquisition, particularly in the minds of youth—who, improvident of the future, regardless of any but the passing moment, and naturally of volatile and gay dispositions, think of present enjoyment only, and therefore too often indulge indolence, trifle away their time in frivolous and childish amusements, or criminally employ it in devising plans of mischief, or in executing schemes of folly. If the hours of youth be thus sacrificed, the succeeding years of manhood will be unproductive of that golden fruit which is the invariable reward of early diligence and application. Accustom yourselves therefore, before those propensities become confirmed by habit, to such constant activity of mind in laudable and literary pursuits, as will counteract their operation and destroy their influence. They are the ruſt of the mind, which, if ſuffered to increaſe or to exiſt at all, will ſoon obſcure its brilliancy, corrode its ſubſtance, and annihilate its ſtrengh.

Laſtly. *Cheriſh religion, and frequently and attentively peruſe the holy ſcriptures.* They will communicate to you the moſt valuable knowledge—the knowledge of yourſelves and of the path which leads to Heaven.

The two moſt important events that can poſſibly engage our attention, which are inevitable, and for the occurrence of which it ſhould be the chief employment of human life to prepare, are death and judgment; becauſe upon that preparation altogether depends our future happineſs or miſery in the next ſtate of exiſtence. The preſent portion of our exiſtence is a ſtate of diſcipline or trial, without which, under the peculiar circumſtances of our condition, as rational beings and free agents, we could not be entitled to reward, or obnoxious to puniſhment; nor could the virtuous energies of our nature be properly called forth into action.

When therefore the brevity and uncertainty of human life are conſidered, the immenſity of reward which is promiſed to piety and virtue, and the dreadful nature of the puniſhment which is threatened for the neglect of them—ſurely the great buſineſs of life ſhould be to prepare for eternity.

Let then all your thoughts, words, and actions, be regulated by the influence of that awful eternity. Reſt your faith upon the doctrines, and regulate your lives by the precepts of Chrift and his Apoftles; and you will affuredly obtain the efteem and approbation of the moft refpectable part of the community, enjoy the moft exhilarating and foothing teftimony of an approving confcience, and finally be received by your Almighty Judge, as good and faithful ftewards of the talents committed to your truft.

In a particular manner moft earneftly do I recommend to you a regular obfervation of all the ordinances of public worfhip, and the exercife of frequent and fervent *private* prayer. Remember that we are fallen and accountable beings, that our thoughts, words, and actions are continually under the infpection of God—that the propenfities of our nature are to evil—that thofe propenfities are too powerful to be controuled by reafon alone—that without the affiftance of divine grace we cannot attain that purity of character which alone can render us acceptable to our Almighty Judge: and that this divine influence is promifed liberally to thofe who fincerely petition for it. "Afk and ye fhall have," faid our Divine Inftructor Jefus Chrift, "knock," as it were at the door of Heaven, "and it fhall affuredly be opened to you."

Prayer preferves in the human mind a conftant fenfe of the omniprefence, omnifcience, and omnipotence of the deity, and of the imperfection, the frailty, and the refponfibility of man. Nor be deterred from the exercise of this indispensable duty, by the idea of labour in its *daily* occurrence. We are not required to offer *long* but *frequent* and *ardent* prayers.—The single petition of the contrite publican "God be merciful to me a sinner!" was favourably received, when the elaborate address of the ostentatious Pharisee was rejected.

Prayer is the great, the blessed medium of intercourse between man and his Almighty Creator.

"Prayer ardent opens Heaven, lets down a stream
"Of glory on the consecrated hour,
"Of man in audience with the deity.
"Who worships the great God, that instant joins
"The first in Heaven, and sets his foot on Hell.

Dedicate, therefore, your early years to the service of your Maker, and you will then find, that as you "grow in age, you will grow in grace," and enjoy the unspeakable satisfaction which arises from the consciousness of a diligent preparation for death, judgment, and eternity.

FASHION.

IN days of yore, when reason held her reign,
And could with ease vain caprices restrain;
When men, accustom'd to one common course,
To fix their minds, requir'd no borrow'd force;
When brutal av'rice did not rule the board,
Nor each his all for trifles could afford;
When splendid luxury was without a name,
And by abundance no one sought for fame;
When but a little was a good supply,
And all with faith on Nature could rely

In this more ancient and more happy age,
The beams of honour ſhone upon the ſtage.

The aged Sire juſt tott'ring to the duſt,
To his fond child conſign'd his ſacred truſt;
With admonitions of his tend'reſt care,
Of folly's wiles with caution to beware.
But ah, degen'rate race! with pleaſure cloy'd!
Of reaſon, wiſdom, prudence, goodneſs void!
What ſpecious charm has lull'd your minds to reſt?
Than your fond Sires, what makes you far more bleſt?
Ah, vainly bleſt, if FASHION rule the day,
Faſhion, a demon clad in falſe array;
An idol, to which thouſands bend the knee,
With anxious hopes from trouble to be free.

Faſhion and lux'ry with their curſed train,
In modern times have long aſſum'd the reign
Have driven reaſon from her rightful throne,
And on her ruins rais'd aloft their own;
Have won the ſmiles of every ſex and age;
All with delight in FOLLY's cauſe engage;
Have burſt the ties of harmony and peace;
And bade the ſtreams of joy and pleaſure ceaſe;
Have oft deſpoil'd a noble, happy mind
Of treaſures ſacred, once by care refin'd.
Such are th' effects of Faſhion's regal ſway,
Perhaps the fate of many a future day.

To prove the fact, to Capitals repair,
And ſeek profuſion on profuſion there.
Explore the throng engag'd in Faſhion's ſphere,
Where all as one, her ſpecious name revere.
Here, ſtruts a Pigmy in his ſumpt'ous lace,
There, from each lattice peeps a crimſon face;
Here, a poor miſcreant, to the world a curſe,
And ſtill ſupported from his father's purſe:
There, trips a Miſs, the fact none have oppos'd,
To public view her modeſty expos'd;
Here, ſtands the Crier at each angle, bold,
At three, P. M. late Faſhions to be ſold;
There, ſtalks an advocate for folly's ſhow,

Pleading with warmth, PRO BONO PUBLICO,
In every ſordid corner you behold
A muſhroom upſtart clad in ſplendid gold;
And parents, children, all as one agree,
To hail EXTRAVAGANCE with ſocial glee.

Are theſe the vices which pollute the age,
And ſtill permitted to pervert the ſtage?
Muſt we at Faſhion's ſhrine obſequious fall,
And liſten to her pleaſing, fatal call?
Deluded world ariſe, nor heed her voice;
Let honeſt prudence be your nobleſt choice;
Extravagance and folly, hand in hand
Too long, alas! have overſpread the land.

To change the ſcene and paint in diff'rent light,
Let ſober Reaſon now reſume her right.
With care let her juſt dictates be obey'd,
And our advancement prove HER ſov'reign aid.
In her embrace, on life's impetuous tide,
Each haſt'nind footſteg ſhe will ſafely guide;
Will guard the fortune of each paſſing hour,
And baniſh care by her coercive pow'r.

To prove that Reaſon is our ſafeſt rule,
Behold the peaſant, taught in Nature's ſchool:
No coſtly gems his daily garb compoſe,
In vain indulgence he ſeeks no repoſe.
In ruſſet gown his ſmiling wife appears,
No cares diſturb, no deep foreboding fears,
As faithful Sol o'ertops the eaſtern hills,
And with his beams expanſive Nature fills;
When the gay lark begins his matin ſong,
To which the ſtrains of cheerfulneſs belong;
In juſt ſucceſſion in the ruſtic art,
Each in his turn, with pleaſure knows his part.
And when at eve that God his luſtre veils,
O'er gloomy cares the cheerful ſong prevails.

From buſy ſcenes and bleſt with pureſt joy,
Lo, the Recluſe in Nature's free employ,

No ſplendid toys his humble cot adorn,
Nor for his plainneſs is he view'd forlorn.
His ſimple habit proves his peaceful mind
For pureſt bliſs and happineſs deſign'd ;
For daily bounties which kind Heav'n beſtows,
To Him who gives, his pure oblation flows.
His gen'rous hand each pilgrim's wants ſupplies,
Nor to the child of ſorrow, aid denies.

Far happier theſe, than thoſe in regal ſtate,
Abſorb'd in lux'ry, and ignobly great ;
Who ſeek for pleaſures which from wealth ariſe,
And for abundance ſtrain their eager eyes.
Who look for honours in the ſplendid ſphere,
And the vain god, extravagance, revere.

The female mind, in idle dreams employ'd,
Too long, alas! has fancy's fruits enjoy'd.
Too long has choſen for its ſureſt guide,
A Ratcliffe's trifle, or a Rowſon's pride.
Go, ſearch the toilet of the ſtudious fair,
Where frightful ghoſts in gloomy horror ſtare.
View the long pile which human greatneſs ſpeaks,
And liſten to a maid's deſpairing ſhrieks:
Where mournful ſpectres hover on the ſight,
And bring to view the ſhades of endleſs night.
Such direful ſcenes employ, with fondeſt care,
The happy moments of our blooming fair.

And now, ye votaries of Faſhion's cauſe,
Adhere to Reaſon and to Reaſon's laws :
Let no vain trifles o'er your firmneſs ſway,
Nor ſeek the luring baubles of the day.
Thus, by your prudence you may daily learn
Between the good and evil to diſcern ;
May know, by tracing Nature's open rule,
What conſtitutes a ſage, and what—a fool.

ANECDOTES.

Some years ſince, not fifty miles from Boſ-ton, lived an induſtrious old lady, who, riſing early one Lordsday morning, gathered her dirty clothes together, and went hard to work, waſhing; which ſhe continued, until a neighbour of hers, miſſing her from church, called at the houſe to know what extraordinary accident had prevented her attendance as uſual; both the old ladies were ſurpriſed—the one at ſeeing her neighbour dreſſed in her beſt clothes and the other infinitely more ſo, at ſeeing her old friend at the waſh tub.

After an eclairciſſement had taken place, the old lady who had ſo ignorantly ſinned, requeſted the other to ſit down, and as ſhe, by her ſad miſtake, had not been to church herſelf, to inform her what was the ſubject, the parſon was preaching on—" he was preaching" ſaid ſhe " on the death and ſufferings of our Saviour." " What!" ſaid the other, " is he dead—well, my huſband don't take the papers, and half Boſton might be burnt down, and I know nothing about the matter."

A YOUNG MAN,

NATIVE of a pleaſant part of New England, having no objections to enter upon a *married life*, hereby makes known his intentions to the young ladies of Carolina. He is about twenty five years of age, of decent profeſſions and fair proſpects—can produce an unſuſpected character—other particulars to be expreſſed on perſonal interview; to approach which, he ſuggeſts the following mode: The lady, whoſe attention may be excited by this propofal, is defired to drop a billet into the box of the poft-office, addreffed to A. B. in which fhe will declare fo much of her mind, as is neceffary to hint the firft avowal of an honourable courtfhip. She will alfo prefcribe her fictitious addrefs, together with the time and place at which he may depofit a letter of more explicit contents. This correfpondence may be continued at the pleafure of the parties, until, by reciprocal underftanding, they may appoint an interview. As his propofitions are religioufly fincere, he expects that her's alfo will be fuch, as far as fhe thinks proper to proceed. He pledges the honour of a gentleman, that, whatever may be her profeffions and difclofures, he will obferve the utmoft diplomatick filence and unremitting fecrecy. She will be indulged, at any ftage of the addreffes, in fufpending the correfpondence whenever fhe chufes. Attention, in conformity to the above, fhall be ftrictly paid for the fpace of fourteen days from this date.

Though an introduction to the acquaintance of a companion, fo novel and unprecedented, may wear with many a theatrical appearance, the writer is confcious of nothing, why it may not be perfectly confiftent with every object of courtfhip. As advertifements of this kind, though really fincere, are too often viewed as mere fcenes of mock-gallantry, he tenders his affurances that this, BONA-FIDE, will be fupported with ferious intention and unaffected candour;

he begs moreover, that the lady who cannot otherwiſe be convinced, would ſo reſpect the propoſition above ſtated, as to make an introductory experiment, iſolated at her own pleaſure, with caution and reſerve.

AN old gentleman, whoſe father attended more to teaching his ſon the methods of accumulating riches than knowledge, lived ſome time ſince in a town in one of the eaſtern ſtates—From application and induſtry, he had amaſſed a property of about 20,000 dollars: although not able either to read or write, he never hired a clerk, but had always been in the habit of keeping his own books. He had invented ſome few characters for the purpoſe of conveying his ideas to himſelf and others: they were formed as nearly ſimilar to the ſhape of the article ſold as the nature of the circumſtance would admit. One day a cuſtomer of his called on him for the purpoſe of ſettling his account, the book of *hieroglyphicks* was handed down, and our merchant commenced with "ſuch a time you had a gallon of rum, and ſuch a time a pound of tea—ſuch a time a gallon of molaſſes, and ſuch a time a cheeſe." "Stop there," ſays the cuſtomer, "I never had a cheeſe from you or any other perſon—I make my own cheeſe." "You certainly muſt have had it," ſaid the merchant, "it is down in my book." The other denied ever buying an article of that kind. After a ſufficient number of pros and cons, upon recollection, he informed him that he believed he had purchased a *grindstone* about that time—"It is the very thing," said the merchant, "and I must have forgotten to put *the hole in the middle.*"

THE PETITION

Of a number of fat and healthy Swine,

Most humbly addressed to the honourable street-commissioners of Philadelphia,

SHEWETH,

THAT your petitioners have at this time very pleasant lodgings in the odoriferous sloughs of Pewter Platter alley, made some time since by laying down water-logs in said alley. But your petitioners are very apprehensive that they shall be disturbed, in consequence of some of their neighbours complaining of bad smells issuing from our habitations, which they fear will produce that ugly demon the yellow fever.—Now, gentlemen, we hope you will not regard either their complaints or their fears, as we know some of them to be very weak nerved people, too easily alarmed about trifles—and do beg that you will grant us the use of our comfortable lodgings, during the remainder of the warm months at least, for which your petitioners will thank you, and as in duty bound will ever pray.

THE RURAL PHILOSOPHER.

Fair Nature's beauties give sublime delight,
To whom alone she gives her charms to prize,

Ten thousand ſweets regale th'attentive ſight,
Which paſs unnotic'd by incurious eyes—

Earth's verdant carpet, lo! how richly wrought,
What grandeur fills the heav'ns from pole to pole;
Theſe ſwell the mind to majeſty of thought,
And ſtrike the fineſt feelings of the ſoul.

How great my theme! how vaſt is Nature's plan,
My muſes power to ſing, alas! how ſmall;
What wiſdom, ſhines from inſect up to man,
What truth and goodneſs viſible in all.

There are who view the ſweetly varied vale,
Yet feel no rapture at the pleaſing ſight,
There are who hear the moon's harmonious tale,
Yet ſee no beauties in the queen of night.

There are who view the flocks, and verdant downs,
The ſummer ſuns, and plenty pouring ſky;
Yet leave their charms to ſhepherds and to clowns,
Nor lift their thoughts, nor ſend their thanks on high.

To me the daiſied bank, the cowſlip field,
The craggy rock, the high o'er ſhadowing hill,
Pleaſure ſublime and ſweet inſtruction yield,
And all my ſoul, with admiration fill.

The blooming hedge row, or the leafleſs tree,
The ſummer's heat, or winter's frozen face,
In ſweet viciſſitude give joy to me,
And fill the ſcene with dignity and grace.

The ſmooth-rind poplar, and the pointed pine,
The mantling wood-bine, and the matted thorn,
In reaſon's ear proclaim a hand divine,
While Nature's plan they perfect and adorn.

The roſe's bluſh, the laurel's glitt'ring green,
The tulip's glow, the crocus' golden rays,
Sweetly diverſify th' enchanting ſcene,
And ſwell the chorus of their maker's praiſe.

The groves and purling ſtreams the muſes pride,
Woods, lakes, and lawns, and all the charms of May,
Can't paſs unſung, when all things ſung beſide,
In graceful concord aid the moral lay.

Learn wiſdom, man! from all thine eye ſurveys,
See! order reigns throughout the ſpacious whole;
That juſt obedience every creature pays,
Should teach, correct, and regulate thy ſoul.

But ah! there are who view th' etherial plains,
Yet hear no muſic in the rolling ſpheres,
Who feel what chanting muſic heav'n ordains,
Nor count how faſt, they number out their years

There are who feel the ſun's diffuſive ray,
Yet unadmiring, view that world of light,
Who praiſe the varied wonders of the day,
Yet ſee no grandeur in the gloom of night.

E'en winter's bell'wing breath whoſe horrid noiſe,
Howls in tremendous tempeſts through the trees,
The Philoſophick ear in peace enjoys
Nor finds leſs pleaſing than the paſſing breeze.

The ratt'ling thunder ſhakes the ſolid world,
And fearful light'nings nature's face deform,
The virtuous mind in no confuſion hurl'd,
Smiles in the tempeſt, and enjoys the ſtorm.

He ſees with wonder, Nature's firſt great cauſe
Hold out the ſcales, and keep the balance e'en;
Though boiſt'rous Eurus burſt his wint'ry jaws;
With all the bluſt'ring turbulence of Heav'n.

The virtuous mind, with equal temper, views
The ſummer's glories, and the winter's glooms,
The ſacred path of conſcious peace purſues,
And looks unterrified on threat'ning tombs.

ELEGY.

Calm is thy reſt, meek ſorrow's child!
  At length thou haſt eſcap'd from grief;
At length, to ev'ry anguiſh throb,
  The final ſigh has giv'n relief.

Yes! thou art happy, ſorrow's child
  Though cold the ſod that binds thy breaſt,
That breaſt ſhall agonize no more,
  No more ſhall heave with woe ſuppreſt.

For ſacred, from each prying eye,
  In ſecret flow'd thy burning tear,
And mournful though thy hapleſs tale,
  'Twas pour'd alone to friendſhip's ear.

Yet, now from riſing anguiſh free,
  How tranquil is thy ſilent ſleep!
How calmly cloſ'd thoſe languid orbs,
  So often uſ'd to wake and weep.

Peace to thy ſhade, for thou wert mild.
  As is the cradled infant's ſigh,
And pure—if ever mortal were,
  As ſouls that ſeek their native ſky.

O'er thy pale form the high graſs waves,
  And willows ſpread funereal gloom,
While eve's ſoft breeze delights to pour
  Its whiſper'd murmurs o'er thy tomb.

And oft at midnight's ſacred hour,
  Forms ſuch as fancy loves ſhall throng
Due honors at the turf to pay,
  And ſoothe thy ſpirit with their ſong.

AN AUTUMNAL REFLECTION.

In fading grandeur lo! the trees
  Their tarniſh'd honours ſhed;
While every leaf compelling breeze
  Lays their dim verdure dead.

E'er while they ſhook a lively length
   Of flowers and fruit and green ;
Now ſhorn of beauty and of ſtrength
   They ſtand a ſhatter'd ſcene.

Ere long the fertile breath of ſpring
   Shall all their charms renew ;
And flower and fruit and foliage bring,
   All pleaſing to the view.

Thus round and round the ſeaſons roll
   In one harmonious courſe,
And ſhed conviction on the ſoul,
   With unremitting force.

Not ſuch is man's appointed fate,
   One ſpring alone he knows,
One Summer, one autumnal ſtate,
   One Winter's dread repoſe.

Yet not the dreary ſleep of death,
   Shall e'er his pow'rs deſtroy,
But man ſhall draw immortal breath,
   In endleſs pain or joy.

Important thought ! Oh, mortal hear
   On what thy fate depends ;
The voice of Wiſdom ſtrikes thine ear,
   And this the voice ſhe sends.

" When virtue glows with youthful charms,
   How bright the vernal ſkies !
When virtue like the Summer warms,
   What golden Harveſts riſe.

When vices ſpring without controul,
   What bitter fruits appear ;
A wintry darkneſs wraps the ſoul,
   And horrors cloſe the year ;

When youths to Virtue's ſhrine repair
   And men their tribute bring ;
Old age ſhall loſe its load of care,
   And death ſhall loſe its ſting."

CITY MANNERS.

I have been completely ſucceſsful, and you muſt ſend me your congratulations immediately.—You thought my huſband could never be brought to ſacrifice what you are pleaſed to term a certainty for an uncertainty; but you are miſtaken; men are different creatures at different times. I believe, nay, I vow I am almoſt certain, they may all be wrought upon by arts leſs ſpecious than thoſe ſo frequently played off upon our ſex. If women would call into uſe but half of their ſagacity, and would ſcrutinize the natural diſpoſitions and propenſities of men, their ſituations in life would more often accord with their own deſires, and feminine graces give a more general poliſh to ſociety. But this muſt be done with care. Men are naturally jealous of authority, and will not tamely ſubmit to any open encroachments upon it; they cannot, therefore, blame us, if we follow their own example, and *wheedle* them out of it, as they ſo often *wheedle* our ſex of what is of a thouſand times more conſequence, our virtue. In this, I am perſuaded, we may always ſucceed: for, notwithſtanding the charge of vanity, ſo univerſally aſcribed to us, I do poſitively declare, and you will not forget that it is a matron who makes the declaration, that the men have a much greater portion of it than the ſuppoſed poſſeſſors. Do be ſo good as to cultivate theſe and ſimilar ſentiments among your acquaintances: I think they might prove beneficial;

and I ſhould receive additional happineſs from the confirmation of my belief.

I have moulded my huſband into the very *thing* I wiſhed him. He already begins to ſee objects through the ſame medium with myſelf; and although he prated a good deal at firſt about the heart-felt pleaſures of the rural life, I ſoon put all ſuch ſimple nonſenſe out of his head by deſcanting upon the elegancies of city enjoyments, the ſtyle in which we ſhould be enabled to live, the choice of our company, and the facility of change; but moſt of all, upon *the profound deference and reſpect* which we ſhould receive from perſons of every rank. This I did not fail to contraſt with our preſent ſituation; and dwelt particularly upon the term happineſs, to which I had often heard him ſay there were as many definitions as there were perſons in the world, and upon the inſenſibility and uncourteous diſpoſitions of his booriſh neighbours.

I am all in raptures at the ſucceſs of my plans; and two or three attempts to go through my uſual houſehold duties, have abſolutely failed; ſo that I do not ſee how I can do any thing better than to inform you that I am ſurfeiting upon anticipated happineſs. I have ſometimes heard men aſſert, that anticipation was preferable to enjoyment; but I believe they will find few of our ſex credulous and viſionary enough to coincide in a doctrine that defeats itſelf. If men had ſenſibility and vivacity enough always to *enjoy the preſent mo-*

ment, I am perſuaded they would never mention the delights of anticipation.

But this, you exclaim, is all idle prating, mere ſpeculation. Granted: we will therefore to the point. My good Proteus has already advertiſed his eſtate, and will probably be able to diſpoſe of it ſoon; then we hie us to the city, and begin to make preparation for living in a ſtyle worthy of my huſband's character and high expectations; then, I truſt, I ſhall be of ſome conſequence in ſociety. I ſhall no longer be puſhed from my own fire by the intruſion of unbidden gueſts, who muſt always be made welcome; nor be compelled to give an exact ſtatement of my family concerns to every impertinent old curmudgeon in the pariſh. In the city, you know every houſe is the lady's; the carriages and ſervants are all at her diſpoſal; ſhe gives all the entertainments, and all viſits are made to her. This, now, is as it ſhould be; and we receive all proper reſpect. Inſtead of being tied to the ſide of your huſband, at all times, walking regularly to church twice on a Sunday, and having nothing to look at but the monotonous countenances which you have ſeen all the days of your life; we are indulged in a promiſcuous intercourſe with the ſexes; plays, theatres, concerts, balls, and galleries of the arts, are perpetually created for our amuſement; and we are led, with admiration and delight, from one novelty to another by a hundred different beaus who are ever at your beck, and who never seem satisfied but when they are *doing you a favour*.

I do assure you, that in cities, the ladies are of infinitely more consequence, in private life, than the gentlemen. They are plodding in their counting-houses the greater part of the day, while we are receiving and paying morning visits, reciprocating civilities, and at all times enjoying the present moment in a manner perfectly agreeable to ourselves. We are often assisted in these amusements by *gentlemen of elegant leisure*, who are the kindest creatures in the world, and who are never insensible to the merit of a fine woman. Several of these gallants have wives themselves, but this does not hinder them from adhering rigidly to the opinion of the "Wife of Bath."*

I must say, and all women, you know, are extremely fond of having their say, that the *liberal opinions* and *genteel customs* that generally prevail in cities, are much to my taste, and afford a striking contrast to the narrow prejudices of a village education. You very well know how much restraint we are obliged to submit to, because we are of what is termed the better sort of people in the country. There can be no other reason in the world for all this, than a thin population. If this were not the case, every body's situation and circumstances would not be precisely known, and the immediate occurrences in every family would not be so familiarly discussed by the common vulgar. This want of population, and the natural auſterity of parents and huſbands, are of very ſerious inconvenience to at leaſt one part of every family. We are ſtrictly enjoined to keep aloof from all others not ſimilarly circumſtanced with ourſelves; and the deſtination of every viſit, or of what is here nick-named party of pleaſure, muſt be previouſly known and approved by the family before it can be finally reſolved upon. In our dreſs, too, we are ſhamefully controlled; and inſtructed to faſhion it ſo as to prohibit all play to the imagination. I really think that things have come to a fine paſs when men are not ſatisfied with the abſolute direction of our perſons. They are not willing now, to allow us even mental freedom; and what they will next invent for our torture, it is impoſſible to conjecture.

But let us not forget, that things are not ſo every where. In the city, this ruſt has quite worn off; and the general poliſh of manners has given to every thing the moſt beautiful appearance. The fancy, and the judgment are left to the guidance of their reſpective poſſeſſors, for they are not always united in the ſame perſon, and the general proſperity of the citizens enables all claſſes to put on the ſame appearance, and to be preſent at all public amuſements. It is not for me to inquire into the cauſes which have produced this delightful ſtate of ſociety; it is ſufficient for me that it is ſo.

Perhaps you may think that the frequent interruptions of health, ſo often experienced in cities, is a circumſtance very much againſt them; but this, I can aſſure you, is an objection more imaginary than real. The houſes of the wealthy are generally ſituated in the wideſt ſtreets, where there is a free circulation of air, and are very ſpacious—their ſtores or compting-houſes, however, are generally down upon the wharves; and if they will always keep themſelves immured in them, where the air will not let them live, they muſt die of courſe, and we are free to better ourſelves the ſooner. This, I am determined, ſhall not keep me from the city one moment;

"For when my tranſitory ſpouſe unkind,
Shall die and leave his woeful wife behind,
I'll take the next good Chriſtian I can find."

You need not laugh at this confeſſion, though it is a frank one; for I will venture to bet you a diſh of my beſt hyſon, it has been made by many an honeſt wife before me. You may poſſibly think, alſo, that it can be no eaſy taſk for a widow, with children, to get a huſband, where there are at all times ſo many charming young girls who are ſeldom diſpoſed to be cruel; but you may diſmiſs ſuch a belief as ſoon as it is conceived, for I do poſitively aſſert, that

"There ſwims no gooſe ſo grey, but, ſoon or late,
She finds ſome honeſt gander for her mate."

It now only remains for me to aſſure you, that we are firmly reſolved upon going to town as ſoon as poſſible, and that I ſhall be very glad to have as much of your company there as you can ſpare.

THOUGHTS ON APPARITIONS.

Ye ſpirits who inhabit worlds unknown !
Terrifi ſpectres ! whither are ye flown ?
Oft have I heard, ye love at this dread hour
To haunt the ruin'd aisle, or moſs grown tow'r :
To flit in ſhadowy forms along the glade,
Or ſtalk gigantic 'midſt the gloomy ſhade.
Yet here alone with ſilent ſteps I tread,
Where broken walls their mouldering ruins ſpread ;
Where the cold aſhes of the fair and great,
Vainly enſhrined, repoſe in awful ſtate ;
Where the dark ivy claſps th' embattled tow'r
And lengthens out a while its final hour ;
But all is ſtill ! no frightful ghoſt appears ;
No ghaſtly phantom its huge form uprears ;
No white rob'd ſpirits glide acroſs the gloom,
No hollow groan low mutters from the tomb ;
But death-like ſilence ſpreads an awe profound,
And darkneſs flings her ſable mantle round.
Then whither are theſe ſhadowy ſpectres fled,
That nightly guard the relics of the dead ?
And where is pale-cheek'd Terror's hideous train,
That o'er the midnight hour is ſaid to reign ?

Ah ! let grim Fear and ſuperſtition tell,
A tale of horror from their murky cell ;
Where by the glimmering taper's pale-blue light,
They paſs, in ſullen mood, the dreary night ;
Starting with frenzied looks at every ſound,
While viſionary phantoms float around,
Yes—they may tell of deeds with horror fraught,
And dreadful ſights that mock the labouring thought ;
Yet will I ſcorn the vain deluding tale,
Nor let their voice o'er Reaſon's ſelf prevail.
But can I ſtill a hardy ſceptick ſtand,
Rejecting truths rever'd in every land ;
While undiſputed facts their force unite,
To prove that ſpirits haunt the ſhades of night ?
Ah no ! I muſt ſubmit—I plead in vain
Imagination's wild deſpotic reign ;
Or ſay that Fear by Fancy's magic aid

May fill with airy forms the dubious shade :
And bid the trembling heart, in manhood's spite,
Start from a wavering bush with pale affright ;
Yes—'tis in vain ! for while with sad surprize,
O'er many a dreadful legend Pity sighs,
Some well-attested facts the mind perceives,
And with discriminating power—believes.

Yet shall I dread at this dark hour to rove,
Amid the solemn stillness of the grove ;
Or where the time-worn battlements arise,
Or the proud turret low in ruin lies ?
I scorn the thought—assur'd that Sov'reign Pow'r
Governs alike the dark, or moontide hour ;
And here as free from rude alarm I stray,
Amid these shades, as in the blaze of day ;
While to thy care, O thou Almighty Friend !
By night, or day, my spirit I commend.

But oh ! my heart delights while thus I rove,
T' indulge the pleasing thought, that some I love,
Who now have gain'd the radiant seats of bliss,
Attend my wand'rings o'er a scene like this.
Oh yes—methinks I feel her presence near,
Whose memory claims affection's grateful tear ;
Whose form so much belov'd, hath still the pow'r,
With sweetest smiles to cheer the darkest hour ;
Dost thou, indeed, my lonely steps attend,
And o'er me now with kind compassion bend,
Anxious with all a mother's love t' impart
A balm to sooth the sorrows of my heart ?
Might I indulge the wish that thou wert near,
Blest spirit might I now behold thee here ;
Such as thou art, array'd in garments bright,
Or such as memory views with fond delight.
I dare believe, my heart with glad surprize
Would linger here till morning beams arise ;
With strong desire that gentle voice to hear,
Whose kindness oft has charm'd my infant ear ;
And, fraught with tenderest love hath lull'd to rest
The little sorrows of my youthful breast.

W

It must not be ! I look around in vain—
Darknefs profound, and awful filence reign
O'er all the gloomy fcene, which feems to lie
Entomb'd beneath the fable-vaulted fky.
Oh ! when fhall this imprifon'd foul of mine
Burst from its dark abode with pow'r divine,
And meet with thofe I love, on that bleft fhore,
Where forrow, pain, and death are known no more.
Oh ! let my foul with hopeful patience fay,
" Thy will be done !" and wait that awful day,
That bids my fpirit wing its wond'rous flight,
From this dark world to realms of pureft light ;
With rapturous joy, to fhare the glorious prize
Of immortality beyond the fkies !

MEDITATION.

The morning dawn'd with beauteous fmile,
  And gaily rofe the radiant fun ;
My eye tranfported, for awhile
  Had o'er the glowing landfcape run,
Whenst from the fouth a cloud arofe ;
I faw with undifturbed repofe.

The mild and foftened rays of light,
  Seem'd on the mountain tops to reft ;
The winding river clear and bright,
  An air ferene, and calm confeft ;
The fields, though all the trees were bare,
Appear'd their fummer veft to wear.

Who could behold the fcene unmov'd ?
  With hafty fteps I bent my way,
And o'er the lawn delighted rov'd,
  And bleffed the giver of the day ;
Why not each moment prove like this ?
I fighed—and yet the figh was blifs.

Returning with a vigorous mind,
  I vow'd the live-long day to range ;
Or 'neath the oak to reft reclin'd,
  When nature might require a change ;

Such dreams and fancies oft amuſe,
While wiſdom's path we fail to chooſe.

Two hours had paſs'd—I now allow'd
My ſcheme of pleasure to purſue;
I roſe; not thinking that the cloud,
Unheeded, was a preſage true;
Alas! with baneful influence wide,
O'er all the ſky it ſeem'd to ſlide.

The ſun had now withdrawn his rays,
The whiſtling winds with fury blew;
And ruffled was the river's glaze,
The heavens each moment darker grew;
Ah! now my hopes were loſt in air,
And vaniſh'd all the proſpect fair.

So when life's opening viſions riſe,
They dazzle and beguile our ſight;
But, ah! the ſweet deluſion flies,
When bliſs has gain'd its utmoſt height,
And leaves us nought but ſorrow's gloom,
To light us to the dreary tomb.

Yet, if we courted hope's bright ray,
A glimmering always might be ſeen,
Painting the ſafe, though thorny way,
To where no ſorrows intervene;
But where in full perfection ſhine,
Love, joy, and happineſs divine!

COMMERCE.

TO be the herald of our own folly, and to proclaim all our latent weakneſſes, requires ſome ſtrength of mind; and I have a thouſand times regretted, ſince my confinement, the exiſtence of any tie which could turn my eye upon myſelf, or awake me from the lethergy into which I have fallen. I know you will diſapprove of this ſentiment, for its impiety, and at any other time, I ſhould fear the reprimand it will certainly bring upon me; but remember, there are times when we are both unable and unwilling to analyze our thoughts, or to ſcan our actions. The agony of my mind, the miſeries which ſurround me, the loſs of my gallant ſon, and the cries of the wretched priſoners for bread, muſt, therefore, be my apology, for my mental or verbal errors.

For what purpoſes were the paſſions of avarice and ambition given to the human mind? Why are mankind ſo generally diſſatisfied with the middle ſtations in ſociety?

I need not inform you how pleaſantly I was ſituated in the county of Dutcheſs, where I had an extenſive farm, kind neighbours, and true friends; where I had been ſucceſſively town-clerk, juſtice of the peace, ſheriff of the county, and member of the legiſlature. I need not dwell upon the eaſe, quiet, and ſubſtantial pleaſures of a country life. You are acquainted with them all, and will therefore ſpare me the pain of an enumeration. But when I tell you that I inherited a great portion of my property, which I was in ſome meaſure bound to hand down to my children, you will not feel leſs ſurprize than I do at the extent of my folly, the abſence of my reaſon, and the force of my credulity.

I am not, however, entirely to blame. Some of my friends, who had embarked in a ſucceſsful trade, were continually urging me to convert my property into caſh, to come to this city, and to enter into the ſhipping-buſineſs. My wife too, who has proved a very ambitious woman, chimed in, and did not fail to magnify the proſpects of ſucceſs. She *longed* to figure in thoſe ſplendid routes and parties, of which ſhe had taſted during our occaſional viſits to town; and ſhe was quite certain I ſhould make more money in one year than we could ſpend in ten. I yielded—came to town—eſtabliſhed a houſe—read price-currents—ſent veſſels to ſea, and was, for ſome time, ſucceſsful; but fortune, like the tide, both ebbs and flows.

A ſingle blow deprived me of a beloved ſon, and an immenſe property. Theſe loſſes were the more ſevere, as they occurred in that ſeaſon of life when we juſt begin to feel the gradual advances of old age. I found, however, a conſiderable relief from my trouble and anxiety, in the friendſhip of Mr. Trick'em, to whom I owed a conſiderable ſum. This gentleman gave me much of his company, and never omitted the kindeſt words; which I attributed to his magnanimity and generoſity, and to the delicacy and tenderneſs of his friendſhip. Indeed he often inſinuated that he was not ignorant of my *ſenſibility or ſituation* and that he feared to leave me long alone, leſt my mind might prey too much upon itſelf. Such inſtances of ſterling virtue occur ſo ſeldom, that they made a great impreſſion upon my mind, and I thought I could not do lefs than acquaint my friend with my exact fituation, in every particular. He feemed much pleafed with my confidenee, advifed me to cheer up, and hinted that a confiderable loan, for a few months, might retrieve my fortune and credit. It was true, he faid, that this money could not be procured for lefs than two and a half per cent a month, but that circumftances would fometimes juftify a much greater premium. I thanked my friend a thoufand times, and immediately called upon Mr. Shark, the broker, to execute his plan. As I had yet a great amount of property in fhips and goods, I found no difficulty in completing the negociation.

The conjectures of Mr. Trick'em were verified. I paid the moft clamorous of my creditors, and appeared at the coffee-houfe, among men of bufinefs as ufual. My profpects began to brighten, and I immediately concluded to pay my *friend* the balance of his account; and the more efpecially as he had hinted that he had a great deal of money to pay within a few days, and knew not how to collect it. Shortly after I had fettled with Trick'em, I found my credit faft declining, and that I fhould be unable to redeem the property which I had depofited with Shark. He did not fpare me, but facrificed enough of my property at auction to fecure his ufury, and gave himfelf no farther trouble about the remainder, or its owner. Juft at this time, when I was in the midſt of all my difficulties, I received word from another *friend*, that Trick'em had informed all my creditors of my embarraſſment, and that he, as one of them, muſt be paid to-morrow, or that he would arreſt me immediately. Mr. Break'em, who gave me this information, further ſtated, that Trick-'em had facetiouſly obſerved to him, that "Ledger thought himſelf under a thouſand obligations to me, but that if the country booby had not been ignorant of *the practices of trade*, he would have known that I could have no *intereſt* in "*keeping him up*" after I had wormed my money out of him; and that it was but natural I ſhould adviſe certain *uſeful friends*, whom his fooliſh confidence had informed me were creditors, to look to him."

I had now, indeed, a full view of *the practices of trade*; and my embarraſſments crowded upon me ſo faſt, that I knew not which way to turn myſelf. I had ſeen ſo much baſeneſs, ingratitude and treachery, that I began to think all mankind were villains, who perpetually prey upon each other; and that their ſeeming virtues were nothing more than different incidents, rendered acceſſary to the grand deſign, by which they might torment and deſtroy with the greater facility. But I will not detain you with the frantick ravings of a mind ſo perfectly killed with care. The denouement approaches faſt.

As the ſhipwrecked mariner clings to the parting veſſel, which he fondly hopes may contain ſubſtance and ſtrength enough to bear him to the ſhore; as the timid virgin, who is about to be ſacrificed to the man whom ſhe hates, ſupplicates the forbearance of her father, and watches his countenance; as the doating wife, who is in momentary expectation of being torn from the arms of a beloved huſband, looks wildly round for the appearance of ſome pitying friend; ſo did your unfortunate kinſman in this trying hour. There were two gentlemen whom I could not but think had ſome friendſhip for me, as I had very eſſentially ſerved them both, more than once. I therefore reſolved to commit the remainder of my property, in truſt, to their good keeping, that I might have ſomething to exiſt upon till I could get my affairs in a train of ſettlement. Theſe *gentlemen* betrayed me, and I was ſent immediately into cloſe confinement, where I am languiſhing in ill health, and ſuffering all the horrors of want.

BUSINESS.

You doubtleſs remember the exultation which I expreſſed when I took my leave of you, among other friends, for the purpoſe of embarking in trade in this city. I am ſure I ſhall never forget the day My feelings now powerfully atteſt the value of the ſalutary advice which you gave me previous to that event. You endeavoured to diſſuade me, by every argument which even paternal care could ſuggeſt, to give up ambitious ſchemes, to content myſelf among thoſe who had proved themſelves my beſt friends, and to fix myſelf for life among the wiſe, the virtuous, and the happy, in preference to thoſe whoſe friendſhips are ſelfiſh, and whoſe vices are contagious. You remember, with what alacrity I ſtruck off my houſe, my lands, and all my moveable property, to the higheſt bidder, that I might ſee in my hands the ſure precurſor of a princely eſtate, and the gift of national honours and emoluments. I have not forgotten the anxiety and chagrin which my unwarrantable anticipation of thoſe "bluſhing honours" pictured in your countenance. But if I be not entitled to your pity for my errors, I hope you will not withhold from me your forgiveneſs, when you are informed of my misfortunes. Do not ſay, that the laſt reſource of every blockhead, is to throw himſelf upon the generoſity of his friends. I know and feel that this is but too often the caſe; but you will do me the juſtice to believe, that there are ſome ſuperior to ſuch baſeneſs, and at leaſt one who will never ceaſe to ſtruggle with fortune till her revolving wheel has once more crowned his board, and compenſated his ſorrows and his toils.

When I firſt came to this city, I expected to have found the merchants open and candid with each other; that they would, at all times, furniſh the new-beginner with correct advice; that they would cheerfully point out to him the men of faireſt character and credit; reciprocate temporary loans, and be honeſt with me at all times. As the very baſis upon which their buſineſs is founded, is mutual confidence and honeſty, I thought I could not but realize this latter expectation. But *experience* is equally beneficial to the confident and ſceptical. If mankind could reſt ſatisfied without reſorting to this laſt, great teſt, how many nations that are now fallen, would have been great and happy! How many individuals would have been in eaſy circumſtances, who are now corrupt, debaſed and miſerable!

I do not wiſh to intrude upon your time and patience, by declaring againſt the long liſt of human infirmities. Your obſervations through life have doubtleſs convinced you of the futility of repining at evils which can never be removed; and your religion has taught you to conſider them as the works of that chaſtening hand which rewards and puniſhes according to its own inſcrutable wiſdom.

When we conſider the inducements which the ſituation of our country holds out to its citizens to embark in trade; its extenſive ſeacoaſt, and happy poſition; the number and activity of its hardy ſeamen; and the univerſal poverty at the expiration of our revolutionary ſtruggle, it ought to create no ſurpriſe that many ſought to remunerate themſelves by commercial adventures, by ſpeculations in the ſcrip of the numerous monied inſtitutions, which became neceſſary to a new nation and a new people, and by large purchases of vacant lands, which were sure to increase in value as the nation increased in population. These causes combined, produced a universal passion for trade; and the splendid success of the early adventurers has been but a too fatal inducement for others to follow, less qualified to succeed, and long after the golden crisis had passed away. The consequence of this mad business has been what many wise men predicted; and future historians will now be obliged to name America with that giddy nation, which had her *Mississippi scheme* and with that avaricious nation which had her *South-Sea Company*.

When we reflect upon the circumstances, we shall not be surprised that our merchants have become cautious and even suspicious. Instead of reciprocating accounts of their success, and the causes that have contributed to it, with frankness to each other, they not unfrequently conceal their own situation even from their own families. Besides every department of trade has now become so overstocked with adventurers, that it has created a universal rivalship and jealousy; and there are at all times, and especially in trade, but too many whose *interests* and natural depravity lead them to betray, rather than protect and advise. Instances of such conduct are by no means rare, and the abuse of confidence has become common.

I need not now inform you, that my object in coming to this city, was to make a rapid fortune. After I had engaged in business. I found my capital was not sufficient to accomplish this, and was forced to have recourse to others in a similar situation. A few days since one of those *friends* called upon me for the same favour, and "broke" the next day, with my money in his hands. A meeting of his creditors is called, he offers them two and six-pence in the pound, which we must take, or he will go upon the limits, live in style, and pay nothing.

I have had the blessed *experience* which every one seems so desirous of, and as I find all my beautiful visions are vanished, I shall endeavour to "back out" in time to save my bacon, and have authorized a person to negociate for my old place in the country, which I shall forever regret that I once relinquished.

PROGRESS OF FEELING.

In the days of my youth, when reason's sweet billow
Scarce swell'd on the stream of reflection and thought,
I sprang with the sky-lark, refresh'd from my pillow,
Nor heeded life's ills, whilst my pleasure I sought.

But soon to my book with a heart palpitating,
The frown of authority bade me attend;
I thought it was hard—yes sure it was grating,
To see my dear sports with my liberty end.

Yet something soon rose, oh! 'twas reading's sweet pleasure,
To calm, to content, to enlighten my mind,
And wond'ring, I smil'd, as I con'd o'er the treasure,
Of fables, of tales, or the Bible refin'd.

Yes, I blefs the dear day when my follies forfaking,
The friend of my childhood confign'd me to fchool,
For fomething like fcience my foul was awaking,
And told me the head o'er the heart ought to rule.

Then the lore of the ancients increas'd the fenfations
Which throbb'd in my bofom, as reafon arofe,
Whilft Poefy fmiling, held out her temptations,
And lur'd me to pluck from her bloffom a rofe.

Ah! the rofe was moft fweet, and much I lov'd dearly,
To tune my wild lyre in feclufion's lone cell,
And oft as the beauties of nature would cheer me,
Enchanted, my fong full of praifes I'd fwell.

But foon, from the fmiles of dear nature a roving,
My heart to the luring of beauty foon fled,
And fhortly I found that the rogue was a loving,
And rul'd—yes, for once, he rul'd over my head.

My ftrains were then fad, and I fung fo fincerely,
That beauty relented, and blefs'd me awhile,
But truly I paid for the bleffing moft dearly,
As fhortly I found that e'en beauty had guile.

So I turn'd quite difgufted from paffion's wild billow,
Nor felt that my lofs was a lofs fo uncommon,
Since fimply 'twas prov'd, as I bound on the willow,
I thought her an angel, but found her—a woman

Oh yes, when the calmnefs of reafon fucceeded,
And painted the follies affection conceal'd,
I blefs'd the dear day when the falfe one receded,
And all the allurements of cunning reveal'd.

Thus tranquil I fmil'd, and now often a ftraying,
Midft folitude's walks, I reflect on mankind,
Whilft haply my fancy is fometimes pourtraying
The changes and chances which round us will wind.

Now lifted by pleafure, now born down by forrow,
In the cafe of ourfelves 'tis we only agree--
So thus, like the reft, will I think of to-morrow,
And care for the world, as the world cares for me.

MY BREAKFAST.

" Good Cook, all ceremony wave,
And, e're I'm famifh'd, let me have
What 'bove all other things I crave,
My Breakfaft.

" Two dozen eggs, and fix fmoak'd fifh,
Of butter'd bread, a moderate difh,
And fome good tea, is all I wifh
For Breakfaft.

" Since I'm fo moderate then, make hafte,
Elfe, honeft Cook, you'll be difgrac'd,
For really, I long to tafte
My Breakfaft.

" Confider Cook, a day and night,
Have pafs'd, fince I, half famifh'd wight!
Have eat, fole fource of true delight!!
My Breakfaft.

" 'Tis ready, fay you, joyous news!
Your pardon then my gentle mufe,
Spite of your charms, I can't but choofe
My Breakfaft.

SLEIGH RIDING.

I envy not the Chariot's ftate,
That idly rolls the proud away,
Give me the pleasures which await
The fmoother flight that wings the Sleigh.

Thus though the tempeft howls around,
And winter whitens all the way,
Wrapt from its rage the bleft are found,
Who fafely truft the gliding Sleigh.

See there the happy lover goes
With ſome fair virgin far away,
Safe in his arms ſhe ſhuns the ſnows,
Delighted with the gliding Sleigh.

Now o'er ſome frozen ſtream afar,
Their nightly courſe they guide away,
While round the pole each flaming ſtar,
Directs the ſwiftly gliding Sleigh.

But hark! the treacherous ſurface round
Breaks, cracks, and thunders every way,
But born to hang, they'll never be drown'd
Who truſt the ſwiftly gliding Sleigh.

MUSIC.

AT a period when real melody is ſo much the ſubject of cultivation, it appears to me very ſingular, that no attempt has been made to reduce to ſome order

THE CRIES OF LONDON.

They ſtill remain in a moſt unmuſical confuſion, for want of ſome perſon to ſuperintend them, and to deliver out to the people their proper cries *in ſcore*, that they may not injure our ears as they do at preſent, by their horrid ſcreaming. This is much to the reproach of an age ſo muſically inclined as the preſent, and I wiſh to rouſe attention to a ſubject which they muſt daily hear on both ſides of their head.

The great errors which have crept into our ſyſtem of *Cries* are principally theſe: the ſame *muſic* is often applied to different words; and we have a great many words ſet to muſic ſo improperly that the " ſound is not an echo to the ſenſe." Not to ſpeak of a great deal of *muſic* by the firſt miſtreſſes of the *Billingſgate* academy, to which there are no words at all, and *vice verſa*, of a great quantity of *words* without muſic, ——of any one may be convinced.

I have ſaid that the ſame muſic is often applied to different words. There is a man under my window at this moment, who cries *potatoes* to the ſelf-ſame tune that I remember when *cherries* were in ſeaſon; and it was but yeſterday a woman invited the public to purchaſe *ſhrimps*, to a tune which has invariably been applied to *ſalt-cod*: as to *ſpinage*, and *muffins*, I have heard them ſo often chaunted in *D*, that I defy any man to know which is which.

Matches too have been tranſpoſed to the key of *periwinkles*, and the cadence which ſhould fall upon *rare*, is now placed upon *ſmelts* and *mackarel*. One could ſcarcely ſuppoſe ſuch abſurdities in London, at a time when every barber's boy *whiſtles* Italian operas, and even the footmen belonging to the nobility give you *Water parted*—at the box-doors. There is another inſtance I recollect in *radiſhes*; every body knows that the bravura part is on the words, *twenty a penny*, but they ſwell theſe notes, and *ſhake* upon *radiſhes*. We have no ears, elſe we could not hear ſuch barbarous tranſpoſitions, which muſt be done by people totally unacquainted with the *gamut*. You may think lightly of this matter, but my family ſhall ſtarve ere

I will buy *potatoes* in the *treble cliff*, or allow them to eat a fallad that has been cried *in flats*.

Soot ho! I will ftill allow to be in *alt*; the fituation of our chimneys juftifies this; but certainly *duft* ought to be an octave lower, although it is notorious, that the unmufical rafcals frequently go as high as *G.* and that without any *fhake*. Is it not clear that *duft* fhould be *fhaked?*

Of *water-creffes*, I muft own the cry has a moft pleafing melancholy, which I would not part with for the flippant triple tune in which we are folicited to purchafe *cabbage-plants*—In *fallad*, the repetition has a good effect—*Fine fallad*, and *fine young fallad*, with a fhake on the laft fyllable of *fallad*, is according to the true principles of mufic, as it ends in an *apogiatura*.

Hot crofs-buns, although they occur but once a year, are cried to a tune which has nothing of that melody which fhould accompany *facred mufic*. There is a flur upon *hot* which deftroys the effect; and indeed gives the whole a very irreverent found. *New cheefe*, I have to obferve, has not been fet to mufic, and is therefore ufually fung as a fecond part to *radifhes*, but the concords are not always perfect. *Duets* are rarely well performed when there is no other accompaniments than the wheels of a barrow.

As I would not wifh to infinuate that all our cries are objectionable, I muft allow that *ground ivy* is one of the moſt excellent pieces of muſic we have; I queſtion much if ever Handel compoſed, or Billington ſung any thing like it. What renders it more beautiful is, that it is a *rondeau*, a very pleaſing and popular ſpecies of air. The repetition of the word *ground ivy*, both before and after the *Come buy my*—has a very fine effect; or, as the critics would ſay, it is *impreſſive* and *brilliant!*

But while I allow the merit of this very natural and popular compoſition, what ſhall I ſay to *cucumbers*? The original tune is entirely forgotten, and a ſort of Iriſh air is ſubſtituted for it. But although I object to this tune by itſelf, I am perſuaded that thoſe who admire the ſublime thunder of a *chorus*, will be highly gratified by a *chorus* of cucumber women in a narrow ſtreet. I have often liſtened to it, when it took my attention from every thing elſe.

Freſh ſalmon is objectionable both on account of the words and the muſic. The muſic was originally part of the celebrated *water piece*, but they have mangled it ſo, that the compoſer himſelf could not recogniſe the original air. Beſides, ſome uſe the word *dainty*, and ſome *delicate*, to the ſame notes, which occaſions an unpleaſant ſemiquaver. Indeed in general the word *delicate* might be as well left out.

Little or nothing of the *bravura* has been attempted in our cries, if we except the *roly-polys*; *green peas* is a very fine inſtance of this ſpecies of compoſition ; I know of nothing in any of our operas which goes beyond it ; it is to be regretted peas don't laſt all the year.

But to go over the whole cries, is altogether impoſſible, elſe I could eaſily prove that we are as much degenerated in this kind of muſic, as we are improved in every other— the barrel-organ men have injured our fiſh and garden-ſtuff women ; for indeed how can a woman, be ſhe ever ſo good a ſinger, liſten to their play-houſe tunes, and whip her aſs along at the ſame time? It cannot be done ; people who have nice ears are moſt eaſily diſturbed by ſounds ; and how can one give the elegant melody of *Windſor beans*, and liſten at the ſame time to *God ſave the King ?*

P. S. If any ſcheme be ſet on foot for the valuable purpoſes which I have mentioned, I beg leave to intimate, that I have lately compoſed a ſet of appropriate airs for each article, from *ſoot* at ſeven in the morning, to *hot ginger-bread* at ten at night ; alſo a ſet of tunes for the watchmen in much better time than they at preſent preſerve. Theſe I ſhall be happy to ſubmit to any committee of *Muſical Cognoſcenti* which may be appointed. If not, I ſhall print them by ſubſcription at *half a guinea* the ſet.

HOPE.

Were fortune's ſmiles inſur'd to man below,
The fear of hovering care he might forego;
Were he aſſur'd that through his journey here,
Fate inauſpicious would not force a tear ;
That joys perpetual would engage his mind,
In nature pure, ſubſtantial and refin'd ;

Inſtead of knowing what he now endures,
Would taſte the bliſs which virtue e'er ſecures.
But doom'd by nature from his earlieſt age,
With num'rous ills and troubles to engage;
To ſtem, with patience, life's impetuous ſtream,
To fancy ſpectres in each ſparkling gleam;
Onward he goes—yet HOPES e'er long to ſee
The world, from threat'ning ills and dangers free.
Yes, HOPE, the anchor of the conſtant mind,
Aſſures that man his wiſh'd for joys *may* find;
That he may know his time with bliſs replete,
His future days in happineſs complete.
If thou would'ſt know that through th' expanded whole,
Fond hope indulg'd revives the ſinking ſoul;
View the lone ſtudent in his early age,
Employ'd in ſearch, while leaning o'er his page.
Fraught with the hope that, by his ſtudious care,
His name on fame's fair record may appear,
He ſtrives with mental force to prove at laſt
Himſelf repaid for labours o'er and paſt.
See the fond mother o'er a darling child,
In every feature ſmiling, placid, mild.
Within her breaſt the ſeeds of hope ariſe,
To future ſcenes ſhe looks with longing eyes;—
Views the dear infant, clinging to her breaſt,
Riſing, fond hope, to be renown'd and bleſt—
Beholds him happy in the world's juſt praiſe,
The child of fortune, born to proſp'rous days.
Lo, the brave tar, the ſport of every wind,
To-day, depreſſ'd—to-morrow, cheer'd in mind;
While toſs'd on waves and toiling at his oar,
Engag'd in thoughts of his dear native ſhore,
Where dwells a wife, whoſe boſom heaves with ſighs,
Around an offspring, liſt'ning to her cries;
Hope cheers his breaſt—he looks with anxious eye,
To climes remote, beneath the weſtern ſky.

THE RETURN OF SPRING.

Ye ſouthern gales, that fan Peruvian groves,
With gentle, am'rous wing,

Awhile ſuſpend your tender loves,
And chide the loit'rer, Spring !
O, gently chide th' unkind delay,
That keeps the nymph ſo long away
From northern climes, whoſe drooping ſwains
I wiſh ſhould hail her on their frozen plains.

Where'er the lingering maid you find,
By ſtream or vocal grove,
Around her waiſt ſoft oſiers bind,
That ſhe may ceaſe to rove,
Then ſwiftly ply your rapid wing,
The captive fair one hither bring,
That all our fields in renovated charms may ſmile,
And flow'rs unnumber'd deck the looſen'd ſoil.

All nature mourns thee, blooming fair—
No more the ſtreams delight :
No more embroider'd vales appear
To check the wandering ſight.
E'en Phoebus darts a fickle ray,
And pours a dull, dejected day,
Refuſing to diſpenſe his ſplendid beams
To looſe the frozen glebe, and thaw the icy ſtreams.

Yet ſad Canadia's ſons, with dread,
Still court the wintry gloom :
For froſt and ſnow on them more pleaſure ſhed,
Than thy enlivening bloom !
With eyes aghaſt they view the plain
Portending thy approaching reign,
And wiſh St. Lawrence' ſtreams may never flow,
But, bound in icy claims, repel their conquering foe.

DOMESTIC HAPPINESS.

'Tis not ſcenes of feſtive pleaſure,
Splendid equipage and dreſs,
Hoarded heaps of glitt'ring treaſure.
Can beſtow true happineſs.

No, the ſweeteſt joy ariſes
From domeſtick dear delights ;

Where the peace that virtue prizes,
With attractive pow'r unites.

Far from ſcenes of ſad vexation,
Happy they who can remove,
To their tranquil habitation,
Bleſt with competence and love.

Where good nature ever ſmiling,
Kindles joy in ev'ry heart;
And affection, grief beguiling,
Sweeteſt pleaſure can impart.

Piety the ſcene adorning,
With a luſtre all divine,
Brings to view the glorious morning,
When their joys ſhall brighter ſhine.

Earth's delights at beſt are fleeting,
Ev'ry pleaſure has its pain;
But when theſe are all retreating,
'Tis to bloom more fair again.

O how lovely is the dwelling,
Where ſuch joys as theſe abound;
Each enjoyment ſure foretelling,
All with glory ſhall be crown'd.

ADDRESS,
Delivered to the Candidates for the Baccalaureate in Union College.

This day cloſes your collegiate life. You have continued the term, and completed the courſe of ſtudies which are preſcribed in this inſtitution. You have received its honours, and are now to go forth as adventurers, unſuſpecting perhaps, and certainly inexperienced, into a faſcinating but illuſive world, where honour flaunts in fictious trappings, where wealth diſplays impoſing charms, and pleaſure ſpreads her impoiſoned banquets. And that too, at a period when the paſſions are moſt ungovernable—when fancy is moſt vivid—when the blood flows rapidly through the veins, and the pulſe of life beats high. Already does the opening ſcene brighten as you approach it, and happineſs, ſmiling but deceitful, paſſes before your eyes and beckons you to her embrace.

Called to addreſs you, at this affecting criſis, and for the laſt time; had I, like the patriarchs of the Eaſt, a bleſſing at my diſpoſal, how gladly would I diſpoſe of it. But I have not; and can therefore only add, to the ſolicitude which I feel, my councils and my prayers.

Permit me to adviſe you then, when you leave this ſeminary, and even after you have choſen a profeſſion, and entered on the buſineſs of life, ſtill to conſider yourſelves only learners. Your acquirements here, though reſpectable, are the firſt rudiments merely of an education which muſt be hereafter purſued and completed. In the acquiſition of knowledge you are never to be ſtationary, but always progreſſive. Nature has no where ſaid to man, preſſing forward in the career of intellectual glory, "Hitherto ſhalt thou come but no further." Under GOD, therefore, it depends upon yourſelves to ſay, how great—how wiſe—how uſeful you will be. Men of moderate talents, by a courſe of patient application, have often riſen to the higheſt eminence, and ſtanding far above where the momentary ſallies of uncultivated genius ever reach; have plucked from the lofty cliff its deathleſs laurel. Indeed, to the ſtature of the mind, no boundary is ſet. Your bodies, originally from the earth, ſoon reach their greateſt elevation, and bend downwards again towards that earth out of which they were taken. But the inner man; that ſublime, that rational, that immortal inhabitant, which pervades your boſoms, if ſedulouſly foſtered, will expand and elevate itſelf, till touching the earth it can look above the clouds and reach beyond the ſtars.

Go then and emulous to excel in whatever is ſplendid, magnanimous and great; with *NEWTON*, ſpan the heavens, and number and meaſure the orbs which decorate them—with *LOCKE*, analyze the human mind---with *BOYLE*, examine the regions of organic matter. In one word, go: and with the great and wiſe, and the good of all nations, and all ages ponder the myſteries of infinite wiſdom, and trace the *EVERLASTING* in his word, and in his works. A wide and unbounded proſpect ſpreads itſelf before you: in every point of which the DIVINITY ſhines conſpicuous, and on which ever ſide you turn your enraptured eyes, ſurrounded with uncreated majeſty, and ſeen in the light of his own glory, GOD appears. He leads the way before you, and ſheds radiance on his path, that you may follow him.

Controul and ſubjugate your paſſions. Originally, order pervaded human nature.—The bosom of man was calm—his countenance serene. Reason sat enthroned in his heart, and to her controul the passions were subjected. But the days of innocence are past, and with them has also past the reign of reason. Phrenzy ensues. He, who was once calm and rational, is now blind and impetuous. A resistless influence impels him. Consequences are disregarded, and madly pressing forward to the object of desire, he exclaims, "My honour, my property, my pleasure;" but is never heard to say, "my religion, my duty, my salvation."

While reason maintained her empire, the passions were a genial flame, imparting warmth to the system, and gently accelerating the circulation of the blood. But, that empire subverted, they kindle into a VESUVIUS, burning to its centre, and pouring out on every side, its desolating lava. The passions, said an inspired apostle, war against the soul: and the same apostle who said this, commands you to overcome them.

Cultivate and cherish the sympathies of your nature. These so blighted by the apostacy, still retain the tints of faded loveliness, and when sanctified in the heart, and unfolded in the life, even of fallen man, they possess a resistless charm, and furnish some faint idea of what he must have been in a state of innocence.

For the exercise of those sympathies, in all the paths of life, you will meet with pitiable objects who will present their miseries to your eye, and address the moving eloquence of sorrow to your heart. Always listen to this eloquence; always pity this misery, and if possible, relieve it. Yes, whatever seas you may navigate, or to whatever part of the habitable world you may travel, carry with you your humanity. Even there divide your morsel with the destitute; defend the cause of the oppressed; to the fatherless be a father, and cover the shivering limbs of the naked with your mantle. Even there, sooth the disconsolate, sympathise with the mourner, brighten the countenance bedimmed with sorrow, and like the GOD of mercy, shed happiness around you, and banish misery from before you.

In all your intercourse with mankind rigidly practice justice, and scrupulously adhere to the truth: other duties vary with varying circumstances. What would be liberality in one man, would be parsimony inanother. What would be valour on one occasion, would be temerity on another. But truth and justice are immutable and eternal principles; always sacred and always applicable. In no circumstances however urgent, or crisis however awful, can there be an aberration from the one or a dereliction of the other without sin. With respect to every thing else, be accommodating, but here beunyielding and invincible. Rather carry your integrity to the dungeon or the scaffold, than receive in exchange for it liberty and life. —Should you ever be called upon to make your election between these extremes, do not hesitate. It is better prematurely to be sent to heaven in honour, than, having lingered on the earth, at last to sink to hell in infamy. In every situation, a dishonest man is detestable, and a liar is still more so.

Truth is one of the fairest attributes of the Deity. It is the boundary which separates vice from virtue—the line which divides Heaven from Hell. It is the chain which binds the man of integrity to the throne of his GOD, and like the GOD to whose throne it binds him, till his chain is dissolved, *his word may be relied on.* Suspending on this, your property, your reputation, your life, are safe. But against the malice of a liar, there is no security. He can be bound by nothing. His soul is already repulsed to a returnless distance from that Divinity, a sense of whose presence is the security of virtue. He has sundered the last of those moral ligaments which bind a mortal to his duty. And having done so, through the extended region of fraud and falsehood, with no bound to check nor limit to confine him, the dreaded enemy of innocence, he ranges; whose lips pollute even truth itself as it passes through them; and whose breath, like the cadaverous mists of Hades, blasts, and soils, and poisons as it touches.

Finally, *cherish and practice Religion.* Man has been called, in distinction from the inferior orders of creation, a religious being, and justly so called. For, though his hopes and fears may be repreſſed, and the moral feelings of his heart ſtifled for a ſeaſon, nature, like a torrent which has been obſtructed, will break forth, and ſweep away thoſe frail works which ſcepticiſm may have erected to divert its courſe.

There is ſomething ſo repulſive in naked infidelity, that the mind approaches it with reluctance, ſhrinks back from it with horror, and is never ſettled till it reſts on poſitive religion.

I am aware that, *that* ſpirit of devotion, that ſenſe of guilt and dread of puniſhment, which pervade the human mind, have been attributed either to the force of habit or the influence of ſuperſtition. Let the appeal be made to human nature. To the poſition of irreligioniſts on this article, human nature itſelf furniſhes the moſt ſatisfactory refutation. Religion is the firſt principle of man. It ſhoots up from the very ſeat of life, it cleaves to the human conſtitution by a thouſand ligaments; it intwines around human nature, and ſends to the very bottom of the heart its penetrating tendrils. It cannot, therefore, be exterminated. The experiment has again and again been tried, and the reſult has always proved worthy of the raſh attempt.

Young as you are, you have witneſſed, with a view to this extermination, the moſt deſperate efforts. But juſt now, a formidable hoſt of infuriated infidels were aſſembled. You heard them openly abjure their GOD. You ſaw them wreaking their vengeance on religion. For a feafon they triumphed.—Before them every facred inftitution difappeared—every confecrated monument fell to duft.—The fervours of nature were extinguifhed, and the lips of devotion palfied by their approach.—With one hand they feized the thunder of the heavens, and with the other fmote HIS throne who inhabited them. It feemed to crumble at the ftroke.—Mounting its fancied ruins, BLASPHEMY waved its terrifick fceptre, and impiously looking up to thofe eternal heights where the Deity refides, exclaimed, "VICTORY!"

Where now are thofe dreaded enemies of our religion? They have vanifhed from the fight. They were, but foon are no more. Nor have the confequences of their exertions been more abiding. A great nation indeed, delivered from the reftraints of moral obligation, and enfranchifed with all the liberties of infidelity, were proclaimed free. But have they continued fo?—No, their minds prefently recoiled from the difmal wafte which fcepticifm had opened before them, and the cheerlefs darknefs which it had fpread around them.—They fuddenly arrefted their ftep.—They retreated, in fadnefs and forrow, from the paths which they had trodden.—They confecratedagain, the temples which they had defiled: they rebuilt the altar which they had demolifhed: they fighed for the return of that religion which they had banished, and fpontaneously promifed fubmiffion to its reign.

What are we to infer from this?—That religion is congenial to human nature—that it is infeparable from it. A nation may be feduced into fcepticifm, but it cannot be continued in it. Why, I would afk, has religion exifted in the world in ages which are paft, why does it exift now, why will it exift in ages to come? Is it becaufe kings have ordained, and priefts defend it? No, but becaufe God formed man to be religious. Its great and eternal principles, are infcribed in characters which are indelible; nor can the violence of infidelity blot them out. Obfcured indeed they may be by the influence of fin, and remain not legible during the rage of paffion. But a calm enfues: the calm of reafon, or the night of adverfity, from the midft of whofe darknefs, a light proceeds which renders the original infcription vifible. Man now turns his eye inward upon himfelf. He reads "refponsibility," and as he reads, he feels a fenfe of fin and dread of punifhment. He now pays from neceffity a homage to religion, a homage which cannot be withheld; it is the homage of his nature.

The queftion is not then, whether you will embrace religion?—Religion you muft embrace—but whether you will embrace revealed religion, or that of erring and blind philofophy. And with refpect to this queftion can you hesitate?

The former has infinitely more to recommend it than the latter. It originated in heaven. It is founded not on conjecture, but on fact. Divinity manifested itself in the person, and shone in the life of its author. True, he appeared in great humility; but though the humility in which he appeared, had been greater than it was, either the sublimity of his doctrines or the splendour of his actions had been sufficient to evince his Messiahship, and prove that he was the saviour of the world. He spoke as man never spoke! Whence did he derive wisdom so transcendent? From reason? No; reason could not give it, for it had it not to give. What reason could never teach, the gospel teaches; that in the vast and perfect government of the universe, vicarious sufferings can be accepted; and that the dread sovereign, who administers that government, is gracious as well as just. Nor does it rest in declaration merely. It exhibits before our eyes, the altar and the victim—the lamb of God, who taketh away the sins of the world.

The introduction of christianity, was called the coming of the kingdom of heaven. No terms could have been more appropriate, for through it man shared the mercy, and from it caught the spirit of the heavens. The moral gloom which shrouded the nations receded before it. The temples of superstition and of cruelty, consecrated by its entrance, became the assylum of the wretched, and resounded with their anthems of grace.

Most benign has been the influence of christianity, and were it cordially received, and universally submitted to, war would ceafe, injuftice be banifhed, and primeval happinefs revifit the earth. Every inhabitant pleafed with his fituation, refigned to his lot, and full of the hopes of heaven, would pafs agreeably through life, and meet death without a figh.

Is the morality of the gofpel pre-eminently excellent? So is its object pre-eminently glorious. Philofophy, confines its views principally to this world. It endeavours to fatisfy man with the grovelling joys of earth, till he returns to that duft from which he was taken. Chriftianity, takes a nobler flight. Her courfe is directed towards immortality. Thither fhe conducts her votary, and never forfakes him, till having introduced him into the fociety of angels, fhe fixes his eternal refidence among the fpirits of the juft.

Philofophy, can heave a figh only, a longing figh, after immortality. Eternity is to her an unknown vaft, over which fhe foars on conjecture's trembling wing. Above—beneath—around is an unfathomable void; and doubt, uncertainty and defpair, are the refult of all her inquiries.

Chriftianity on the other hand, having furnifhed all neceffary information concerning life, with firm undaunted ftep, croffes death's narrow ifthmus, and boldly launches forth into that dread futurity which borders on it. Her path is marked with glory. The once dark, dreary region, brightens as fhe approaches it, and benignly fmiles as fhe paffes over it. Faith follows where fhe advances ; till reaching the ſummit of everlaſting hills, an unknown ſcene, an endleſs variety of lovelineſs and beauty preſents itſelf, over which the raviſhed eye wanders, without a cloud to dim or a limit to obſtruct its ſight. In the midſt of this ſcene, rendered luminous by the glory which covers it, the city—the palace—the throne of God appears ! Trees of life wave their ambroſial tops around it ; Rivers of ſalvation iſſue from beneath it. Before it, angels touch their harps of living melody ; and ſaints in ſweet reſponſe, breathe forth to the liſtening heavens, their grateful ſongs ! the breezes of Paradiſe waft the ſymphony, and the bending ſky directs it to the earth. The redeemed of the lord catch the diſtant ſound, and feel a ſudden rapture. It is the voice of departed friendſhip---friendſhip, the loſs of which they mourn upon the earth, but which they are now aſſured will be reſtored in the heavens ; whence a voice is heard to ſay, "Fear not ye, death cannot injure you ; the grave cannot confine you ; through its chill manſion grace will conduct you to glory. We wait your arrival---haſte, therefore come away !" All this chriſtianity will do for you. It will do more than this : it conſecrates the ſepulchre, into which your bodies, already touched by death, will preſently deſcend. There, mouldered into duſt, your fleſh ſhall reſt in hope. Nor will the ſeaſon of its humiliation laſt forever ; chriſtianity, faithful to her truſt, appears for its redemption. She approaches and ſtands before the tomb : ſhe ſtretches out her ſceptre and ſmites the ſepulchre. Its moſsgrown covering rends aſunder. She cries to the ſilent inhabitants within---her energizing voice echoes along the cold, damp vaults of death, renovating ſkin and bones, and duſt, and putrefaction. Corruption puts on incorruption, and mortal immortality. Her former habitation, thus refined and ſublimated by the reſurrection, the exulting ſoul re-enters, and thenceforth the meaſure of her joy is full!

Here thought and language fail me. Inſpiration itſelf deſcribes the glories of futurity by declaring them indeſcribable. "Eye hath not ſeen, ear hath not heard, neither hath it entered into the heart of man to conceive, the things which are prepared for the people of God." What ideas are theſe! how muſt the ſoul exult at the proſpect, and ſwell at the amazing conception!

As chriſtianity exhibits the moſt enrapturing motives to the practice of virtue, ſo it urges the moſt tremendous conſiderations to deter from vice. She declares, ſolemnly and irrevocably declares, "That the wages of ſin are death." And to enforce her declaration, ſhe points to the concluding ſcene of nature: when, amidſt a departing heaven and a diſſolving world, the ſon of man ſhall deſcend, with the voice of the archangel and the trump of God, to be glorified in his ſaints, and take vengeance on his enemies!

Such is the goſpel---and this goſpel I deliver to you. It is the moſt invaluable gift; and I ſolemnly adjure you to preſerve it inviolate forever. Through whatever part of God's creation you may wander, carry this with you. Conſult it in proſperity ; reſort to it in trouble ; ſhield yourſelf with it in danger, and reſt your fainting head on it in death.

More efficacious than the fabled ring---it conſecrates its keeper ; preſerves his life, and eternizes his memory. While you prize and preſerve this gift, your happineſs is ſecure. The world may be convulſed around you, the elements diſſolve, and the heavens depart, ſtill your happineſs is ſecure——but ſhould you ever in an hour of raſhneſs, be tempted to caſt it from you ; remember that with it, you caſt away your ſalvation. Ii ts the laſt hope of ſinful, dying man. This gone—all is loſt ! Immortality is loſt—and loſt alſo is the ſoul who might otherwiſe have inherited and enjoyed it.—Under theſe impreſſions, go forth into the world—and may God go with you.

MOON-LIGHT.

Now leaning o'er this elevated ſteep !
To view the glimmering ſplendours of the deep,
Lo ! o'er the waves, the moon's refulgent light
Shines in full glory, and diſpels the night !
While through the vaſt expanſe, the ſtarry hoſt
Seem in her brilliant path obſcurely loſt !
Bleſt beam ! which to the fainting trav'ller's eyes
Appear'ſt in beauty through the boundless ſkies,
To guide his midnight footſteps through the gloom,
And light him wand'ring to his native home.

Who, long through wilds and difmal terrours loft
Beholds thy glory on fome ftormy coaft,
Chearful, he fmiles ! nor thinks his journey long,
The rocks re-echo to his paffing fong !
While from the clouds appears thy friendly ray
Through the tall trees, to point his doubtful way

MODERN SONNET.

Penfive at eve, on the hard world I mus'd
And my poor heart was fad : fo at the moon
I gaz'd—and figh'd and figh'd ! for ah ! how foon
Eve faddens into night. Mine eye peruf'd
With fearful vacancy, the *dampy* grafs
Which wept and glitter'd in the *poly* ray
And I did paufe me on my lonely way
And mufed me on thofe wretched ones who pafs
O er the black heath of forrow—But alas !
Moft of *myfelf* I thought : when it befell
That the footh fpirit of the *brezy* wood
Breath'd in mine ear—" All this is very well"—
But much of *one* thing is for *no* thing good
Ah ! my poor heart's inexplicable fwell !

TO SIMPLICITY.

O ! I do love thee, meek *fimplicity !*
For of thy lays the lulling fimplenefs
Goes to my heart, and fooths each small diftrefs,
Diftrefs though fmall yet haply great to me !
'Tis true on lady fortune's gentleft pad
I amble on ; yet though I know not why
So fad I am !—but fhould a friend and I
Grow cool and *miff*—O ! I am *very* fad !
And then with fonnets and with fympathy
My *dreamy* bofom's myftic woes I pall,
Now of my falfe friend plaining plaintively
Now raving at mankind in general :
But whether fad or fierce, 'tis fimple all
All very fimple, meek *fimplicity !*

A MOONLIGHT WALK.

Allur'd by Cynthia's ſilver ray,
With wand'ring ſteps alone I ſtray,
Where solemn ſilence unmoleſted reigns ;
Afar from riot's noxious light,
T'enjoy the ſacred calm of night,
And liſt'ning catch her ſweetly plaintive ſtrains.

From far the ſoft reſponſive ſong,
Born on the zephyr floats along,
Nor ought is heard to interrupt the lay,
Save where the wearied peaſant ſleeps,
Secure while Tray the portal keeps,
Whoſe hollow notes extend their lengthen'd way.

Or where the ſolemn bird of night,
Exulting in the azure light
Bids echo's voice repeat the drowſy theme,
Or crickets chirp beneath the thorn,
Whoſe twigs the glitt'ring gems adorn
That ſport reflected in the limpid ſtream.

Paſs'd is the fervid heat of day,
Now bluſt'ring ſtorms arefar away ;
Beneath the covert of the brambles ſhade,
The glow-worm's ſhining lamp is ſeen,
'Ting'd faintly with a ſilver green,
Spreading its radiance in the moonlight glade.

Sweet is the lonely moonlight ſcene,
When all is tranquil and ſerene,
And weary nature ſinks in calm repoſe :
Yet many a downy pillow bears,
A head perplex'd with tort'ring cares,
That vainly ſeeks a reſpite from its woes.

Contentment flies the gilded dome
And chuſes for her envied home,
The humble roof where peaceful virtue dwells ;
She there diſplays her richeſt ſtores,
And in the wounded boſom pours,
Her ſoothing balm——and anxious fear diſpels.

Z

Grant me, O gentle Nymph thy ſmile,
Life's path uncertain to beguile,
And round my lot diffuſe thy cheering ray;
Let peace of mind and joy ſerene,
Calm as this ſilent lovely ſcene,
Sooth ev'ry grief——and wipe each tear away.

CORYDON AND MIRA.

On the banks of a ſmooth flowing ſtream,
There ſat a young, beautiful ſwain,
Diſappointment in love was his theme,
And he ſent forth this ſorrowful ſtrain.
" Oh Mira, delight of my eyes
" What maiden with thee can compare,
" Alas! love-ſick Corydon dies,
" By thy cruelty, hard hearted fair.

" What though, I am lowly and poor,
" Others rich, and in rank rather high,
" Thou wilt not find one that has more,
" Of love, and affection that I.
" Oh Mira, can thouſands of gold,
" Can even the mines of Peru,
" Can greatneſs indifflrent or cold
" Ever equal the heart that is true.

" How happy! before I had ſeen,
" Thy bluſh, like the roſes of morn,
" Thy air—that of beauty's ſweet queen,
" Or the dimples thy cheeks that adorn:
" Thy ringlets, that flow with ſuch grace,
" Thy boſom a lily ſo white,
" Heard thy voice which more muſic conveys
" Than Philomel ſongſter of night.

" Before that unfortunate day,
" The hours mov'd ſwiftly along,
" With the ſhepherds ſo cheerful and gay,
" I danc'd to the pipe and the ſong.
" Now Flora and Zephyr in vain,
" Attending the ſpring of the year,
" Deck with flow'rets, and verdure the plain,
" They all diſmal as winter appear.

" In vain where the rivulet flows,
" At the foot of the ſycamore tree,
" As usual I ſtrive to repoſe,
" Alas ! there's no comfort for me.
" If in woods or in myrtle alcoves,
" I wander, or thoughtful recline,
" The birds while they warble their loves,
" Cauſe with envy my breaſt to repine.

" Through the grove every breeze ſeems to ſigh,
" How ſtrongly it dwells on my mind,
" Ah ! Corydon why do'nt you die,
" Thy Mira is falſe and unkind.
" Then die hated youth—life's career,
" Arreſt in a watery grave,
" O'er thy fate ſhe may ſhed a ſad tear,
" Though the lover ſhe ſcorned to ſave."

He ſung, and the flocks on the plain,
Felt compaſſion on hearing his moan ;
From the bank where he ſat, wretched ſwain !
He aroſe and walk'd leiſurely home !
He to hang himſelf *afterwards* choſe,
But in vain ſent to neighbours around
For a halter to end all his woes—
So he lives ſtill—quite merry and ſound.
Yet fortune look'd on him with frowns,
With Cupid he oft was at ſtrife,
'Till an Old Woman *worth ninety pounds*,
So pleas'd him, he made her his wife !

ODE TO THE RIVER OCCOQUAN.

Loſt in a pleaſing wild ſurprize,
I mark thy fountains round me riſe,
And in an artleſs current flow,
Through dark and lofty woods below,
That from the world the ſoul confine,
And raiſe the thought to things divine ;
Withdrawing as from either ſhore
They bend their giant ſhadows o'er
Each dull and low deſire of art,
And with new feeling wake the heart.

O ſacred ſtream ! a ſtranger I,
Would ſtay to ſee thee paſſing by,
And mark thee wand'ring thus alone,
With varied turns ſo like my own !
Wild, as a ſtranger led aſtray,
I ſee thee wind in woods away ;
And haſting through the trees to glide,
As if thy gentle face to hide.
While oft in vain thou would'ſt return,
To viſit here thy native urn :
But like an exile doom'd no more
To ſee the ſcenes he lov'd before,
You wonder on, and wind in vain
Diſpers'd amid the boundleſs main ;
Here often on thy borders green
Perhaps thy native ſons were ſeen,
Ere ſlaves were made, or gold was known,
Or children from another zone
Inglorious did, with axes rude
Into thy noble groves intrude ;
And forc'd thy naked ſon to flee,
To woods where he might ſtill be free.
And thou ! that art my preſent theme,
O gentle ſpirit of the ſtream !
Then too perhaps to thee was giv'n,
A name among the race of heav'n ;
And oft ador'd by nature's child
Whene'er he wander'd in the wild ;
And oft perhaps beſide thy flood,
In darkneſs of the grove he ſtood ;
Invoking here thy friendly aid
To guide him through the doubtful ſhade
Till over-head the moon in view
Through heav'ns blue field her chariot drew
And ſhew'd him all thy wat'ry face,
Reflected with a purer grace ;
Thy many turnings through the trees
Thy bitter journey to the ſeas.
While oft thy murmurs loud and long
Awak'd his melancholy ſong ;
Which thus in ſimple ſtrain began,
Thou queen of rivers, Occoquan !

THE MOTHER.

OH! I am rich; the Mother cries,
And clafps her infant to her breaft.
Bends o'er his feebly clofing eyes,
Till fweetly footh'd he finks to reft.

Oh! I am rich; Golconda's mines,
From all their ftores could ne'er impart
Such pure, fuch exquifite delight,
As that which rufhes on my heart.

Such vivid joy my bofom fwells,
I fcarce believe the impreffion true;
I fcarce believe, whilft fancy tells,
'Tis my own baby that I view.

Oh! yes thou art indeed my own;
Why do thefe tears of rapture ftart?
I feel a thrill before unknown,
I feel the mother at my heart.

To me thou ow'ft thy life my child!
And daily is the boon renew'd:
Yet thanklefs babe! thou haft not fmil'd,
To blefs thy mother for thy food.

Ah! when that fmile of calm content
Firft o'er thy little cheek fhall play,
So fweet thy gratitude 'twill paint,
That every care 'twill overpay.

No other fhares my tender care
That fmile muft blefs no others view;
The foft carefs I cannot fpare,
To me, my babe, alone, 'tis due.

Yes, there is one my beauteous boy
To thy embraces has a claim,
My bofom's Lord, who feels the joy,
To own a Father's facred name.

Too keenly now the nerves of fenfe,
Vibrate to each impreffion true,

E're long they'll joy alone dispense
And give these pleasures ever new.

Soon shall thy feeble eye, which now
Scarce can endure the blaze of day ;
Turn with delight the dawn to view,
And drink with joy the genial ray.

And soon thy little ear shall prove
The diff'rence of each varied tone,
Soon shall thy mother's voice of love
Be by thy tender organs known.

Each day new pleasures shall appear,
Each hour new charms shall bring along ;
Soon shall I catch with eager ear,
The half formed accents of thy tongue.

O'er scenes, with such endearments fraught,
Oft shall I bend with raptured eyes,
Catch the first rudiments of thought,
And mark each new idea rise.

With hopes like these my fancy glows,
By language faintly poorly shewn,
The transport which a mother knows,
A mother can conceive alone.

Yes, I am rich ; ah ! why those cries ?
Come let me hush my boy to rest,
Close, close, sweet babe thy little eyes,
And sink to slumber on my breast.

ADDRESS TO THE POLAR STAR.

Star of the north, how oft have I alone
In midnight walks ador'd thy golden throne ;
Remote from vulgar fires thou dost retain
Thy sphere forever in the starry plain,
Fix'd to the pole thou never dost remove
Far from the planet that preserves thy love ;
But to this orb, thy faithful fires confine
True to thy trust with constancy divine.

To the Stockholders of Banks.

Obſerving that uncommon intereſt and exertion are making to get into the Directory, and that ſeveral different liſts of names have been recommended to your conſideration; we, believing ourſelves to be as well qualified as others to perform what we deem the *intereſting buſineſs* of that inſtitution, diſdain all underhand methods of recommending ourſelves through the medium of others, and come openly forward to offer ourſelves. And that you may correctly underſtand our motives for ſoliciting your ſuffrages, we will briefly and candidly ſtate our pretenſions.

We are not great, overgrown merchants, whoſe large capital is ſufficient to ſupply all our wants, nor are we young merchants nor regular tradeſmen, for whoſe benefit, it is *erroneouſly* ſuppoſed, Banks were inſtituted; but we are men who know and have felt the ſalutary influence of the banking ſyſtem, who have made moſt of what we poſſeſs through its agency, who have been and ſtill are ready at all times to *accommodate* our friends when it can be done *conveniently*. It is true, that ſome of us do not hold many ſhares, but yet we are monied men, and are conſtantly occupied in money matters; ſtock, and notes of every kind are perpetually coming before us, and going from us; and, as ſometimes we deal largely and *ſpeculate boldly*, the additional ſum of 27,000 dollars regular diſcount, and 30, or 40,000 dollars beſides, will be extremely acceptable and uſeful to us. We ſhall lay ourſelves out to be as *accommodating* as poſſible to our *friends* and *regular cuſtomers*; and that we may be particularly ſo to them, we ſhall make it a point to reject all other paper that may interfere with our immediate intereſt; this will be doing the poor diſappointed devils no injury, becauſe the funds which *we* draw out of the inſtitution will enable us to ſerve them at ſecond-hand. To be ſure we only pay ſix per cent. ourſelves, but the extreme anxiety and exertion which it coſts us to get into this ſituation, the trouble which we and our *brokers* are at to diſcover the ſituation and wants of others, and our zeal to relieve their diſtreſſes, cannot be conſidered as overpaid at an intereſt of three per cent. per month: beſides by ſo doing, we prevent the inſtitution from being troubled with ſmall matters, which ought not to take up their time and attention, and take all the trouble and riſk upon ourſelves.

We hope theſe obſervations will be attentively conſidered, and if they be, the reſult muſt be favourable to us. Conſider all you who wiſh to be *favoured* and *accommodated*, what would be the conſequence if only actual notes given for value received were to be diſcounted? Why it would be ſaid that fewer Banks would be ſufficient to anſwer every fair and uſeful purpoſe of trade and commerce, and in that caſe, many large ſums of the ſtockholders money now in the hands of *judicious* individuals, and employed in the moſt *active* and *intereſting* manner; would be withheld, and who can ſay what would be the conſequences. The *friendly* practice of reciprocating names and notes would ceaſe, and that decent and religious cuſtom called *ſhaving* would be generally neglected.

Obadiah Gripe.
Timothy Snatch.
Judas Holdfaſt.
Peter Lather-well.
Simon Cloſe-cut.

ODE.

Tell me, where's the vi'let fled,
Late ſo gaily blowing,
Springing 'neath fair Flora's tread,
Choiceſt ſweets beſtowing ?
Swain the vernal ſcene is o'er,
And the vi'let blooms no more !

Say, where hides the bluſhing roſe,
Pride of fragrant morning,
Garland meet for beauty's brows ;
Hill and dale adorning ?
Gentle maid, the ſummer's fled,
And the helpleſs roſe is dead !

Bear me then to yonder rill,
Late ſo freely flowing,
Wat'ring many a daffodil
On its margin glowing.
Sun and wind exhauſts its ſtore ;
Yonder riv'let glides no more !

Lead me to the bow'ry ſhade,
Late with roſes flaunting ;
Lov'd reſort of youth and maid,
Am'rous ditty chaunting.
Hail and ſtorm, with fury ſhow'r ;
Leafleſs mourns the rifled bow'r !

Say where bides the village maid,
  Late yon cot adorning,
Oft I've met her in the glade,
  Fresh and fair as morning?
    Swain, how short is beauty's boon!
    Seek her in her grassy tomb!

Whither roves the tuneful swain,
  Who, of rural pleasures,
Rose and vi'let, rill and plain,
  Sung in softest measures?
    Maiden, swift life's vision's flies,
    Death hath clos'd the poet's eyes!

TO MARY.

The blust'ring winds are hush'd on high,
  The darken'd clouds are all withdrawn,
And stealing to the western sky
  The evening shades move o'er the lawn.

The woodland pours its sweetest song
  That softly sinks as day retires;
And as it dies the vale along,
  A harmony of soul inspires.

Calm as this closing hour of day,
  And blest with harmony as sweet;
May Mary's seasons glide away,
  And peace and joy her wishes meet;
And may no dark relentless storm
Her tranquil happiness deform.

A WINTER PIECE.

" *Dread* WINTER *comes at last to close the scene.*"

————————Yes winter comes!
'Tis but a moment since the smiling Spring
On Zephyr's downy wing rejoicing came,
And op'd and kiss'd the coyly blushing rose.
Then nature from her sleep awoke serene,
And dress'd herself anew.—At his approach
Tall hills of snow ran down with gratitude;

The lofty mountains rais'd their melting heads,
And in the face of heaven, wept for joy:
The little riv'lets ran to find the ſea,
And join'd to ſwell the thankful ſong of praiſe.
But ah! their joy was ſhort! their ſongs have ceas'd;
All nature ſleeps again: dread Winter's here
The Lapland Giant comes with pendant ice,
Chill horror ſhooting from his gelid chin;
Nor lakes, nor ſeas, can ſtop his rough career:
He builds his bridge acroſs old ocean's breaſt.
Affrighted, Sol retires with haſty ſtrides,
And dares not obliquely downward look,
On his once conquer'd, now his conquering foe.
The earth is all in weeds of mourning clad,
To wail the loſs of her departed friend:
Th' unconquer'd evergreen is left alone,
And nods defiance to the northern blaſt.

This mirror paints the fate of changing man.
This moment *youth*, with all its op'ning charms,
In playful mood, ſits laughing in his face:
His ſwelling heart now beats with ſanguine hope
Of ſatisfying bliſs, and full-blown joy:
He hugs himſelf in his fantaſtic dream,
And thinks that nought can blaſt the vernal flow'r:
But, while anticipation gilds the wing of hope,
The frigid hand of Time with furrows deep
His forehead ploughs; and blights the pleaſing view.
"Then let fair Virtue's ſeed in youth be ſown;
"'Twill prove an evergreen in hoary age,
"And flouriſh in the winter of our years:—
"'Twill waft us to the realms of peace and love,
"To taſte th' ecstatic bliſs of ſaints on high:
"There happineſs will ſpring without alloy,
"And ſeraphs chaunt their *never ending ſtrains*."

EPITAPHIUM CHYMICUM.

Here lieth to *digeſt*, *macerate*, and *Amalgamate* with Clay,
In *Balneo Arenæ*,

Stratum ſuper Stratum,
The *Reſiduum*, *Terra damnata* & *Caput Mortuum*
Of BOYLE GODFREY, CHYMIST, and M. D.
A Man, who in this Earthly *Laboratory*,
Purſued various *Proceſſes* to obtain
Arcanum Vitæ,
Or, the Secret to live:
Alſo, *Aurum Vitæ*,
Or, the Art of getting, rather than making Gold.
Alchymiſt like,
All his Labour and *Projection*,
As *Mercury* in the Fire, *Evaporated* in *Fumo*.
When he *diſſolved* to his firſt Principles,
He *departed* as poor
As the laſt Drops of an *Alembic*;
For Riches are not poured
On the *Adepts* of this World.
Though fond of News, he carefully avoided
The *Fermentation*, *Efferveſcence*
And *Deſcripitation* of this Life.
Full Seventy Years his *exalted Eſſence*
Was *Hermetically ſealed* in its *Terrene Mattraſs*
But the radical Moiſture being *exhauſted*,
The *Elixir Vitæ* ſpent,
And *exſiccated* to a *Cuticle*;
He could not *Suſpend* longer in his *Vehicle*,
But *precipitated Gradatim*, *Per Campanam*,
To his Original Duſt.
May that Light, brighter than *Bolognian Phoſphorus*, preſerve him for the *Athanor*, *Empyreuma*, and *Reverberatory Furnace* of the other World.;
Depurate him from the *Fæces* and *Scoria* of this,
Highly *Rectify* and *Volatilize*
His *ætherial* Spirit,
Bring it over the *Helm* of the *Retort* of this Globe,
Place it in a proper *Recipient* or *Chryſtaline* Orb,
Among the Elect of the *Flowers of Benjamin*;
Never to be *ſaturated* till the General *Reſuſcitation*,
Deflagration, *Calcination*,
And *Sublimation* of all Things.

F I N I S.